BILINGUAL
SCHOOLING

and the
Survival of Spanish
in the
United States

BILINGUAL SCHOOLING

and the Survival of Spanish in the United States

A. BRUCE GAARDER

NEWBURY HOUSE PUBLISHERS / ROWLEY / MASSACHUSETTS

Library of Congress Cataloging in Publication Data

Gaarder, Alfred Bruce.
  Bilingual schooling and the survival of Spanish in
the United States.

  (Studies in bilingual education)
  Bibliography: p.
  1. Education, Bilingual–United States.   2. Spanish
Americans in the United States–Education.   I. Title.
LC3731.G3   371.9'7   76-45740
ISBN 0-88377-065-2

Cover design by Wendy Doherty

NEWBURY HOUSE PUBLISHERS, INC.

 Language Science
Language Teaching
Language Learning

ROWLEY, MASSACHUSETTS 01969

Printed in the U.S.A.   First printing: May 1977
                                         5   4   3   2   1

CONTENTS

	Glossary of special terms and abbreviations	vii
	Overview	1
1	Rationale of bilingual education in the United States	7
2	Organization of the bilingual school	21
3	Teaching the bilingual child: research, development and policy	35
4	The first seventy-six bilingual education projects	49
5	Teaching Spanish in school and college to native speakers of Spanish	61
6	The golden rules of other language acquisition by young children	77
7	Teacher training for Spanish-medium work in United States schools	81
8	Political perspective on bilingualism and bilingual education	95
9	Language maintenance or language shift: the prospect for Spanish in the United States	129
10	Bilingual-bicultural education and cultural pluralism: the special case of the Mexican Americans	153
11	The dilemmas of cultural pluralism	175
12	La centralidad del idioma español común	185
13	Análisis crítico de *Peregrinos de Aztlán*	191
14	Las consecuencias del bilingüismo colectivo	225
15	Establishment of the *Liga nacional defensora del idioma español*	231

NEWBURY HOUSE SERIES
STUDIES IN BILINGUAL EDUCATION

Sponsored by
The International Center for Research on Bilingualism
Laval University
Quebec City, Canada

BILINGUAL EDUCATION IN A BINATIONAL SCHOOL
by William F. Mackey

THE LANGUAGE EDUCATION OF MINORITY CHILDREN
Selected Readings
Edited by Bernard Spolsky

BILINGUAL EDUCATION OF CHILDREN: The St. Lambert Experiment
by Wallace E. Lambert and G. R. Tucker

A SOCIOLINGUISTIC APPROACH TO BILINGUAL EDUCATION
by Andrew D. Cohen

BILINGUAL SCHOOLING AND THE SURVIVAL OF SPANISH
IN THE UNITED STATES
by A. Bruce Gaarder

THE AMERICAN BILINGUAL TRADITION
by Heinz Kloss

BILINGUALISM IN EARLY CHILDHOOD
Edited by William F. Mackey and Theodore Andersson

BILINGUAL SCHOOLS FOR A BICULTURAL COMMUNITY
Edited by William F. Mackey and Von N. Beebe

Glossary of Special Terms and Abbreviations

AID	Agency for International Development
CIA	Central Intelligence Agency
el español común	The broad spoken and written style used in common by the people of all Spanish-speaking countries for schooling, business, newspapers, magazines, the church, public discussion and other formal and semi-formal purposes. Commonly called "world standard Spanish."
EMT	English mother tongue
ESL	English as a second language
FL	Foreign language
FLES	Foreign language (teaching) in the elementary schools
Inservice	Refers to additional, usually part-time, training for teachers while they are employed, i.e., in service as teachers.
K	Kindergarten
N-EMT	Non-English mother tongue
Title VII	The Bilingual Education Act, federal legislation which supports bilingual schooling
USIA	United States Information Agency

OVERVIEW

Two themes run through these essays: *bilingual schooling* and *the role and prospects of the Spanish language in the United States*—which is almost, but not quite, the same as *the education of non-English mother tongue children, especially those who speak Spanish,* and *the possibility of a flowering of Hispanic culture in this country.* Eleven of the essays are written in English; four are in Spanish.

Bilingual education can be viewed either as a small matter of pedagogy in another language and limited to the school building, or as a broad sociological innovation centered in the school but finding its strength and exerting its strongest effects far beyond the school grounds among adult speakers of that language. Likewise, the Spanish language here can be thought of as one among at least a hundred non-English tongues in this country, spoken part of the time by a mere five per cent of the population, or it can be viewed as the northernmost part of a Spanish-language area beginning at Tierra del Fuego, with more than 165 million speakers and an extraordinarily high birth rate. These essays always emphasize the larger view.

The range of topics is correspondingly broad: for bilingual schooling, the rationale, school organization, teaching methods, preparation of teachers, and relationships with the community; for the Spanish language, the question of its dialects versus *el español común,* how to teach Spanish to its native speakers, the self-destructive nature of collective bilingualism, cultural pluralism, and the possibilities of establishing a stable, diglossic relationship between Spanish and English; and finally, utopianly, an account in Spanish of the recently established

1

Liga nacional defensora del idioma español, the first such effort for Spanish in the United States. At every point what seems most significant is the pattern of conflicting attitudes toward these matters—the politics more than the pedagogy.

The essays were written over a period of ten years. Some have been revised; in other cases, notes are used for updating or to reveal significant contrasts between then and now. That there has been a marked evolution in the thinking about these topics can be illustrated by reference to the rationale set forth in defense of bilingual schooling. The earliest pieces draw heavily on experimental research to justify it. Ten years later that strategy was still useful but had been overshadowed by the flat assertion that every people has the incontrovertible right to rear and educate its children in its own image. This includes its own language.

That the bilingual education movement is a rapidly evolving one is revealed by two other notable changes over the period of ten years. Its earliest proponents believed that to increase the number of bilingual persons and the domains of usage of both tongues—with no differentiation between students who choose to learn another language and an ethnic minority which has no choice but to learn English too—was obviously a good thing, a blessing. Ten years later the realization was dawning that, blessing or not, collective (as opposed to academic) bilingualism is a phenomenon which tends strongly to destroy itself. The other change, of psychological rather than linguistic import, is the extent to which the largest group of Spanish speakers, the Chicanos, have moved from a quasi-rejection of their communality with Mexicans to one of strong identification with them, including the indigenous origin on this continent thousands of years ago.

There have been a few minor deletions from the original versions in order to avoid repetition, for example, references to the original rationale of bilingual education.

The question raised again and again throughout the book remains unanswered at its end: Is there among the ten million speakers of Spanish in the United States enough loyalty to their culture and language to strengthen and maintain them, or is bilingual schooling only another passing educational innovation, a short-term expedient aimed at social justice and the melting pot?

This is not a book about the Spanish-speaking peoples of the United States. Occasional references to their histories and cultures and to them as peoples—the Mexican-Americans (Chicanos), the Puerto Ricans, the Cubans, the Spanish, and other Spanish-Americans—are made solely to elucidate the theme of bilingual schooling related to language survival. Even so, a few words of general information seem indicated for the reader who knows nothing of this important segment of the population in the United States.

The largest group, the Mexican-Americans (or Chicanos, as they increasingly prefer to be called) numbers perhaps six million (Advisory Committee; Census Bureau; Galarza et al.). Ethnically one with the people of Mexico—of indigenous American continental stock with a strong admixture of Spanish and other European elements—they can, as they choose, view themselves as having origins here many thousands of years ago, or as having origins here since the first explorations in the American Southwest by Spaniards in the sixteenth century (and in any case before the settlement of Jamestown). A key date in their history is 1848, when after the war between Mexico and the United States the treaty of Guadalupe Hidalgo affirmed annexation from Mexico of much of what is now the Southwest of the United States. Although there are Mexican-Americans in every one of the United States, the large majority are in California, Arizona, New Mexico, and Texas, with strong concentrations in Illinois, Michigan, Kansas City, and other places. Although many are still rural and small-town dwellers, they now increasingly and predominantly are located in cities, notably Los Angeles, El Paso, San Antonio, and Chicago.

Although erroneously stereotyped as a closely homogeneous people (Catholic, Spanish-speaking and of Hispanic culture, poor, of peasant origin) they are notably heterogeneous in every respect, and this is increasingly true. That they have been victims of discriminatory practices in respect to education, housing, and political and economic considerations is notoriously true and has been documented repeatedly (Galarza et al.; Brussell; Carter; Grebler; House of Representatives; McWilliams; U.S. Commission on Civil Rights; U.S. Senate). They do commonly and notably speak Spanish, basically the Spanish of Mexico. Most—except in many cases the very old, the very young, recent immigrants, and the most economically depressed—also speak English.

The next largest group, the Puerto Ricans, numbers perhaps two million in the continental United States (although since all Puerto Ricans are citizens of the United States there is continual shifting to and from Puerto Rico). Puerto Ricans are concentrated principally in the northeastern cities of New York, New Jersey, Massachusetts, Connecticut, and Pennsylvania, but with strong contingents in the Chicago area, and lesser ones in all of the other states (House of Representatives; U.S. Senate 1967; National Puerto Rican Development and Training Institute).

The Puerto Ricans are an Hispanic people, their language is Spanish and their culture in every respect has owed most—until very recent times—to Spain. Ethnically they represent a number of stocks, including the indigenous *jíbaros* and immigration indirectly from Africa. To a very notable extent they are proudly free of the compulsion to discriminate on the basis of skin color or race. For our purposes here a key date in their history is 1898, when their country was taken over by the United States. Since that date they have undergone increasingly severe and disruptive cultural and economic influences from the United States (Cebollero). Consequently, and because of the limited economic resources of their island country and a dense population, there have been two movements: (1) toward increasing Spanish-English bilingualism both in Puerto Rico and on the mainland, and (2) toward emigration to the United States in search of employment. Puerto Ricans have strong traditions of respect for and use of Spanish in education, law, religion, government, the press, etc., but in the United States, where so many forces tend actively to deplore, denigrate and destroy Spanish and little formal effort is made to sustain it, their Spanish, like that of the Mexican-Americans, is strongly influenced by contact with English. One result of discriminatory practices against the Puerto Ricans in continental United States is the unusual ineffectiveness of the schools which they attend.

The third largest group, the Cubans, is estimated to number a million persons, principally located in Florida and the other southeastern states but notably also in the northeastern cities and with small contingents in all other areas of the nation. Two key dates are 1898, when their island homeland came under the domination of the United States, and 1959, when the triumph of the Cuban revolution led to large-scale emigration to the United States. Significantly, to a large extent the emigrants were of the educated, upper and middle socioeconomic classes in Cuba. Consequently there were soon established Spanish newspapers and journals, and organizations which have tended to preserve among them a strong sense of the prestige of Spanish and their Hispanic culture. Even so, although the potential for maintenance of Spanish is comparatively greater among the Cubans, and despite the early introduction of bilingual education for their children in the Miami (Dade County), Florida public schools, it cannot be said that the long-range prospect of Spanish among them is more favorable than elsewhere in the United States.

The remaining million, largely from Latin America, are dispersed throughout the United States with only small identifiable enclaves from a single country, notably in the vicinity of New York City, Washington, D.C., and San Francisco.

REFERENCES

Advisory Committee for the Education of the Spanish Speaking and Mexican Americans. *Annual Report to the Assistant Secretary/Commissioner of Education.* Washington, D.C.: U.S. Office of Education (1973), pp. 7-8.

Brussell, Charles B. *Disadvantaged Mexican American Children and Early Educational Experience,* (J. A. Forester and E. E. Arnaud, eds.) Austin, Texas: Southwest Educational Development Corporation (1968).

Carter, Thomas. *Mexican Americans in School: A History of Educational Neglect.* New York: College Entrance Examination Board (1970).

Cebollero, Pedro A. *A School Language Policy for Puerto Rico.* Superior Educational Council of Puerto Rico. Educational Publications Series II, No. 1 (1945).

Census Bureau. *Persons of Spanish Origin in the United States, March 1971 and 1972.* P-20, No. 250. Washington, D.C.: U.S. Government Printing Office (1973).

Galarza, Ernesto, Herman Gallegos, and Julian Samora. *Mexican-Americans in the Southwest.* Santa Barbara, California: McNally and Loftin (1969), p. 4.

Grebler, Leo. *The Mexican Americans.* New York: The Free Press (1969).

House of Representatives. *Bilingual Education Programs—Hearing Before the General Subcommittee on Education of the Committee on Education and Labor* (on H.R. 9840 and H.R. 10224). Washington, D.C.: U.S. Government Printing Office (1967).

McWilliams, Carey. *North from Mexico: The Spanish-Speaking People of the United States,* 2d ed. New York: Monthly Review Press (1961).

National Puerto Rican Development and Training Institute. *A Proposed Approach to Implement Bilingual Education—Research and Synthesis of Philosophical, Theoretical and Practical Implications.* New York: National Puerto Rican Development and Training Institute, 2150 Third Avenue (1973).

U. S. Commission on Civil Rights. *The Unfinished Education—Report II, Mexican American Educational Series.* Washington, D.C.: U.S. Government Printing Office (1971).

U. S. Senate. *Bilingual Education—Hearings Before the Special Subcommittee on Bilingual Education of the Committee on Labor and Public Welfare* (on S. 428), Parts 1 and 2. Washington, D.C.: U.S. Government Printing Office (1967).

U. S. Senate. *Hearings Before the Select Committee on Equal Educational Opportunity. Part 4—Mexican American Education.* Washington, D.C.: U.S. Government Printing Office (1971).

1

RATIONALE OF BILINGUAL EDUCATION IN THE UNITED STATES

ABSTRACT   *This essay begins with the original rationale present-*
ed before the Special Subcommittee on Bilingual Education of the
Committee on Labor and Public Welfare, United States Senate, May
18, 1967. It gives the reasons first used to justify making the non-
English mother tongue a medium of school instruction, in addition to
English, in the United States. It adduces pertinent research in support
of using the mother tongue and reveals certain anomalies or absurdities
in the American educational system. The essay then summarizes other
pertinent research findings, particularly those related to the testing of
intelligence.

There were in 1960 about 5 million persons of school age (6-18) in the United
States who had a non-English mother tongue. It is reliably estimated that over 3
million of this group did in fact retain the use of that tongue. In this group of
school children who still use the non-English mother tongue, there are 1.75 million
Spanish-speakers, about 77,000 American Indians, and slightly over a million from
some 30 additional language groups: French, German, Polish, Czech, Yiddish,
Ukrainian, and many others. The situation is not known to have changed notably
since 1960. These are the children we are concerned with, plus another million or
so in the same category under 6 years of age and soon to enter the schools. They
are necessarily and unavoidably bilingual children.

Bilingualism can be either a great asset or a great liability. In our schools millions of these youngsters have been cheated or damaged or both by well-intentioned but ill-informed educational policies which have made of their bilingualism an ugly disadvantage in their lives. The object of this testimony is to show the nature of the damage that has been done and suggest how it can be remedied in the future.

Bilingual education means the use of both English and another language—usually the child's mother tongue—as mediums of instruction in the schools. It is not "foreign language teaching" but rather the use of each language to teach all of the school curriculum (except, of course, the other language itself). There are five main reasons which support bilingual education. The first three apply to the child's years in the elementary school:

1.   Children who enter school with less competence in English than monolingual English-speaking children will probably become retarded in their school work to the extent of their deficiency in English, if English is the sole medium of instruction. On the other hand, the bilingual child's conceptual development and acquisition of other experience and information could proceed at a normal rate if the mother tongue were used as an alternate medium of instruction. Retardation is not likely if there is only one or very few non-English-speaking children in an entire school. It is almost inevitable if the non-English language is spoken by large groups of children.

2.   Non-English-speaking children come from non-English-speaking homes. The use of the child's mother tongue by some of the teachers and as a school language is necessary if there is to be a strong, mutually reinforcing relationship between the home and the school.

3.   Language is the most important exteriorization or manifestation of the self, of the human personality. If the school, the all-powerful school, rejects the mother tongue of an entire group of children, it can be expected to affect seriously and adversely those children's concept of their parents, of their homes, and of themselves.

The other two reasons apply when the bilingual child becomes an adult:

4.   If he has not achieved reasonable literacy in his mother tongue—ability to read, write, and speak it accurately—it will be virtually useless to him for any technical or professional work where language matters. Thus, his unique potential career advantage, his bilingualism, will have been destroyed.

5.   Our people's native competence in Spanish and French and Czech and all the other languages and the cultural heritage each language transmits are national resources that we need badly and must conserve by every reasonable means. I will return later to most of these points.

There is a vast body of writing by educators who believe that bilingualism is a handicap. The evidence seems at first glance to be obvious and incontrovertible.

There is a clear, direct chain relationship between language competence, formal education, and economic status among Americans whose mother tongue is not English. The children speak Spanish, or Navajo, or French, and they do poorly in school: therefore (so goes the argument), their bilingualism is to blame. Many researchers have established a decided correlation between bilingualism and low marks on intelligence tests, but what no research has shown is that bilingualism, per se, is a *cause* of low performance on intelligence tests. On the contrary, studies which have attempted to take into account all of the factors which enter the relationship show that it is not the fact of bilingualism but *how* and *to what extent* and *under what conditions* the two languages are taught that make the difference. (If this were not true, how could one explain the fact that the governing and intellectual elite in all countries have sought to give their children bilingual or even multilingual education?) Much of the literature on bilingualism does not deal at all with bilingual education. Rather it shows the unfortunate results when the child's mother tongue is ignored, deplored, or otherwise degraded.

The McGill University psychologists, Lambert and Peale (now Anisfeld) have shown that if the bilingualism is "balanced," i.e., if there has been something like equal, normal, literacy developed in the two languages, bilingual 10-year-olds in Montreal are markedly superior to monolinguals on verbal and nonverbal tests of intelligence and appear to have greater mental flexibility, a superiority in concept formation, and a more diversified set of mental abilities. It is their judgment that there is no evidence that the supposed "handicap" of bilingualism is *caused* by bilingualism, per se, and that "it would be more fruitful to seek that cause in the inadequacy of the measuring instrument and in other variables such as socioeconomic status, attitude toward the two languages, and educational policy and practice regarding the teaching of both languages" (Lambert and Peale).

There is an educational axiom, accepted virtually everywhere else in the world, that "the best medium for teaching a child is his mother tongue." What happens when the mother tongue is so used? A recent study (1966) made in Chiapas, Mexico, by Dr. N. Modiano for the New York University School of Education shows the results that can be expected. The Modiano research examined the hypothesis (implicit in current educational policies throughout the United States) that children of linguistic minorities learn to read English with greater comprehension when all reading instruction is offered through English than when they first learn to read in their non-English mother tongue.

The investigation involved all students attending 26 schools in three Indian *municipios* in Chiapas. All students were native speakers of either Tzeltal or Tzotzil, two of the indigenous languages of Mexico. Thirteen were Federal or State schools in which all reading instruction was offered in Spanish. Thirteen were National Indian Institute Schools in which literacy was developed in the mother tongue prior to being attempted in Spanish. The purpose of the study was to determine which group of schools produced the greater measure of literacy (specifically, greater reading comprehension) in the national language, Spanish.

Two indications of reading comprehension were obtained. First, all teachers were asked to designate "all of your students who are able to understand what they read in Spanish." Approximately 20 per cent of the students in the all-Spanish Federal and State schools were nominated by their teachers as being able to understand what they were asked to read in Spanish. Approximately 37 per cent of the students in the bilingual Institute schools were nominated by their teachers as being able to understand what they read in Spanish. This difference favors the bilingual approach beyond the .001 level of probability.

Then, a carefully devised group reading comprehension test was administered to all of the selected children. The children's average score in State and Federal schools was 41.59; in the bilingual Institute schools it was 50.30. The difference between these means was found to be significant at beyond the .01 level of probability. Within each of the three *municipios* mean scores in Institute schools were higher than in Federal and State schools. Thus, not only did the teachers using the bilingual approach nominate more of their students for testing, but their judgment was confirmed by the fact that their students scored significantly higher on the group test of reading comprehension (Modiano).

In Puerto Rico, in 1925, the International Institute of Teachers College, Columbia University made a study of the educational system on that island where English was the major medium of instruction despite the fact that the children's mother tongue is Spanish. The Columbia University group undertook a testing program to measure pupil achievement in all grades and particularly to explore the relative effectiveness of learning through each of the two language mediums. To test reading, arithmetic, information, language, and spelling they used the Stanford Achievement Test in its regular English version and in a Spanish version modified to fit Puerto Rican conditions. Over 69,000 tests were given.

The results were displayed on charts so as to reveal graphically any significant difference between achievement through English and achievement through Spanish. Both of these could be compared on the same charts with the average achievement of children in schools in the continental United States. I will summarize the findings in two sentences:

1. In comparison with children in the continental United States, the Puerto Ricans' achievement through English showed them to be markedly retarded.

2. The Puerto Rican children's achievement through Spanish was, by and large, markedly superior to that of continental United States children, who were using their own mother tongue, English.

The Columbia University researchers, explaining the astonishing fact that those elementary school children in Puerto Rico—poverty-stricken, backward, "benighted," beautiful Puerto Rico—achieved more through Spanish than continental United States children did through English, came to the following conclusion, one with extraordinary implications for us here:

Spanish is much more easily learned as a native language than is English.

The facility with which Spanish is learned makes possible the early introduction of content into the primary curriculum.

Every effort should be made to maintain it and to take the fullest advantage of it as a medium of school instruction.

What they were actually saying is that because the writing system of Spanish matches the phonetic sound system better than English does, speakers of Spanish can master reading and writing very quickly and can begin to acquire information from the printed page more easily and at an earlier age.

The conclusion is, in sum, that if the Spanish-speaking children of our Southwest were given all of their schooling through both Spanish and English, there is strong likelihood that not only would their so-called "handicap" of bilingualism disappear, but *they would have a decided advantage over their English-speaking schoolmates, at least in elementary school, because of the Spanish writing system.* There are no "reading problems," as we know them, among school children in Spanish-speaking countries (International Institute).

And their English could be better too, but that's another story.

American Samoa, with about 20,000 people, is an example of what it means when children, in communities which have a high degree of linguistic solidarity, are required to study through a language not their own. In American Samoa the home language of the native people is Samoan, and they cling to it tenaciously, even to the extent of providing their children both after-school and weekend instruction in Samoan. In the villages there are also "pastor's schools" conducted in Samoan. In 1963 the Science Research Associates high school placement tests were given to 535 graduates of the Samoan junior high schools, i.e., pupils who had completed the ninth grade. The median grade placement score was 5.8, i.e., close to the end of the fifth grade. Only 21 of the 535 pupils scored 9.0, i.e., in the ninth grade, or better. Most of the 21 had studied in the United States or had other unusual advantages. The author of one report judged that one obstacle to the learning of English was the Samoans' pride in their own culture.

The most obvious anomaly—or absurdity—of our educational policy regarding foreign language learning is the fact that we spend perhaps a billion dollars a year in the United States to teach the languages—in the schools, the colleges and *etc* universities, the Foreign Service Institute, the Department of Defense, AID, USIA, CIA, etc. (and to a large extent to adults who are too old ever to master a new tongue)—yet virtually no part of the effort goes to maintain and develop the competence of American children who speak the same languages natively. There are over 4 million native speakers of French or Spanish in our country and these two languages are the two most widely taught, yet they are the ones for which our government recognizes the greatest unfilled need (at the levels, for example, of the Foreign Service of the Department of State and the program of lecturers and technical specialists sent abroad under the Fulbright-Hays Act).

The establishment of bilingual education programs in our schools could be expected to increase and improve, rather than lessen, emphasis on the proper teaching of English to children who speak another mother tongue. Under our present policy, which supports the ethnocentric illusion that English is not a "foreign" language for anyone in this country, it is almost always taught as if the bilingual child already knew English. Our failure to recognize the mother tongue and thus to present English *as a second language* helps to produce "functional illiteracy" in almost 3 out of every 4 Spanish speakers in Texas.

In a bilingual education program, English would be taught from the child's first day in school, but his concept development, his acquisition of information and experience—in sum, his total *education*—would not depend on his imperfect knowledge of English. Bilingual education permits making a clear distinction between education and language; i.e., between the content of education and the vehicle through which it is acquired.

I use the example of two window panes, the green-tinted Spanish one and the blue-tinted English one, both looking out on the same world, the same reality. We tell the little child who has just entered the first grade, "You have two windows onto the world, the Spanish one and the English one. Unfortunately, your English window hasn't been built yet, but we're going to work on it as fast as we can and in a few years, maybe, it'll be as clear and bright as your Spanish window. Meantime, even if you don't see much, keep on trying to look out the space where the blue one will be. And stay away from the green one! It's against our educational policy to look through anything tinted green!"

The influx of Spanish-speaking Cuban refugee children into Florida in recent years brought about the establishment of two model bilingual education programs in the Dade County (Miami) public schools. The first is essentially a period a day of Spanish-language arts instruction at all grade levels for native speakers of Spanish. It was established, according to educators there, "because it did not seem right not to do something to maintain and develop these children's native language." The second program is a model bilingual public elementary school (Coral Way) which is now (May, 1967) finishing its fourth year of operation. This highly successful school provides us with information on three points of great importance in the present context:

1. At the fifth-grade level the children have been found—insofar as this can be determined by achievement testing—to be able to learn equally well through either of their two languages. (This is a level of achievement that cannot be expected in even our best college-level foreign language programs.)

2. Since half of the children are Cubans and half begin as monolingual speakers of English, each learning the other's language and his own, it is apparent that a truly comprehensive bilingual education program can serve not only the non-English mother tongue children *who must necessarily become bilingual,* but also the ordinary monolingual American child who speaks nothing but English and *whose parents want him to become bilingual.*

3. The strength of the program lies in the high quality of the teachers of both languages (all of them native and highly trained speakers of the language in which they teach) and the fullness of the support they get from the school administration and the community.

The implications of these three points are momentous.

RECOMMENDATIONS

1.   That comprehensive programs of bilingual education in self-selected schools and for self-selected pupils at all school grade levels be supported.

2.   That the opportunity to profit from bilingual education be extended to children of all non-English-speaking groups. All are now losers under our present educational one-language policy: at worst they become hopelessly retarded in school; at best they lose the advantage of mastery of their mother tongue.

3.   That adequate provision be made for training and otherwise securing teachers capable of using the non-English tongue as a medium of instruction.

4.   That there be provision for cooperative efforts by the public schools and the non-English ethnic organizations which have thus far worked unaided and unrecognized to maintain two-language competence in their children.

5.   That provision be made for safeguarding the quality of the bilingual education programs which receive Federal financial assistance.

It should be noted that the rationale in 1967 made the case for "bilingualism" with no hint of one of the main themes of this book: the totally different significance and dynamics of the many kinds of bilingualism and the consequent folly of treating them all alike (see Chapter 10). Meanwhile, by 1975 additional research findings—old and new—have strengthened the thesis of bilingual education and brought about its reformulation: Failure to give a full and proper role in education to the non-English mother tongue child's language and culture amounts to a denial of equal educational opportunity. The following reports of research seem to substantiate that statement.

ILOILO, THE PHILIPPINES

The Iloilo experiment begun in 1948 in the Philippines is instructive. Children in an experimental group received all instruction in reading, arithmetic, and social studies through Hiligaynon, their mother tongue. From grade three on all their instruction was through English. The experimental group surpassed a control group taught through English alone in all three areas by the end of the second grade and continued to surpass the control group at the end of the third year. At the latter point they also did better than the controls in oral English and only slightly less well on written English tests. The experimentals' lead continued, but only in social studies, through the sixth grade (Carroll). The point to note here is that the Hiligaynon-speaking children were not in constant contact with other children from a different people and a different culture and language which dominated their own. In such a situation the importance of the mother tongue instruction is even greater in terms of its psychological effects.

CONNECTICUT

In one of the most careful studies known, Perry A. Zirkel in 1970-71 evaluated bilingual education in grades 1-3 of the public schools in four Connecticut cities: Hartford, Bridgeport, New Britain, and New London. Using the model of experimental and control groups of Puerto Rican pupils—equated insofar as possible in number, grade level, school attended, age, sex, language dominance, and socioeconomic status—he pretested the children with the nonverbal Goodenough-Harris Draw-a-Man test, the Manuel Inter-American Test of General Ability (which has parallel forms in Spanish and English dealing with listening comprehension, numerical skills and nonverbal abilities), and the Inferred Self-Concept Scale. Post-testing, following approximately a school year of teaching, was with the Manuel tests and the self-concept scale, plus a statistically validated home interview with the parents.

Most significantly, Zirkel attempted to assess in advance by observation and interview what was meant in each of the four places by "bilingual education" and found:

a "true bilingual" group with the major part of the instruction through Spanish, plus an English-as-a-second-Language (ESL) component, at Bridgeport and Hartford;

a "quasi-bilingual" group which employed Spanish-speaking aides who gave instruction through Spanish approximately five per cent of the school day, with some ESL daily, at New Britain; and

a "quasi-bilingual" group with Spanish-speaking "resource teachers" who offered 30-60 minutes of instruction in Spanish to small groups of Spanish-speaking children "pulled out" of their regular classrooms for that purpose, with no ESL, at New London.

Analysis of student outcomes at each of the two grade levels followed a covariance design, the criterion variables being general academic ability in Spanish, the same in English, and self-concept.

The results of the true bilingual group were that the "experimental group generally surpassed the control group at both levels . . . the differences . . . were statistically significant with regard to self-concept at Level I and with regard to academic ability in both Spanish and English at Level II" (Zirkel, p. 88).

For the quasi-bilingual groups (which at the pretest point were considerably higher than the Bridgeport subjects) the analysis disclosed "slight and non-significant differences between the experimental and control groups with respect to the selected student outcomes" (Zirkel, p. 108).

As for the home interview, conducted and analyzed with statistical rigor, the parents of children in the true bilingual model "were found to be significantly more interested, involved, and in favor of the school program at the end of the school year than were the parents of the control group" (Zirkel, p. 108). Although the pupils following the true model were the only ones "whose self-concept score increased from pretesting-to-posttesting unadjusted by analysis of covariance . . . the overall trend for Spanish-speaking pupils in the early grades seemed to be one of a decreasing self-concept level" (Zirkel, p. 112).

REPUBLIC OF SOUTH AFRICA

Two reports from the Republic of South Africa are particularly illuminating. Malherbe tested 18,000 pupils in three types of schools: monolingual Afrikaans, monolingual English, and bilingual Afrikaans-English. He found the pupils in bilingual schools surpassed the pupils in monolingual schools with respect to language attainment in both English and Afrikaans, geography and arithmetic (Malherbe).

Later Malherbe reported that the percentage of people speaking both English and Afrikaans (in the Republic of South Africa) dropped from 73% in 1951 to 66% in 1960 as a result of separating Afrikaans- and English-speaking children at school and students at universities in separate institutions. The government, dominated by Afrikaaners, had realized that Afrikaans-English *bilingualism leads to English monolingualism and had adopted a policy of limiting bilingual education in order to protect their own tongue* (Malherbe).

EVIDENCE RELATED TO THE TESTING OF INTELLIGENCE

Intelligence testing is a kind of microcosm of all education, and data related to such testing of non-English-speaking children can help to clarify the issues associated with bilingual education. Those data are less ambiguous, more rigorous, than data from comparisons of teaching practices, because the key variables in intelligence testing are fewer and are more easily controlled.

The case to be made here is not simply that our intelligence (I.Q.) tests are unfair because they are culture-bound and because it has been found that "intelligence" (once thought to be stable throughout one's life) can be increased. That kind of unfairness to all pupils, whatever their language, has been demonstrated. Rather, the emphasis here is on the special unfairness to Spanish-speaking children of Anglo-culture-bound tests presented in English by English-speaking persons.

1. The basic evidence is that as determined by standard, English-language I.Q. tests, the number of Spanish-speaking children (Chicanos) in California who have been classified as educable mental retardates (EMRs) has been so large in proportion to the rest of the school population as to present a statistical impossibility—unless one postulates a theory of racial inferiority.

Educable Mentally Retarded (California) (Leary, 1970)

	Blacks	Chicanos	Others
Student population	8.9%	15.2%	75.9%
EMRs (65,000)	25.5%	28.3%	46.2%

Further data of the same kind are supplied by Philip Ortego (1970).

I.Q. Scores for Chicanos and All U.S. Children

I.Q. Score	% of all U.S. Children	% Chicanos
below 75	5	13
75-90	25	50
90-100	50	25
above 100	20	12

2. The second point is that if the Chicano child's "intelligence" is measured by the use of nonverbal instruments in order to avoid some of the problems arising from his lack of competence in English, his intelligence quotient increases notably. In a review of the literature on this point James Vasquez quotes Forester and Arnaud who report on the testing of 97 Chicano children in St. Paul, Minnesota with both the English-language, Stanford-Binet I.Q. test and the nonverbal Point Scale of Performance Tests. On the former the mean of their scores was 83.77; on the latter it was 101.06.

3. There is further increase in the I.Q. scores of N-EMT children if nonverbal (or translated verbal) tests are used and if they are administered in the children's mother tongue by native speakers of that tongue. Evidence of bias persists, nevertheless, because attempts thus far to produce tests which are equally culture-free for all students have failed "inasmuch as they can only measure phenotypic behavior, which by definition, is the product of learning in a specific social and cultural setting" (Vasquez, p. 161, quoting Jane Mercer).[1]

4. It follows from the above three points that I.Q. tests completely fair to N-EMT children must necessarily be based on the specific social and cultural setting of the N-EMT children and must be administered in the non-English tongue by a qualified person who is one of its native speakers. Furthermore, since I.Q. scores—contrary to what was once commonly believed—depend heavily on the testee's total previous experience, including formal learning, the children's education, especially during their early years while the capacity and need to learn are greatest and English cannot yet have been completely mastered, must be in substantial measure through the mother tongue. However much the I.Q. testing program alone might be improved in ways indicated above, the failure to provide equal educational opportunity (insofar as formal schooling is concerned) for Spanish-speaking children would be as great as ever in any classroom where the medium is exclusively English and the teacher other than a Spanish speaker well trained to teach through Spanish.[2]

The data presented in this section show that despite the schools' and the examiners' efforts to be fair in the use of standardized English-language, English-administered, or American culturally conceived tests to determine intelligence and measure achievement in Spanish-speaking children, there is inevitably discrimination resulting from four incongruencies:

the children's inadequacies in English;

the school's failure to exploit fully their potential in Spanish;

the cultural *mismatch* of the testing instruments used;

the cultural *bias* of the instruments.[3]

A significant inference may be drawn from the above exposition. Whereas in the construction and administration of measures of intelligence considerable effort is now made in order to avoid cultural bias and to eliminate the verbal factor (and, as we have seen, with only limited success), in the normal course of teaching *no such care can possibly be taken*: most formal teaching and learning is necessarily verbal, and the book and other teaching materials are deliberately infused with cultural content (bias) designed to inculcate the "American heritage" (a tall, Anglo-Yankee Uncle Sam; the landing of the Pilgrims; the winning of the West; Damn the torpedos, full speed ahead! Charge!—up San Juan Hill; "I shall return"; the melting pot, etc.). The I.Q. testing procedures, unfair as they are to N-EMT children, represent the English-language school and school teachers at their very best. It follows that the normal course of teaching cannot but be much more harmful to N-EMT children.

Furthermore, to suppose that the situation could be corrected by adding to our school history books the exploits of the non-English mother tongue peoples is to miss the point: instruction would still be in English and imparted almost wholly by English mother tongue teachers.

IMPORTANCE OF THE EARLIEST CHILDHOOD YEARS

The assertion made in the preceding section relative to the crucial early years of a child's life, when the capacity and need to learn are greatest, can be documented. A review of pertinent research, by Dr. Theodore Andersson in "Bilingual Education and Early Childhood," a paper prepared for the First Annual International Multi-Lingual Multi-Cultural Conference, San Diego, California, April 2, 1973, is the basis of the following summary statement and its documentation.

There is weighty evidence that during the early childhood years, from birth to age eight or thereabout, as much as 80% of each individual's intellectual capability is developed. The development does not take place at the same rate during those years. Rather, the rate is greatest at the beginning, after birth, and declines steadily.[4]

The implications of these findings seem clear. (1) School policy is harmful to the child to the extent that it delays the child's learning or lessens his access to significant learning experiences. Such delay and lessening are inevitable if the school makes English the sole medium of instruction for a N-EMT child whose command of English is inferior to his command of the mother tongue. There is evidence too abundant to be worth citing of school policy in the American South-

west which results in Mexican-American children being required to enroll for a
"pre-primary year" and of their subsequent retention an extra year in grade one
while their ability to use English is supposedly catching up with the demands upon
that ability made by the school. (2) The second implication is that the child's
learning (his access and involvement in significant experiences) should proceed
apace from birth onward, through the language in which he is best equipped to
learn. This will commonly be the mother tongue, not simply because he commands
it as he does not command English, but because it has been the medium of the
affective side of his life, of his very consciousness of being human. (It is of course
true that some N-EMT children also know English in some measure, and some are
evidently more proficient in English than in the mother tongue by the time they
enter school. In these cases the choice of the school medium of instruction must
still take into consideration such factors as affectivity and whether or not the
child belongs to a "visible" minority. (3) The third implication is that both the
school and the parents should be aware of the potentially harmful effect of upset-
ting and disturbing the normal course of a child's development by misguided
emphasis on changing his speech from his mother tongue to the official tongue.
A common example of this are the well-intentioned parents who insist on using
their own "broken," heavily accented English as the language of the home. This
can have the effect of counteracting the model of native English pronunciation
and syntax provided by the child's school teachers who are educated native
speakers of English.

THE QUESTION OF HUMAN RIGHTS

The most profoundly significant rationale for bilingual-bicultural schooling is the
simple proposition that every people has the fundamental human right to rear and
educate its children in its own image and language.

NOTES

1. Forty-seven randomly selected Spanish-speaking "retarded" children, half from
urban, half from rural backgrounds in California were reexamined in the Spanish language by
Spanish-speaking psychologists, and it was found that 42 of the 47 scored above the I.Q.
ceiling of the mental retardate classification. Thirty-seven scored 75 or higher; over half scored
80 or above; 16% scored 90 or more. This was part of the evidence presented in *Diana, et al.
vs. (California) Board of Education* which led U.S. District Court Judge Robert E. Peckham to
rule on February 5, 1970 that thenceforth school officials would be required (a) to explain
any disproportionate assignment of Spanish-speaking children to classes for mental retardates,
and (b) to have prepared an I.Q. test normed to the California Spanish-speaking child
population; and that such children should be tested in both Spanish and English and be
allowed to respond in either tongue.
     Researcher Leary (cited herein) reports on one girl who scored 30 on the English
version Stanford-Binet Intelligence Test and then scored 79 when retested in a Spanish version
of the same test. Leary reports than when Victor Ramirez, a school psychologist, tested nine
children in Spanish (all of whom had been labeled "mentally retarded" after being tested in

English) all but one of the nine moved out of the EMR category (Leary, op. cit., p. 1). Researcher Ortego has reported that when a group of Chicano EMRs in Los Angeles were retested through Spanish, the group's average score increased by 13 points, and one student showed an improvement of 28 points (Ortego, op. cit., p. 28).

   2. Dr. Jane R. Mercer studied Chicano children in Riverdale, California and found that their I.Q.s, as determined by standard, commonly used tests, correlated positively with the extent to which they and their families showed certain characteristics commonly associated with "Anglos." The five "characteristics" were:

   living in a house with 1.4 or fewer persons per room;

   the mother's expectancy that the child would continue formal schooling beyond the high school;

   head of the household with ninth-grade education or higher;

   English spoken all or most of the time in the home;

   family ownership of the home (or buying it).

Chicano children with five of these characteristics had I.Q.s averaging 104.4; with four of the characteristics, I.Q.s averaging 95.5; with three, averages of 89; with two, 88.1; with one or none, I.Q. averages of 84.5. These data indicate strongly the bias of the I.Q. tests in relation to socioeconomic status and acculturation to English and the English-speaking community. (From Jane R. Mercer, "Current Retardation Procedures and the Psychological and Social Implications on the Mexican American," paper prepared for Southwestern Cooperative Education Laboratory, Albuquerque, New Mexico, April 1970.)

   3. "Mismatch" means simply that one culture covers or emphasizes some areas which the other ignores, and fails to emphasize areas which are important to the other. Thus:

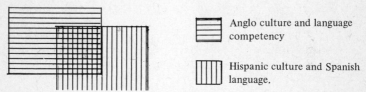

Anglo culture and language competency

Hispanic culture and Spanish language.

"Bias," on the other hand means (for example) the load of pejorative connotations attached to terms like *mestizo* and *Mexican.* (During this writer's youth in New Mexico, Spanish speakers commonly called themselves *mexicanos* while talking Spanish, but in English, the word *Mexican* was considered to be insulting.) In northern New Mexico and Colorado, Spanish speakers still resist and resent being called Mexicans or *mexicanos.*

   4. The findings of Benjamin Bloom indicate that half of a child's total intellectual capability is developed by age four, and 80% by age eight. (Benjamin Bloom, *Stability and Change in Human Characteristics,* New York: John Wiley & Sons, 1964, p. 68.)

   The findings of Burton L. White and his research team at Harvard University have led them to change the focus of their study from age six to ages zero to three. (From "Fundamental Early Environmental Influences on the Development of Competence," in Merle E. Meyer, *Third Symposium on Learning: Cognitive Learning,* Bellingham, Washington: Western Washington State College, Feb. 1972.)

REFERENCES

Carroll, John B. "Modern Languages," *Encyclopedia of Educational Research,* ed. Robert L. Ebel et al. New York: MacMillan (1969), p. 868.

International Institute of Teachers College. *A Survey of the Public Educational Systems of Porto Rico.* New York: Bureau of Publications, Teachers College, Columbia University (1926).

Lambert, Wallace, and Elizabeth Peal. "The Relation of Bilingualism to Intelligence," *Psychological Monographs: General and Applied, No. 546.* Washington, D.C.: American Psychological Association, 1333 16th St., N.W., 76 (1962), p. 27.

Leary, Mary E. "Children Who Are Tested in an Alien Language–Mentally Retarded?" *The New Republic,* May 30, 1970.

Malherbe, E. G. *The Bilingual School.* London: Longmans, Green (1946).

–––. "Commentaries," *Description and Measurement of Bilingualism: an International Seminar,* ed. L. G. Kelly. Toronto: University of Toronto Press (1969), p. 325-27.

Modiano, Nancy D. "Reading Comprehension in the National Language: A Comparative Study of Bilingual and All-Spanish Approaches to Reading Instruction in Selected Indian Schools in the Highlands of Chiapas, Mexico." Doctoral dissertation, New York University (1966).

Ortego, Philip D. "Montezuma's Children," *The Center Magazine* (Nov.-Dec. 1970), 3, No. 6, p. 27.

Vasquez, James. "Measurement of Intelligence and Language Differences," *AZTLAN,* vol. 3, No. 1 (1973), pp. 155-63. This summary draws heavily on the Vasquez review. The cited material is from J. A. Forester and E. E. Arnaud (eds.) *Disadvantaged Mexican American Children and Early Educational Experience.* Austin, Texas: Southwest Educational Development Corporation (1968), p. 53.

Zirkel, Perry A. *An Evaluation of the Effectiveness of Selected Experimental Bilingual Education Programs in Connecticut.* West Hartford: The University of Hartford (1972).

2

ORGANIZATION OF THE BILINGUAL SCHOOL

ABSTRACT   *This is an effort to identify and weigh the principal factors which determine school organization and classroom practices when two languages are used as mediums of instruction. It shows the great differences between adding the mother tongue and adding another tongue, and between one-way and two-way bilingual schooling. Classroom practices are discussed, such as the use of one or both languages by a single teacher, allotments of time, and the treatment given each language. There is a brief discussion of the nature of language and of language learning.*

A *bilingual school* is a school which uses, concurrently, two languages as mediums of instruction in any portion of the curriculum except the languages themselves. Thus, for example, arithmetic taught in both English and Irish, or arithmetic in English and history in Irish, or all subjects (except Irish and English) in both tongues would constitute bilingual schooling. English through English and all other subjects in Irish would not. The teaching of a vernacular solely as a bridge to another, the official language, is not bilingual education in the sense of this paper, nor is ordinary foreign language teaching.

Bilingual schools of several kinds and varied purpose are now and have long been in operation worldwide. This paper assumes that there are at present sound

21

reasons, which will become increasingly more compelling, for establishing many more such schools and seeks to set forth some guidelines for their organizers. The reasons for *adding the mother tongue* as a teaching medium are:

a.   to avoid or lessen scholastic retardation in children whose mother tongue is not the principal school language

b.   to strengthen the bonds between home and school

c.   to avoid the alienation from family and linguistic community that is commonly the price of rejection of one's mother tongue and of complete assimilation into the dominant linguistic group

d.   to develop strong literacy in the mother tongue in order to make it a strong asset in the adult's life.

For *adding a second tongue* as a teaching medium the reasons are:

a.   to engage the child's capacity for natural, unconscious language learning (Andersson, 1960; Penfield, 1956; and Stern, 1963, chapter 11)

b.   to avoid the problems of *method, aptitude,* etc., which beset the usual teaching of second languages

c.   to make the second language a means to an end rather than an end in itself (Stern, chapter 9)

d.   to increase second language experience without crowding the curriculum

e.   plus other well-known reasons which do not concern us here: to teach the national language, to provide a lingua franca or a *world status* language, for cultural enrichment, and economic gain.

The literature on bilingualism gives virtually no information on the organization of bilingual schools. Furthermore it generally omits consideration of the teaching-learning process itself: what happens in the classroom—the interaction of teacher, pupils, methods and materials—and the theories of language and language learning underlying those happenings. This paper gives central importance to what happens in the classroom, and it is largely based on such a body of theory (Moulton, 1963). The position taken here is that however desirable—or undesirable—bilingual schooling may be, its effectiveness can neither be assessed nor assured without full consideration of school organization and classroom practices.

The chart on page 23 shows some basic features that differentiate bilingual schools (Stern, 1963, Part II; UNESCO, 1953).

The dynamics and pedagogy are not at all the same in a school which adds the mother tongue as in one which adds a second tongue. In the *two-way* model both the mother tongue and the second tongue are added.

Organization is here viewed as process and product. That is to say, organization is taken as (a) the process or course of action followed in bringing a bilingual school into existence and (b) as the educational structure which follows upon and is to some extent determined by (a). The view taken here is that the most important factors entering into the structure of bilingual schools are the time allowed for

One-way school: one group learning in two languages	Two-way school: two groups, each learning in its own and the other's language
Second tongue added	Mixed classes
Unequal time and treatment: Irish in southern Ireland; Russian in non-Russian USSR; most bilingual schools in Latin America; English in Nigeria; French in Madagascar; English in Wales in some schools; French or Spanish in grade 12 in nine Virginia high schools (1967).	*Unequal time and treatment*: Spanish-English, Laredo, Texas; English-Swedish, Viggbyholmsskolan, Sweden; German-American Community School, Berlin-Dahlem.
Equal time and treatment: In some Welsh-English schools, one language alone on alternate days.	*Equal time and treatment*: English-French, Ecole Active Bilingue—Ecole Internationale de Paris; L'Ecole Internationale SHAPE, St. Germain; the European School, Luxembourg.
Mother tongue added	Segregated classes
Unequal time and treatment: Hiligayon in the Philippines; Welsh in Wales, in some schools.	*Unequal time and treatment*: (no example known)
Equal time and treatment: (no example known)	*Equal time and treatment*: Spanish-English, Miami, Florida (mixed classes in grades 4-6).

each of the languages, the treatment and use of each language and whether the language which is added to the previously existing system is the mother tongue or not. Other factors, too, can make a great deal of difference to the school's effectiveness, e.g., whether individual teachers teach in one or in both languages, whether one or two languages are employed within an individual class period, the relative socioeconomic status of native speakers of each of the languages and the relative prestige of each (Carroll, 1963; Fishman, 1966).

ORGANIZATION AS PRODUCT

A bilingual school which can be used to illustrate the major organizational patterns and the problems of bilingual schooling is the Coral Way Elementary School in Miami, Florida.[1] In operation since 1963, in a neighborhood broadly representative of all economic levels but mostly lower middle class, it is a six grade school with normally four classes at each grade level and a total of approximately 720 pupils. Half of the pupils enter the school as monolingual speakers of English; half are native speakers of Spanish (Cubans), some of whom know bits and pieces of English. Coral Way Elementary is a *two-way* bilingual school, since each group learns through its own and the other's tongue. Since Coral Way has segregated classes (the language groups are not mixed in grades 1-3 and only to a limited extent in grades 4-6), it is in effect two *one-way* schools. For the Cubans (in this United States setting) Coral Way adds the mother tongue; for the Anglos[2] it adds

Spanish, a second tongue. It gives as nearly as possible *equal time and treatment* to the two mediums. Finally, since either of the two halves, the Anglo or the Cuban, could function alone as a *one-way* school with complete effectiveness, Coral Way exemplifies all the organizational possibilities except that of *unequal time and treatment.*

Equal Time, Equal Treatment

Equal time, equal treatment means curriculum-wide (except for the languages themselves) use of both languages as mediums. Coral Way presents all subjects in grades 1-3 through the mother tongue for approximately half the day, and all are taught again through the other tongue during the following half. These are segregated classes. There is, however, free interchange of both languages for physical education, art, music and supervised play, during which periods the groups are mixed.

There are two sets of teachers, native English and native Spanish (four teachers in all, one for each of the four classes at each grade level), plus four bilingual teaching aides. The aides perform two kinds of teaching task: they are responsible for the physical education, art, music and supervised play; and they give special help to slow learners and transfer students. Even more importantly, they allow the regular teachers free time every day for consultation and planning for the purpose of coordinating the two halves of each child's program.

The Coral Way bilingual school program was initiated in grades 1-3 simultaneously, work in the second language being increased by stages until by approximately mid-year each child was receiving half of his instruction through each of the languages. After the initial year (1963-64) this procedure was followed in the first grade only. As noted above, in grades 1-3 new concepts and skills are learned first through the vernacular and then reinforced by being taught again through the second tongue. This is not slavish imitation of the first teacher by the second one, but rather the presentation of the same content and concepts in a fresh, somewhat different way by a teacher with the varied perspective of another country[3] and another language. In the fourth and fifth grades (the third year of operation of the school) it was found that the pupils' command of the second language was such that they could learn through it alone without need of a duplicate class in the vernacular.

Despite the carefully coordinated dual-perspective double teaching of each subject, the basic methodological principle is that of expecting the instructors in each language to act in the classroom as if that were the only language in the world and the children's entire education depended on it. This means that work in one language is not presented in terms of or with reference to the other one.

One of the most difficult problems at Coral Way arose from the need to provide the same curricular time allotments as in other Miami schools. Although the reinforcing procedure gives maximum second language experience with minimum crowding of the curriculum, some time inevitably goes to the second language per se. This reduces the amount of extra-curricular activities during school hours.

MINUTES IN THE SCHOOL DAY

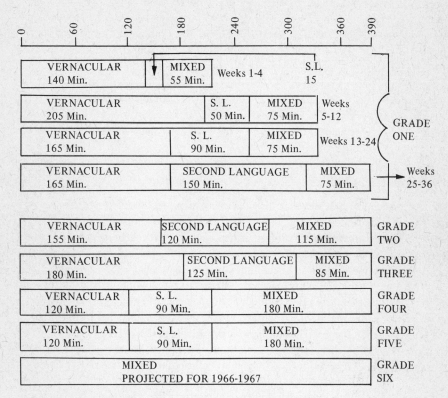

TIME DISTRIBUTION PATTERN–Coral Way Elementary School

Vernacular and *second language* (S. L.) mean the use of these as mediums of instruction. *Mixed* in grades 1-3 means physical education, art and music only. In grades 4-6 *mixed* also means combined classes of Anglos and Cubans alternating 3 weeks of each grading period working through English only, and 3 weeks working through Spanish only, in all subjects.

    The most crucial teaching problem is the proper initiation of pupils (in grades 1-3 during the first year of the school and in grade one thereafter) to the second language. The same problem occurs with latecomers and with transfer pupils who enroll initially above grade one. The Coral Way solution has two special features: (a) close coordination of each day's second language experience with the preceding experience in the vernacular, and (b) careful structuring of the second language experience so that although the teacher-class interaction gives the impression of complete spontaneity, the teacher's portion is in fact worked out in advance to introduce and review constantly a specified corpus from the form and order systems and from the lexicon of the new tongue. Detailed linguistic sequences for

English and Spanish *as second languages* were developed in order to meet the needs of the several content areas of the curriculum. The oral lesson material is supplemented by a great many pictures of objects and activities. As an additional precaution to assure a good second language beginning without detracting from the other curricular areas, the school day is lengthened one hour during the last twelve weeks in grade one, and one hour throughout the year in grade two. In grade one the second language is taught by the regular second medium teacher. Transfer pupils get special help with their second language from the aides. These pupils sit with their grade-mates all day except during the regular class in the second language, when they receive semi-private instruction from the aides. This special help, 30-45 minutes daily, may be required for only a few weeks or it may go on for an entire year.[4]

Indications of Success

There are several indications that the Coral Way bilingual school has been successful. The introduction at the fourth and fifth grade levels of mixed classes in each language without reteaching in the other was based on the teachers' judgment that learning had become equally effective through either language alone. Those Anglo pupils who entered Coral Way in the first grade in September 1963 (and who therefore have been exposed for the longest time to the possibly harmful effects of receiving half of their schooling through a foreign tongue) have been the object of close attention. On the Stanford achievement tests, administered in the spring of 1966, their median percentile ranking was as follows: paragraph meaning, 85; word meaning, 93; spelling, 99; arithmetic reasoning, 93; and arithmetic computation, 60. Their median score on the Otis Alpha test of mental maturity was 89. These pupils are not a selected group. Thus far the scores of the Cubans on these tests (all given in English) are generally lower than those of the Anglos, despite the fact that fluency in English is a prerequisite for taking them. Expert observers have noted that the Anglo children acquire excellent pronunciation of Spanish, while the English of some of the Cuban children shows interference from Spanish. This is attributed to the fact that the former group hears nothing but native Spanish, while in the homes of the latter one hears a good deal of heavily-accented English spoken by adult immigrants.[5]

It is scarcely surprising that the Cubans' scores on tests of achievement given through the medium of their second language are lower than those of the Anglos. A fair comparison could be made only if both groups were tested through both languages. Extensive testing of Puerto Rican children by the International Institute of Teachers College, Columbia University, using comparable Spanish and English forms of the Stanford achievement tests showed this to be true (International Institute of Teachers College, 1926). (See note at end of chapter for later data.)

Unequal Time, Unequal Treatment

Unequal time, unequal treatment for each of the languages characterizes most bilingual schooling throughout the world. Typically, the added language (i.e., taught in addition to the national, official or regular school language), whether it is the mother or the other tongue, is kept in a subordinate position. This is commonly true of the mother tongue, as when rising nationalism forces the introduction of history through Spanish in Mexican French-language schools, or when African vernaculars are introduced in the early primary grades as a mere bridge to the eventual exclusive use of English. It is true of the other tongue, as in the USSR where several hundred high schools were to teach some academic or scientific subjects—especially physics and mathematics—through English, French or German, (*New York Times,* 1964) or in the United States, where there is a movement currently under way (1967) in a few high schools and colleges to teach such courses as history and geography through the medium of the second language to advanced students of that language.

One of the most promising unequal time and treatment programs in the United States is for schools where some of the students at each grade level have in common a mother tongue other than English. The program is simple. Instead of ignoring or deploring the children's home language the school provides regular instruction in and through it for something like a period a day in all grades. The course material may be, for example, Spanish language arts and literature[6] or it may be a sampling of all areas of the regular school curriculum. The latter seems better, for it takes virtually no time away from the regular curriculum and has the added advantage of employing the language as a means to ends other than achievement in the language itself. The latter system also contributes more to curriculum-wide literacy in the mother tongue.

The question of time and treatment, equal or unequal, is central to the larger question of the alleged handicap of bilingualism most often reported in the literature in school situations where the mother tongue is the subordinate language, given markedly unequal time and treatment, ignored completely, or even made the object of official censure. There is increasing awareness that the cause of any handicap may not be the existence of bilingualism per se, but school policy regarding the teaching of both languages and sociological factors extrinsic to the school itself (Jensen, 1962; Lambert, 1962).

ORGANIZATION AS A PROCESS

Wherever bilingual education is to be an innovation great care should be exercised to inform and orient all sectors of the community—particularly parents, pupils and all persons officially concerned with the school—to the rationale, procedures and goals of the program. In addition to general meetings of all parents, separate grade-level meetings have been found desirable.

The teachers should have native-like command of the language taught, with academic preparation and experience through that medium. In order to maximize the dual perspective pupils can get from bilingual schooling, the teachers should be native speakers educated in the country where the language is native. A special feature of the Coral Way program commends itself to this writer. During the summer preceding the opening of the school and the two following summers a six-week workshop on teaching methods and materials and for program planning was conducted for the Coral Way teachers. The first summer there was a required course in descriptive linguistics and another in the structure of the English language, for all teachers. As noted above, the use of teacher aides frees time every day for the regular teachers to coordinate work in the two languages.[7]

Regarding teaching materials little can be said in the brief space of this essay. In some vernaculars books and other materials are inadequate or non-existent. As for the added second language, if suitable texts are available from the language's home country a healthful biculturism can result from the chance to use them in addition to texts prepared for use in the country where the school is situated, but overemphasis or exclusive use of books based on a foreign environment can divorce the school from the reality of the child's home and community.

The course of action to be followed to bring a bilingual school into existence should be set with full awareness of the essential differences between teaching the mother tongue and teaching a second language.

Deep Grammar

The native speaker of a language (including the native speaker-teacher) usually has no awareness of the *deep grammar* (Twaddell, 1962) of his own language, i.e., the interdependent systems of phonology, morphology and syntax which comprise it, and the extent to which the native speaker-child brings virtually complete, thought-less mastery of the systems to school with him at the age of six. As with his own regional accent and the complex body motion which accompanies his own speech, he doesn't know or knows only vaguely that the deep grammar is there and is concerned in the classroom with the niceties of usage (Say "as a cigarette should," not "like a cigarette should."), with grammatical nomenclature (This is a verb, and this is its direct object.) and with orthography (*i* before *e* except after *c*). Usage, nomenclature and orthography, whatever their importance, are of the surface alone; they are applied on top of the deep, thoughtless mastery which the native speaker-child acquired at home.

Grammatical nomenclature and the niceties of usage are at best a sort of polish on the surface of the deep grammar, the language itself. This polish can be applied quite effectively when the pupils speak an acceptable variant of the subject language, especially if theirs is the same variant as the teacher's. The polish is largely ineffective with the speaker of an unacceptable variant; the configuration of his deep grammar is so different that the polish, applied in the traditional ways, doesn't even touch the surface. Finally, there is the situation of the child who is not a speaker of the language to which the teaching is applied. In the sense of the figure used here, he has no deep grammar in the new language, hence no surface to be polished.

The point is that for pupils who speak unacceptable variants of their school language (e.g., English-based Jamaican Creole or Liberian Pidgin English) just as for pupils who are learning a second or foreign language, the normal materials and methods and orientation of the mother tongue class are not very effective.

Another common weakness in the teaching of a second language derives from the assumption that language is composed of words and that teaching is therefore teaching words. The grain of truth in this assumption gives the child no clue to any of the structural or paralinguistic differences among, for example, these utterances (which would be enormously more complex if presented orally, as they must be to the neophyte):

1.   I haven't seem him for five years.

2.   Hace cinco años que no lo veo.
      (It makes five years that not him I see.)

3.   Seit fünf Jahren habe ich ihn nicht mehr gesehen.
      (Since five years have I him not more seen.)

Yet visits to the classrooms reveal teachers who, irrespective of the materials that are being used, are concerned largely with the *names of things* and word-correspondence from language to language.

Next, there is the teacher who is overly aware of the traps described above, particularly the importance of developing in the child a sense and command of the stuff of language itself, what we are calling deep grammar. Here the most serious weakness lies in over-structuring the course materials at too early an age, i.e., too early and overt dependence upon pattern drills based on contrastive analysis of the two languages, or upon the strict sequencing of the order of presentation of the features of the new language. Such drills and sequencing are not in themselves bad. The harm seems to come when their use requires that children 3-7 years old focus their attention on the language itself rather than beyond language, on their involvement in events or situations. The way out of the dilemma is suggested above in the description of Coral Way. If the child is to acquire the intuitive sense of deep grammar which he lacks, the teacher must know how to give it to him in ways which, however structured and systematized they may be, have the appearance and effect of complete spontaneity. For as Penfield says, speaking of the child's learning of a second tongue, " . . . language is not a subject to be studied nor an object to be grasped. It is a means to other ends, a vehicle, and a way of life" (Penfield, 1956, 257).

Finally, there is the question of whether or not to allow teacher and pupils to use both of the languages of a bilingual school during a given class period (as opposed to confining each to its own class periods or its own part of the day). In the United Nations Nursery School in Paris children three to five years old are mixed without regard to mother tongue and the teachers use both languages, a sentence in one then the same sentence in the other, especially at the beginning of the year with three-year-olds. This practice is implicitly justified on the grounds that two thirds of the school population is transient and that the children need above all security and understanding. Four- and five-year-olds are allowed to hear each language alone for increasingly longer periods of time (Dartigue, 1966). But the weight of opinion seems to favor the one-language-one person principle.

Unquestionably a young child learns a second language quickly and effectively if it is the unavoidable means to his full-time involvement in all the affairs of
his life. Much less than full-time involvement will suffice for him to learn the new
language. The minimum time, the optimum kind of involvement, and the affairs
most conducive to this learning process *in a school* are still largely unknowns.
Water falling drop by drop into a bucket will fill it, unless, of course, the conditions are such that each drop evaporates before the next one strikes.

NOTE

A three-year study of the Coral Way experimental bilingual program was completed
in 1967 as a doctoral dissertation at the University of Miami (Richardson), to
evaluate its effectiveness during the first three years of operation, school years
1963-64, 1964-65, and 1965-66.

There were three separate groups in the study and each group included
Spanish- and English-speaking pupils in both the experimental school and control
school. Group A pupils in the experimental school were in the first grade at the
beginning of the program and continued through grades two and three; Group B
pupils were in the second grade and continued through grades three and four; and
Group C pupils were in the third grade and continued through grades four and five.
English-speaking pupils in the control school and Spanish-speaking pupils in other
schools were compared with Spanish-speaking pupils in the control school.

In October of each of the first four years of the bilingual program the Stanford achievement tests—in English—were given to all pupils in the study. The Otis
Alpha test was given in the third grade and the California Mental Maturity test was
given in the fifth grade. Both of these tests are also in English. The second language
ability of the pupils in the experimental program was measured by the Cooperative
Inter-American Reading Tests (Manuel) with both Spanish and English versions,
which were given to all pupils in the bilingual program in May of 1964, 1965, 1966,
and 1967. These tests do not measure competence in speaking or listening.

The conclusions of the doctoral study deal only with the first three years of
the six-year program. It was expected that the achievement of the same pupils
would again be assessed at the end of the six years.

The three experimental groups, A, B, and C, were compared with control
groups A, B, and C in the areas of paragraph meaning, word meaning, spelling,
arithmetic reasoning, and arithmetic computation. One hypothesis was that there
would be no significant difference in achievement in the language arts and in
arithmetic, at the same grade levels, between English-speaking and Spanish-speaking
pupils in the experimental school and the same two groups in the control school.
*Both English-speaking and Spanish-speaking pupils in the bilingual program per-
formed as well on the criterion tests as did their corresponding groups who had
studied the regular curriculum in the monolingual control school.* These results
show that the experimental program of study was relatively as effective as the

regular curriculum in paragraph meaning, word meaning, spelling, arithmetic reasoning, and arithmetic computation for both English- and Spanish-speaking pupils. Stated otherwise, neither group achieved less as a result of receiving instruction in its native tongue during only one half of each school day, or as a result of being asked to learn through two different languages. In addition, both groups of pupils made good progress toward learning a second language.

Another hypothesis tested was that there would be no significant difference between pupil progress in ability to read, understand, and deal with academic content in the native language and in the second language as measured by the Cooperative Inter-American Reading Tests. The reading tests were given to all pupils in the experimental school in May of each year. Following the final year of the doctoral study they were given once more, in May of 1967.

Each administration of these tests, in 1964, 1965, and 1966, revealed statistically significant differences between the ability of both groups of pupils to learn through their native and their second language. However, as might be expected, the difference for both groups diminished each year. The fourth testing, in May of 1967, showed for the first time no significant differences between the achievement through Spanish and through English for Groups A, B, or C of the Spanish-speaking pupils.

The Inter-American Reading Tests showed that for the *English*-speaking groups there were still significant differences between their achievement through English and their achievement through Spanish at the end of the fourth year. As noted above, the difference decreased each year. It was intended that the tests would be given again in May of 1968.

It should be borne in mind that, except for the bilingual aide work in music, art, and physical education and their lunch and playground periods, the Cuban pupils and the American pupils were not in class together in the early grades. Beginning in the 1966-67 school year, however, and continuing in 1967-68, some groups of pupils in grade five and entire classes in grade six were in class together and the curriculum was no longer presented to them twice, once through each language. Instead, for alternating spans of varying length, e.g., three weeks, the children learned in a given curricular area in each language alone. This means that the administrators and faculty of Coral Way believed as early as 1966 that despite the differences noted above, a good deal of learning could be entrusted to the pupils' second language alone, whether English or Spanish.

NOTES

1. The Coral Way project was established with Ford Foundation support. The director of the Ford Foundation Project was Dr. Pauline M. Rojas.

2. A term widely used to differentiate native English speakers from native speakers of Spanish.

3. The Spanish medium teachers at Coral Way were born and educated in Cuba.

4. Similar concern for developing readiness for second language work in the newly-enrolled pupil is reported from the Ecole Active Bilingue (Ecole Internationale de Paris), L'Ecole Internationale SHAPE St. Germain, and the German-American Community School, Berlin-Dahlem. See Stern, op. cit., 58, 59, 61.

5. These data and much of the other description of Coral Way school were furnished by Mr. Lee Logan, the school principal. His help is here gratefully acknowledged. An incidental fact of interest is that the annual cost at Coral Way attributable to its being a bilingual school is about $17,000 in excess of what it would cost as a monolingual school. This is a four per cent increase of the school's annual budget. The extra money goes to pay the teaching aides and to buy Spanish language teaching materials.

6. See Chapter 7.

7. In the opinion of the Coral Way principal, Mr. Lee Logan, the first requisite for success is that the school principal have the privilege of selecting every menber of the staff. The second requisite is that aides be employed as noted in text.

REFERENCES

Andersson, Theodore. The optimum age for beginning the study of modern languages. *International Review of Education,* 6 (1960), p. 298-306.

Carroll, John B. Research problems concerning the teaching of foreign or second languages to younger children. In *Foreign languages in primary education: the teaching of foreign or second languages to younger children* (Report on an International Meeting of Experts 9-14 April, 1962, International Studies in Education), H. H. Stern, ed. Hamburg: UNESCO Institute of Education (1963), p. 72-80.

Dartigue, Esther. Bilingualism in the nursery school. *French Review,* (1966), 4.

Fishman, Joshua. Bilingual sequences at the societal level. In Carol J. Kreidler (ed.), *On teaching English to speakers of other languages* Series II. Champaign, Illinois: National Council of Teachers of English (1966), p. 139-144.

(The) International Institute of Teachers College. *A survey of the public educational system of Porto Rico.* New York: Bureau of Publications, Teachers College, Columbia University (1926), p. 93-149.

Jensen, J. Vernon. *Bilingualism—Effects of Childhood Bilingualism.* (Reprinted from *Elementary English,* Feb. 1962, p. 132-143; April 1962, p. 358-366). Champaign, Illinois: National Council of Teachers of English (1962).

Lambert, Wallace and Elizabeth Peal. The relation of bilingualism to intelligence. In Washington, D.C.: American Psychological Association, *Psychological Monographs: General and Applied,* No. 546, 76, No. 27 (1962).

Manuel, Herschel T. *Cooperative Inter-American Reading Tests.* Austin: Guidance Testing Associates, 6516 Shirley Avenue.

Moulton, William G. *Linguistics and Language Teaching in the United States, 1940-1960,* Utrecht, Netherlands: Spectrum. Also available from Superintendent of Documents, U.S. Government Printing Office, Washington, D.C. 20402 (1963).

New York Times, October 11, 1964.

Penfield, Wilder and L. Roberts. *Speech and Brain Mechanisms.* Princeton: Princeton University Press , chapter 9 (1956).

Richardson, Mabel W. "An Evaluation of Certain Aspects of the Academic Achievement of Elementary Pupils in Bilingual Program," Miami: University of Miami, unpublished doctoral dissertation (1967).

Stern, H. H. (ed.). *Foreign Languages in Primary Education: The Teaching of Foreign or Second Languages to Younger Children.* (Report on an International Meeting of Experts 9-14 April, 1962, International Studies in Education), Hamburg: UNESCO Institute of Education (1963).

Twaddell, W. Freeman. Does the FL teacher have to teach English grammar? *PMLA,* 57, 2, (May 1962), p. 20.

UNESCO. *The Use of Vernacular Languages in Education.* (Monographs on Fundamental Education—VIII), Paris: UNESCO (1953).

3

TEACHING THE BILINGUAL CHILD:
RESEARCH, DEVELOPMENT AND POLICY

(A workpaper presented at the Conference for the Teacher of the
Bilingual Child, University of Texas, June 10, 1964).

ABSTRACT   *This piece focuses on the classroom and the bilingual
child, suggests a varied program of research and experimentation
needed to strengthen bilingual schooling, and identifies many of the
variable factors which must be considered. It calls for research not as
neutral assessment of the "product" of teachers' efforts, but as a
means of controlling and assessing the teaching-learning "process" and
working developmentally toward exemplary programs. References to
related research and studies serve to orient researchers interested in
bilingual schooling.*

We do not need to observe the careers of such brilliant men as Julian Green,
Salvador de Madariaga, and Joseph Conrad to know that bilingualism can be an
invaluable intellectual and social asset. Innumerable cases attest to this truism.
Nor do we need to observe many bi-illiterate speakers of two languages to know
that in some cases bilingualism correlates negatively with a full measure of personal
development. This paper assumes that whether the bilingualism of a child is to be
a strong asset or a negative factor in his life depends on the education he receives

in both languages (Anastasi and Cordova). The child in this case is the native-born American youngster whose mother tongue is not English. The concern is for both that mother tongue and English. Since it has been public school tradition in the United States either to ignore that mother tongue or to discourage its use, this paper is concerned chiefly with research efforts designed to strengthen and maintain it, on the further assumption that strengthening and maintaining the mother tongue will contribute powerfully and directly to the development of the personality and intellect and in turn increase the student's ability to learn English and through English.

On these assumptions the most important issue is unmistakable: At what age, by what means, to what degree, and in what relationship to his studies in English, should the child achieve literacy in his mother tongue?

An international "Committee of Experts" convened by UNESCO in 1951 to discuss the use of vernacular languages in education declared that "It is axiomatic that the best medium for teaching a child is his mother tongue" (UNESCO). The committee included in its report a world-wide survey showing that it is indeed generally conceded that every child should begin his formal education in his mother tongue. Nevertheless, educational practice in the United States supports the "ethnocentric illusion" that for a child born in this country English is not a foreign language, and virtually all instruction in schools is through the medium of English. It would seem, therefore, that among the research projects most needed is a series of classroom-based studies to test as a hypothesis that statement which the rest of the world considers axiomatic.

CLASSROOM-BASED RESEARCH

This research would be undertaken simultaneously in a number of situations, described typically below, and with the conditions approaching those noted in each case.

Basic plan for bilinguals

In actual practice, there are anomalies in the foreign language development policies in American education which approach the fraudulent. One of these is the situation in the American high school which results, for example, in the bilingual French-English speaking child's making the lowest grade in the French class. This anomaly, a commonplace whether in French or Spanish or German, is easy to explain if not to justify: the teacher has only a smattering competence in the foreign language and her attempts to communicate in it embarrass both herself and the native speakers in her class. I have heard teachers explain this inability to communicate with Mexican-American pupils in New Mexico by saying that the Spanish they taught and spoke was "Castilian." In addition the teacher is using a book and methods geared exclusively to the supposed needs of the monolingual majority of the class. Consequently, the bilingual students, who in most cases have more "knowledge" and mastery of the tongue than the teacher or the classmates will ever have, sit confused, neglected, and too often conclude that there is something wrong with the language they speak and with themselves for speaking it. (For extended discussion of "the language they speak," see Chapters 13 and 14.)

The same anomaly pervades the thing called FLES and every other level of language teaching: the United States government encourages a multi-million-dollar expenditure annually for language development (in both the "common" and the "neglected" languages) (GPO) but no part of the effort is directed specifically to the further development of those same languages in the more than one in ten Americans who already have a measure of native competence in them. Rather the generally unformulated, national policy is at best to ignore, at worst to stamp out, the native competence while at the same time undertaking the miracle of creating something like it in monolinguals.[1]

Development, rather than research, is called for here: application of long-known methods in many and varied experimental settings at every level, K to 16, to make each student's bilingualism all that it can be. Specifically, the experimentation here recommended focuses exclusively on the development of a high level of literacy in the non-English mother tongue (N-EMT). This is not "foreign language" or "second language" study as these are traditionally conceived and organized and does not involve monolingual speakers of English except as noted in item 6 below. In brief, each "experiment" is simply the provision of at least one class daily in mother tongue study and study through the mother tongue for all N-EMT students.

Some specific suggestions are in order, to help avoid the worst of the mistakes that mar experimentation of this kind.

1. The teacher should be a vigorous literate native speaker of the standard variant and, if possible, of the student's variant of the language. For work at the upper elementary school level and above, the teacher should have learned *through the medium of the N-EMT* the subject matter to be taught. His competence could be determined and his certification based on the results of proficiency tests such as those the Modern Language Association of America has prepared for the five common languages. Pennsylvania and New York have already used these tests for this purpose. For languages lacking such standardized tests, examination of teacher candidates could be by examining committees.

2. The N-EMT pupils would for the most part follow the normal curriculum in English. Their schedules would be adjusted, however, to provide at least one period daily in the N-EMT.

3. The N-EMT would be the exclusive medium of instruction in all N-EMT classes. From the beginning, instruction would be focused on the language per se only a minimum part of the time. The major emphasis would always be on the regular subjects of the curriculum, mathematics, science, the social studies, etc., learned through the medium of the non-English language.

4. Only native "speakers" of the non-English language would be admitted to these classes, with the single exception noted in item 6 below. The minimum

requirement for classification as a native "speaker" would be sufficient proficiency in listening comprehension to understand normal conversation and simple explanations.

5.   Given the widely varying background of such native speakers, there might be need for a pretest for placement purposes. Such a test for speakers of Spanish has been developed by the public schools of Albuquerque, New Mexico.

6.   At the high school level monolingual students who are learning the same second language could be admitted to these classes of native speakers as a special honor if they demonstrate unusual aptitude for such learning.

7.   When administratively possible, double academic credit should be granted: for the foreign language study per se, and for the work in the subject field taught through the foreign language. For example, a class in geography studied in Polish could earn credit in Polish and in geography.

8.   One class period daily would suffice for this instruction. Experimentation could be directed to the question of whether three weekly periods would be enough to develop a high enough level of literacy.

9.   Experimentation of this kind could begin without loss at any academic level, with any number of students from 2 to 35 in a class. If the number of non-English mother tongue speakers in a school is quite small, the children may well be grouped on levels of competence without too much regard for grade level. Thus, pupils in grades 1, 2, and 3 could be together, or those in 3, 4, and 5, or those in 4, 5, and 6.

10. The section in this paper on *Contrastive analyses—teaching materials* is pertinent here. Particularly important is the emphasis on learning through the language rather than concentrating solely on the language itself.

Basic to the two-language development program under discussion is the need to reinforce the non-English ethnic group's self-image as speakers of their native language. Irrespective of the extent to which their speech deviates from "cultivated standard"—and in some cases there may be virtually no deviation—they are likely to regard their language as somehow inferior, unsuited for use in one or more domains strongly dominated by the official language, and themselves as weakly representative speakers of the tongue. Here the concept of linguistic relativity, sometimes exaggeratedly espoused by descriptive linguistics, should be strongly emphasized. Whatever the speaker's dialect and idiolect it should not be suggested that he is to give it up and thereafter speak and write in another, different, "better" way. (Common observation shows that he will never forget it and will be able to return to it at will throughout his life.) Rather he is to learn *another,* a third language or language style which will be more appropriate and effective in other situations in which he might aspire to take part.

Basic Plans for Bilingual Schools
(See Chapters 2, 3, 7.)

VARIABLES AFFECTING LANGUAGE LEARNING

In Montevideo, Uruguay, there have long been K-6 second-language schools. Crandon Institute is a specific example. The case is cited from personal observation by Miss Elizabeth Keesee, Specialist for Foreign Languages, United States Office of Education. These schools have the following characteristics:

a.   All instruction is (for example) in English at all levels.

b.   Classes of about 30 students under the charge of a single teacher.

c.   All playground and out-of-class speech in Spanish. (Virtually all students are native speakers of Spanish or prefer that tongue.)

d.   Parents and students highly disposed to foreign language learning.

e.   Most students from upper or upper-middle socioeconomic class.

f.   All teachers natively competent in the school language and well trained for their work.

g.   Production of highly literate, native-like use of English in all students.

There are similar schools in Texas where all or virtually all of the pupils are native speakers of Spanish and where English is the sole medium of instruction. The analogy with the Montevideo situation weakens at items *d, e,* and *f,* which, it may be reasonably hypothesized, contributed much to the achievement of item *g.* These three variables should be investigated, with the object of modifying the school situation so as to offset or overcome pupil deficiencies attributable to them (Lambert, Gardner).

ANALOGY AND INFERENCE VS. ANALYSIS

A major question besetting foreign language teachers is the shifting inter-relation between learning by analogy and learning by analysis at each stage or maturity level from infancy to adulthood. "Traditional" language teaching methods have relied heavily on analysis; "audio-lingual" methodology purports to depend heavily on analogy. If all pupils began language learning in grade one there would be no problem. Since there are in fact beginning groups at ages 6 to 25 and older, one pattern cannot fit them all. An approach to this problem could be made by a study of the *age of onset and relative strength at each age level* of the components of language learning aptitude isolated by Carroll and Sapon, the motivational and attitudinal factors described by Lambert and his associates, plus ability to reason by analogy and inference basic to all first language learning. Armed with the results of such study the language teacher could better adjust his dosage of analogy (pattern drill, overlearning) and analysis (rules, explanations) to suit his learners.

Since analogical reasoning (I walked, I talked, *ergo*, I runned) and inferential determination of meaning (for example each of us knows thousands of "words" but only a few score or hundreds were learned consciously by dictionary or other word study) are basic to first language learning and in lesser degree to second language mastery, there is need for a study of these two processes and for the development of teaching procedures which will (1) make students aware of their function, (2) give step-by-step practice in the conscious application of both processes, and (3) exploit both processes at every point in the language course (Lagrone et al.).

FOREIGN LANGUAGE, LITERARY STUDIES, AND OTHER ACADEMIC FIELDS

The traditional curricular pattern in American colleges and universities—and in secondary schools offering more than two years of foreign language study—has produced a mutually supporting relationship between language study and only one other academic field: literary studies. This has meant that following the "introductory" and "intermediate" courses (and sometimes a bit of "advanced composition," or "conversation"), the only further formal courses involving foreign language have been courses in the corresponding literature. This practice leaves out of account the possibility that some students might wish to do advanced study in a foreign language applied to specialization in an academic field other than literature.

Notable deviations from the language-to-literature tradition are found in those institutions which offer work in the "neglected" languages. It is not unusual for the courses in such languages as Chinese, Arabic, or Persian to have been introduced at the insistence of "area" specialists as a means of strengthening advanced offerings in their fields (Axelrod and Bigelow). This is not the case with the more commonly taught languages.

It seems particularly important to provide for bilinguals at the college level the opportunity to capitalize on their non-English language by professional specialization, in, for example, political science, international law or relations, anthropology, or economics, related specifically to foreign regions where that language is spoken. This would require developing the same strong, mutually-reinforcing relationship between foreign language study and other fields as now exists only for literary studies. A good deal of preliminary work along this line has been done at Goucher College in Baltimore for majors in International Relations and Political Science, including the expansion of library holdings, indices of periodicals, preparation of a tape library of speeches, etc., presentation of portions of courses through the foreign language, requirement of oral and written reporting in the language, and portions of tests and final examinations to be written in the language (Corrin).

COOPERATION WITH ORGANIZED ETHNIC GROUPS

Nationwide there are ethnic groups, societies, churches, and parochial schools with a strong commitment to the maintenance and development of competence in a language other than English. Judged in the light of a policy which considers competence in modern foreign languages as a national asset, the efforts of these groups should be strongly encouraged, supported, and coordinated where feasible with those of the public schools. Within the limited context of this paper the salient needs are two:

1. Language materials and instruction-through-language materials for such teaching.
2. Standardized tests suitable for use in grades 4, 6, 8, 10, and 12 to measure achievement in the four language skills.

COMMUNITY- AND REGION-BASED RESEARCH
Studies of Dialect Variation

Any effort to develop the full potential of the bilingualism of native American speakers of a language other than English could profit from answers to two questions:

1. What is the range of dialect variation within the entire community of American speakers of that language?
2. How does the dialect variant of the particular group of speakers under consideration differ from the standard variant which they want to learn?

This information is essential to the production of teaching materials, particularly for use in secondary schools and above. The most casual observation will show marked differences, for example, between the Spanish spoken in the northern Rio Grande Valley and that of San Antonio. Are these regional differences marked enough to warrant different teaching materials for students in the two areas?

Languages in Contact

Much needs to be done to clarify the changing status of the two languages in contact in the bilingual at every level. Of particular interest in the context of this paper—apart from basic linguistic surveys of each bilingual speech community—are linguistic *interference, borrowings,* and *switching.* These matters are treated in great detail by Haugen and Weinreich, and both authors suggest many approaches to research. Pertinent to these issues is Fishman's observation that " . . . if a strict domain separation becomes institutionalized such that each language is associated with a number of important but distinct domains, bilingualism can become both universal and stabilized even though an entire population consists of bilinguals interacting with other bilinguals."

SOCIOLOGICAL STUDIES OF PEOPLES IN CONTACT

Because it is constantly changing, the dynamics of a two-language community—whether a neighborhood, an entire town or a region—can never be sufficiently studied. Research of the kind done by Oscar Lewis and his associates in Tepoztlan (Mexico) if performed in the typical American setting where two peoples, each with its own mother tongue, come in contact exclusively through only one of those languages, the socially dominant one, would help the teacher, the school administrator, and the policy makers to act more wisely. To be most useful this research should show both the anthropologist's concern for the dynamics of belief and behavior systems under stress and in contact, and the scientific linguist's awareness of language as a factor in interpersonal and inter-group relationships.

Research on the conflict of two languages within the individual personality requires first that the investigator realize that for a child whose mother tongue is not English, English is a foreign language. The difficulty of grasping this point is typified in the Kohut-Lerea research reported here in the reference to Wallace Lambert and Elizabeth Peal. These highly sophisticated researchers, referring to the 25 Polish-, three Norwegian-, and two Greek-speaking children they worked with, said, "The bilingual subjects in this study acquired a dual language system because of exposure to a second language in the home."

ATTITUDE FORMATION

The work of Wallace Lambert and his associates indicates strongly that the mastery of a second language depends on two independent sets of factors, intelligence and aptitude on the one hand, and on the other hand a complex of motivation and attitudes vis-à-vis the people and culture represented by the second language. Lambert's social-psychological theory of language learning affirms that " . . . the learner's ethnocentric tendencies and his attitudes toward the other group are believed to determine his success in learning the new language (Lambert 1963). Here Lambert refers particularly to "success" in the degree that identifies the learner with the second language community, i.e., including native-like mastery of phonology. In the light of this theory there is in the American Southwest, Louisiana, and Canadian-French New England marked ethnocentrism, an authoritarian orientation and unfavorable attitudes in both the English and non-English groups of speakers. There is more than a suggestion of a cruel dilemma if Lambert's "integrative" attitude (studying as if one desired to become a member of the other group) is required in order to produce the highest degree of second language mastery. In this case the research need is prompted by the fact that psychologists are currently working on the problem of changing attitudes. It therefore suggests itself that studies and experiments directed toward the formation of more favorable attitudes and motivations in the Lambertian sense might be fruitful.

BILINGUAL DOMINANCE CONFIGURATION

Without denying the likelihood that most speakers of a given age and socioeconomic level in an area of stable population will speak alike, it must be recognized too that members of a minority group, speakers of a subordinate language, in a period of linguistic transition where youngsters sometimes cannot communicate with their grandparents, in areas of marked urban vs. rural differences (some of them traversed annually by uneven waves of illiterate or semi-literate foreign national migrant speakers of the same tongue) subjected on every side to forces of acculturation, all attending schools of greatly varying excellence and where all instruction is given in a dominant language, all part of an increasingly mobile society—the members of such a minority group may also differ widely among themselves in their use of both their native language and the dominant one. That is to say, their bilingualism will show wide variations in pattern, quite apart from the relative excellence of their use of the language. They will differ with respect to their *active or passive* control of the language (Does the "bilingual" think in the language? Does he both understand and speak it? Can he write? Or only read?); with respect to the *situation* where the language is used (Home? Church? Club? Work? With his children? Or only with his parents? With his boss as well as his subordinates? In public?); and with respect to *topics and styles* of usage (Can he discuss religion, the malfunctioning of his automobile, his profession, in both languages? Can he send and receive at each stylistic level as well in one language as in the other?) Are there technical or stylistic gaps in his vocabulary? All of the above is to say that there is immediate need for the construction of a survey instrument which will determine the *bilingual dominance configuration* of a given group or individual (Fishman, 1964).

It is important to know the "dominance configuration" of any bilingual group that becomes a subject of study, for at least three reasons:

1. With such knowledge those charged with the education of the bilingual child or adult are better equipped to appraise him and prepare a course of study for him.

2. The dominance configuration, determined periodically and combined with tests of language proficiency, would be the surest means of determining changes in the status of language maintenance and language shift in bilingual speech communities.

3. It seems likely that an accurate index of bilingual dominance would be a powerful weapon in support of the position that "balanced" bilinguals will not score below monolinguals in tests of both verbal and non-verbal intelligence. Armed with an adequate instrument for determining the bilingual dominance configuration, it would be possible to replicate, in effect, in any of our bilingual areas, the Peal-Lambert study of bilingual ten-year-olds in Montreal which gave strong evidence that *if the children are*

equally well educated in both languages, i.e., "balanced" bilinguals, they are superior in both verbal and non-verbal intelligence to monolinguals, and also appear to have greater mental flexibility, a superiority in concept formation, and a more diversified set of mental abilities.

RESEARCH BASED ON THE BILINGUAL INDIVIDUAL
Interviews-in-depth of "balanced" bilinguals

Despite conditions of learning which do not favor the development of highly literate "balanced bilingualism" in Americans who enter school with a mother tongue other than English, some individuals do achieve this goal. It is hypothesized that a study of a representative sample of such persons would produce information of value to educators concerned with the bilingual child. The need here is for a survey instrument with which to conduct interviews-in-depth of adults identified as "highly literate balanced bilinguals." "Balance" in this case cannot be expected to mean absolute parity, since this is always impossible. Rather it would mean a relatively equal number of important domains associated with each language, and relatively equal literacy in each. The difficulty of identifying such persons except by personal observation suggests that this research might follow the development of the index of bilingual dominance configuration noted elsewhere in this paper.

STUDIES OF SECOND-LANGUAGE ACQUISITION

There is urgent need for a study of second-language acquisition under "natural" (coordinate) conditions at at least three age levels, infancy, six years, and 15 years to determine the sequence of learnings in the three language systems: phonology, morphology and syntax. Each such study should be conducted with the assistance of a person competent in descriptive linguistics in order to note the complete process of developing phonemic discrimination (Weir). By "natural" conditions is meant total immersion in the second language environment in a school and play situation, e.g., a monolingual American child placed in a French-language boarding school in France. Such a study could provide invaluable insights into the sequencing of second language learning materials.

Along with this day-by-day study of the acquisition of a second language to the point where the basic structures of the language have been mastered, there is need for longitudinal studies of the development of the bilingual children through the twelfth grade.

BILINGUALISM AND A THIRD LANGUAGE

There is much informal, usually subjective, evidence to support the belief that bilingualism acquired by natural means facilitates the learning of a third language. It is also quite common to be told that the second language should be taught in such a manner as to facilitate the later acquisition of a third. This latter is especially so because although most Americans have little opportunity in school to study any language other than French, German, or Spanish, many might find in later years a greater need for Chinese, Polish, or Twi. The research indicated in this connection is on two levels:

1.   Development of objective evidence (possibly through case studies of individuals) of the relationship of bilingualism to third language learning and the conditions and mechanisms by which the relationship manifests itself.

2.   Application of those conditions and mechanisms to the formal school learning of a second language in order to facilitate maximally the learning of a third one.

TEACHING MATERIALS

The immediate need is for a study of the range of dialect variation. Thereafter, work should begin on an analysis of the standard form contrasted with each dialectical variant to facilitate the production of teaching materials. The third step would be the teaching materials themselves (Brault) designed for presentation through that language and with at least the following features:

1.   intensive oral drill from recorded patterns;

2.   extensive reading and listening to recorded literature;

3.   extensive use of sound films on technical and other subjects to broaden the student's horizon and sense of his own possibilities;

4.   controlled composition;

5.   increasing emphasis on learning through the language rather than learning the language as an end in itself.

In order to deal with the most notable stylistic variations, there is need for a body of materials (in both printed and recorded form) consisting of short selections—usually paragraphs—of exposition, narration, dialogue, etc., graded by difficulty and each presented in variant forms corresponding to the levels of style distinguished in Joos' *The Five Clocks.* It is not suggested that such materials would fill the stylistic gaps in the vocabulary of "unbalanced" bilinguals but they could be used to develop an awareness of those levels.

NOTE

1. See the introductory statement, Title I, Sec. 101 of the NDEA "Findings and Declaration of Policy": "The Congress hereby finds and declares that the security of the Nation requires the fullest development of the mental resources and technical skills of its young men and women. . . . This requires programs that will . . . correct . . . the existing imbalances in our educational programs which have led to an insufficient proportion of our population educated in . . . modern foreign languages . . ."

REFERENCES

Anastasi, A., and F. Cordova, "Some Effects of Bilingualism upon Intelligence Test Performance of Puerto Rican Children in New York City." *Journal of Educational Psychology,*
44, No. 1 (January, 1953). These researchers reached the typical conclusion: "Whether
or not bilingualism constitutes a handicap, as well as the extent of such a handicap,
depends upon the way in which the two languages have been learned. . . " p. 3.

Axelrod, Joseph, and Donald N. Bigelow. *Resources for Language and Area Studies* (A Report
on an Inventory of the Language and Area Centers Supported by the National Defense
Education Act of 1958), Washington, D.C.: American Council on Education (1962).

Brault, Gerard S. *Cours de langue française destiné aux jeunes Franco-Americains,* Philadelphia:
University of Pennsylvania (1963). Also pertinent is the research of Ruth I. Golden
reported in *Effectiveness of Instructional Tapes for Changing Regional Speech Patterns*
(final report on U.S. Office of Education Title VII project No. 559), Detroit (Michigan)
Public Schools (1962).

Carroll, John B. "A factor analysis of two foreign language aptitude batteries," *The Journal
of General Psychology,* 59 (1958), pp. 3-19.

Carroll, John B., and Stanley M. Sapon. *Modern Language Aptitude Test* (MLAT). New York:
Psychological Corporation (1958).

Corrin, Brownlee Sands. *Research on Values and Uses of Foreign Languages for Instruction
and Study in the Social Sciences* (Political Science and International Relations),
Baltimore: Goucher College (1962).

Fishman, Joshua (1964). The problem of devising an instrument to determine the "bilingual
dominance configuration" has been analyzed in Dr. Fishman's unpublished paper,
"Domains of Language Behavior in Multilingual Settings," (Yeshiva University, 1964).
Uriel Weinreich proposed a dominance configuration on a different basis: op. cit. pp.
74-80. Lambert and Peal judged bilingual "balance" by combining an association
fluency test, a picture vocabulary test and other measures. Also see Lambert's article
"Measurement of the linguistic dominance of bilinguals," *Journal of Abnormal and
Social Psychology,* 50 (1955), pp. 197-200.

Gardner, Robert C., and Wallace F. Lambert. "Motivational Variables in second-language
acquisition" in *Canadian Journal of Psychology,* 13 (1959), pp. 266-272.

GPO. *Report on the National Defense Education Act—Fiscal Years 1961 and 1962,* U.S.
Department of Health, Education, and Welfare, Office of Education, publication
OE-10004-62, U.S. Government Printing Office, Washington, D.C. (1963).

Haugen, Einar. *Bilingualism in the Americas: A Bibliography and Research Guide.* American
Dialect Society Publication, University of Alabama Press (1956).

Joos, Martin, *The Five Clocks. International Journal of American Linguistics,* 28, No. 2, Part
V (1962).

Lagrone, Gregory, Andrea McHenry, Patricia O'Connor, et al. "Developing Reading Skills,"
in *Teacher's Manual for Español: Hablar y Leer,* New York: Holt, Rinehart and
Winston, 1962, pp. ix-xiv. Aaron S. Carton (with Nancy Magaud) "The Method of
Inference" in *Foreign Language Study.* New York: The Research Foundation of the
City University of New York (1966).

Lambert, Wallace. "Psychological Approaches to the Study of Language," *The Modern
Language Journal,* XLVII, No. 3 (March, 1963), p. 114.

Lambert, Wallace, and Elizabeth Peal, "The Relation of Bilingualism to Intelligence"
Psychological Monographs: General and Applied, No. 546, 76, No. 27, 1962
(American Psychological Association, 1333 16th St., N.W., Washington, D.C.). Cf. also
Louis Lerea and Suzanne M. Kobut, "A Comparative Study of Monolinguals and

Bilinguals in a Verbal Task Performance," *Journal of Clinical Psychology,* XVII, No. 1 (January, 1961), pp. 49-52.

Lambert, Wallace, Robert C. Gardner, R. Olton, and K. Tunstall. *A Study of the roles of attitudes and motivation in second-language learning.* Mimeographed. McGill University 1961. For an overview of the relation between intelligence and socioeconomic status see Kenneth Eells, Allison Davis, Robert J. Havighurst, Virgil E. Herrick, and Ralph W. Tyler, *Intelligence and Cultural Differences.* Chicago: The University of Chicago Press (1951).

Lewis, Oscar. *Life in a Mexican Village: Tepoztlan Restudied.* Urbana, Illinois: University of Illinois Press (1963). Oddly enough, although Tepoztlan is a bilingual community Lewis gives virtually no attention to the language problem. For the linguist's orientation to these matters cf. John J. Gumperz, "Types of linguistic communities," and Joan Rubin, "Bilingualism in Paraguay," both in *Anthropological Linguistics,* 4, No. 1 (January 1962), pp. 52-58.

UNESCO. *The Use of Vernacular Languages in Education* (Monographs on Fundamental Education—VIII), UNESCO, Paris (1953), p. 11. Other studies of particular interest in this regard and basic to the topic of this paper are: Pedro A. Cebollero, *A School Language Policy for Puerto Rico.* Superior Educational Council of Puerto Rico. Educational Publications Series II, No. 1 (1945); and H. H. Stern, (ed.) *Foreign Languages in Primary Education: The Teaching of Foreign or Second Languages to Younger Children.* Report on an International Meeting of Experts (9-14 April, 1962); International Studies in Education, UNESCO Institute for Education, Hamburg (1963). Contains a chapter "Research problems concerning the teaching of foreign or second languages to younger children" by John B. Carroll.

Weinrich, Uriel. *Languages in Contact, Findings and Problems.* New York: Publication of the Linguistic Circle of New York, No. 1 (1953); also the Hague: Mouton,(1963).

Weir, Ruth Hirsch. *Language in the Crib.* The Hague: Mouton and Co. (1962). See also Werner E. Leopold's classic study *Speech Development of a Bilingual Child.* 4 vols., Evanston, Ill.: Northwestern University Press (1939-50).

4

THE FIRST SEVENTY-SIX
BILINGUAL EDUCATION PROJECTS

ABSTRACT   *The essay provides an analytical scheme and criteria for judging the probable effectiveness of bilingual schooling projects, applies the scheme and criteria to the first seventy-six such projects funded by the Office of Education under the Bilingual Education Act, and offers some comments and criticism of the entire program.*

This essay examines certain salient features of the plans of operation of the first seventy-six bilingual schooling projects supported by grants under the Bilingual Education Act. It reveals what appears to be, in a large majority of them, such inadequate attention—time, resources, and understanding—to the other tongue, as compared to the attention paid to English that, on the whole, the concept of bilingual education represented by these plans of operation seems to be something less than the legislation and its advocates intended. I say "appears" and "seems" because the analysis was made from close reading of the official plans of operation, plus addenda and other correspondence in the files of the U.S. Office of Education, plus returns from a questionnaire sent to the project directors, rather than from direct observation of the projects in action. The qualifiers are required too because the development of language competency in children takes several years, and at this writing only the first half-year of the five years of the supporting grants has elapsed.[1]

The Congress couched its extraordinarily generous and innovative legislation in support of dual-language public schooling in terms that permit both the ethnocentrists and the cultural pluralists to see what they want to see in the Act. It could mean the merest token obeisance to the non-English mother tongue (N-EMT) and the culture it represents, or it could—as a fictitious example—support production for one of the American Indian tribal groups of a full panoply of teaching materials in their language for all the school subjects, the complete training of a corps of native speakers of that language and full implementation of the resulting curriculum from kindergarten through the twelfth grade, plus schooling for the parents in their native tongue. English, of course, could never be excluded.

The Office of Education has interpreted bilingual education officially to mean the use of two languages, one of which is English, as mediums of instruction . . . for the same student population, in a well-organized program which encompasses part or all of the curriculum, plus study of the history and culture associated with a student's mother tongue.

As one might expect, of the 76 projects some—quite within their rights—proposed the use of the child's mother tongue for purposes of instruction as a "bridge" to English, to be crossed as soon as possible and then eliminated entirely or virtually so in favor of English as the sole medium. With these our special quarrel is that the bridge seems usually to be a one-way affair with no encouragement to pass back and forth freely, and is sometimes so short as perhaps not to reach the other side of the abyss. Most of the projects have planned to give a much more substantial role to the mother tongue as a medium of instruction in the regular school subjects. Many profess to aim for equal emphasis on the two languages and seek to develop in their pupils equal competence in the two. Here it is evident in most cases that, whether consciously or unconsciously, the emphasis is very far from equal.

In the plans of operation of all of the projects, there is a profession of emphasis on the "history and culture" of the child who has a mother tongue other than English. They want to strengthen his "sense of identity," his "self-concept." Here—as will be seen later in this essay—the disparity between aims and means is enormous. Every project attempts to provide improved and intensified instruction in English. This component, in most cases the principal focus of the project plan, cannot be described in this limited essay. Finally, each plan provides in-service training for its project teachers and aides, and occasionally, for other personnel. Suffice it to say, for the purpose of this brief overview, that the in-service training included in most cases a short orientation session before the fall term began, and periodic sessions are held during the academic year focused on the other culture, the teaching of English as a second language, and the teaching of and through the N-EMT. The important point to note is that this work is conducted in the great majority of the cases by the local project director or the bilingual coordinator.

A brief overview of the entire program would show 76 separate projects in 70 different cities, each project to be funded for 5 years if work is performed satisfactorily.

Breakdown of Projects

Language (in addition to English)		Projects
Spanish		68
Spanish and Sioux	1	
Spanish and Pomo	1	
Spanish and Keresan and Navajo	1	
Spanish and Chinese	1	
Mexican-Americans	58	
Puerto Ricans	7	
Puerto Ricans and one other		
language group	2	
mixed Spanish-speaking	2	
Cherokee		2
Chinese (Cantonese)		1
(plus the one noted above)		
French		1
Japanese		1
Navajo		1
(plus the one noted above)		
Portuguese		2
		76
In elementary schools only		54
In secondary schools only		8
In both		14

Most projects have begun the first year very modestly, with only one or a few classes of pupils at one or two grade levels only. Some are more ambitious. All expect to expand year by year for five years.

Total first year cost of 76 projects	$7,500,000
Average cost	98,684

Are the "other-medium" teachers (those expected to teach some or all of the regular school subject areas through the children's mother tongue) adequately prepared for bilingual schooling? There is evidence that most of them are not. In most of the plans of operation the qualifications of the staff are carefully set forth. Forty-nine call for mere "bilingualism," or "conversational ability" in the other tongue. Six want "fluent" bilinguals; at least one specifies the ability to read, write, and speak the two languages; some say the teachers will be "hopefully" or "preferably" bilinguals. On the other hand, eleven either identified or demanded well-qualified people; and in fifteen there is at least one person educated abroad and some were seeking one or more such teachers. The ethnic groups differ markedly in respect to teacher qualification, with the highest requirements found among those with easiest access to literacy, notably the Portuguese, Chinese, French, and Puerto Ricans.

In about 20 cases the plans contain no requirement that the director and other key project leaders be more than "bilingual," and in at least 28 cases not even that limited knowledge of the non-English tongue is demanded. Again, in a score of cases the specific requirements for the director and other key persons in respect to competence in the other language and the culture it represents are high.

The above and following comments on teacher adequacy should be read with the knowledge that to a large extent the projects expect to depend on the teaching services of aides, sometimes called para-professionals, "bilingual" individuals usually drawn from the community, rarely required to be literate in the non-English tongue, and paid disproportionately low wages. Sometimes the aides work with bilingual teachers. In other projects only the aides are expected to be bilingual, and the regular teachers, the "master" teachers are Anglos. Much can be said in favor of bringing into the schools persons who represent fully the usually under represented ethnic minorities. But if those representatives obviously have less professional status, less training, less authority and receive less money than the teachers, the other-medium side of the project is getting less than a full, fair trial.

One plan calls for 40 bilingual aides at two dollars per hour to "encourage and energize the parents." In another plan of operation for grade one (and eventually grades 1-3) the aides alone are to be bilingual, their English must be "demonstrably competent," but they need only "conversational competency" in the other tongue. Yet the hope is that they somehow are to be given "the factual basis to permit a useful comparison and analysis of the differences between Spanish and English as spoken languages in the classroom" and are expected to prepare teaching materials. In still another case the merely bilingual kindergarten and preschool aides will be given in-service training in language development in both tongues in "contrasting usage, translation, relationships, vocabulary development, concept development, and pronunciation," and they are expected to "improve the oral language facility" of both pupils and parents.

What is mere, hopeful, even fluent bilingualism or "conversational ability" in two languages? Since most of the projects plan to use their own local teachers, and since the American school system has provided virtually no opportunity for child speakers of non-English languages to maintain and develop those languages—indeed, it has commonly discouraged and denigrated such speaking—the merely bilingual person is a product of the very kind of schooling which bilingual education aims to correct. Members in most cases of social groups with strong oral traditions rather than literary ones, given a first chance at literacy at age 15 in the ninth grade under Anglo foreign language teachers who seldom speak the child's tongue and invariably use books designed for Anglo beginners, how many such bilinguals will have read as many as five books or written 50 pages in their mother tongue? There is indeed the possibility of college study of the tongue, and in some few cases the *vita* notes such college work. The most favored case recorded notes that each teacher has at least 21 college semester hours of Spanish. An elementary school teacher with a college major in a foreign language is a rarity indeed, and none turned up in the data. Nor is the weakness lessened by the assurance of two directors (who had set no special requirements for their bilingual aides) that the secretary is expected "to read and write" and "translate the materials." A third plan of operations sets no requirements beyond "bilingualism" for the teachers, but specifies that the project secretary must be proficient in writing both languages: "Accurate spelling and punctuation is a priority need for the secretary."

A quick look at what the other-medium teachers and aides are usually expected to do affirms the weakness of their training. "They are expected to teach through the non-English tongue such subject fields as mathematics, science, the social studies, and language arts." There is a common belief that the person who speaks two languages can say anything in one that he can say in the other. That is simply not true. The most common situation finds such a speaker facile in one or more "domains" of usage in one language, and in other domains in the other. Perhaps small talk and intimacy in one, business and formality in the other. Facility in the terminology of a game or a sport or a technology in one language, expression of religious feeling in the other. Arithmetic in only one. Professional matters in only one. Everyday affairs can probably be conducted in either, but no one can stand up and invent authentic translations of mathematics teaching terminology or the terminology of any other school subject.

"They are expected in most of the projects to create or assist in the creation of teaching materials in the non-English tongue." Little need be said here to make the point. It is currently lauded pedagogy to encourage teachers to choose freely among teaching materials and adapt them as needed in order to adjust to the pupils' individual differences, but how many teachers can be expected to write their own books? A few project plans of operation gave examples of locally produced writing in the other tongue. Some were well done. Most are exemplified by the following:

A formal letter:
Hemos estado trabajando bajo considerable obstáculos con respeto a la escritura de la proposición. . . . La fecha . . . adelantada dos días para darles el beneficio de discusiones . . . .

A printed announcement:
Si Ud. desea conversar con el professor, por favor márquelo en el espacio destinado a ello. . . . Su firma justificará que Ud. revisó la libreta de notas. . . . Poner una nota es algo muy importante en la Escuela, además de ser el deseo de las Escuelas Públicas de _____ , a fin de interpretar mejor a los alumnos y ayudar así a los padres. . . . Para un avance satisfactorio, es indispensable una asistencia regular y a tiempo. . . . *Hábitos De trabajo* Significa que siempre debe estar preparado con sus materiales y tareas, siga y escuche las direcciones que se le dan.

A formal letter to the parents:
. . . Uds. puede ayudar a su niño tener éxito en el colegio.

A formal printed announcement:
Hablando diariamente, escuchando, leyendo y escribiendo, son las pericias del idioma inglés. . . . Substantivos vívidos y verbos como *canyon* y *amontonar* se acentúan.

Educational theory about success in school:
El suceso de un niño. . . .

Teaching materials:
Si alguien en un carro quiere que vaya con el, tenga cortes, pero marchase y no entre su carro.
Maria, agarra tres pelotas. Ensename dos modos para decirme que tienes tres pelotas.

Formal publication:
Advancemos: Mano en Mano

Must one be a pedant to be disturbed by these examples of inordinate influence from English and violation of the structure of Spanish? I think not, for the implication in all but possibly one of the Title VII project plans is that the other-language medium, whether Spanish, Cantonese, French, or whatever, will be its "standard" form. No one has yet claimed that San Francisco Cantonese, the Portuguese of Providence, and the Spanish of San Antonio are separate linguistic systems whose exquisite aberrations should be polished and respected and set apart from the vulgar standard by their own contrastive analyses. One plan states that its bilingual teacher aides will be trained in "standard South American Spanish." The exception noted calls for someone to prepare "material in barrio Spanish," but not to the exclusion of standard writings.

In one plan the measurement of behavioral objectives includes listening to tapes of three sentences each in Castilian Spanish and British English and repeating them in "Mexican Spanish" and "United States English." This particular plan of operation emphasizes speech and drama at the junior high school level.

Since almost all of the project plans require the same bilingual teachers to be responsible for both the non-English and the English side of the program, these teachers are expected to represent and present authentically, fully, fairly, two cultures: that of the United States and that of the non-English mother tongue child's forbears. In most cases they must somehow interpret a third culture, the amalgam, because the Puerto Ricans in continental United States, and Mexican-Americans and Franco-Americans find that their cultural patterns are in essential ways different from either of the two parent cultures.

It is at the bastion of biculturalism rather than at the bastion of language alone that bilingual education will succeed or fail, and it is here that the doubts gnaw most painfully.

First of all, is it fair to expect a product of the amalgam, a product of the educational system and policy which bilingual education seeks to correct, to represent fairly and powerfully both of the parent cultures? Does not bicultural-ism—a word which appears repeatedly in the projects' aims—imply double perspective, not the perspective of two eyes, but of two pairs of eyes? The use of the same persons to explicate both cultures—rather than two sets of persons, one for the English medium and United States culture, one for the non-English medium and the culture it carries—is matched in a number of project plans by the decision to have the teachers and aides themselves produce the classroom materials dealing with the other history and culture. In some projects the history books and others in this area will be translations of United States, English-language texts.

The following examples illustrate some of the ambivalence and uncertainty regarding the other-tongue history and culture:

> One project means to establish in the children "a detachment towards the Spanish and English languages to enable the student to function in either his native or Anglo-Culture (sic) whenever he so chooses." Can language be thus successfully detached from culture?

> One program "encompasses bilingualism with diglossia," by which is meant ". . . the socio-cultural context in which language learning takes place." But "many children's books have been translated into Spanish" (not, it should be understood, by the project's personnel) and "children's songs, singing games, and rhythmic activities will be translated into Spanish. . . ."

> In one plan the Mexican-American child is expected, on completion of the "Texas Government and History" course through Spanish, to demonstrate "respect for himself as an individual by over (sic) acceptance of various levels of ability and differing physical characteristics in others." Could this be the same as acceptance of one's lot?

> "Cultural readings for literature, interdisciplinary materials from the social sciences and science materials will be translated (to Spanish) and modified for language instruction." Yet the purpose of these culturally oriented materials is supposedly to develop pride in the child's own heritage, to give him a new point of view, not merely the same one presented through another language.

> In still another project, the teacher responsible for bicultural activities must have a high degree of competency in both tongues "because of requirements of both accurate and idiomatic translations."

As noted, the applicant for a Title VII bilingual education project has the right to propose the degree of emphasis on the non-English language and culture that his wisdom dictates. This is not the same, however, as declaring intention to do one thing and then, unwittingly, describing conditions which can be expected to frustrate that intention.

> One project expects to develop the ability of all children, both N-EMT and EMT (English mother tongue), to pursue ordinary school subjects in either language, but it will teach the language arts and mathematics to N-EMT children in that tongue only enough to avoid retardation.

One project seeks "to develop his [the child's] ability to function in and through two languages" and develop his "competence needed to employ two linguistic systems separately and consciously as mediums for speaking (reading and writing) and thinking in the total curriculum. . . ." But in the third year of the project, reading in Spanish will be included only if sufficient funding is available and community approval can be determined, and such subjects as mathematics will be taught in English only. Two other projects are virtually identical in this respect.

A hint of some notion of the concept of diglossia comes in one plan of operation which seeks to develop "coordinate bilingualism." The plan states that ". . . those areas in which the student must succeed in high school and college—for example, mathematics—will be taught in English . . ." and "those areas which the student associates with his own background, for example, native literature . . ." will be taught in Spanish.

One project means to "develop curriculum authentic in respect to Mexican-American culture," but for the program development specialists there is a formal requirement of expertise in setting "behavioral objectives" and no such requirement as a knowledge of Spanish.

One project aims at a "true, balanced bilingual program," but "English will become the major medium of instruction during the second grade."

In one of the plans, which provides work through the N-EMT in language, mathematics, and the social studies, only the aides are bilingual. The children show that they are learning "by responding in classes where the real teacher is Anglo to or through translators (sic) if necessary."

The plans of operation of the 76 projects are not entirely clear about the amount of time that will be devoted each day to instruction using the N-EMT as the medium. There is uncertainty on this point because the expression "bilingual program" sometimes means both tongues, sometimes only the N-EMT. Thus, in one, the "bilingual" part is four hours daily, but the breakdown, during the first quarter year, is three hours of ESL, and one of history taught through English and the N-EMT; and during the second quarter there are two hours of ESL, and two hours of history divided between the two languages. At least four programs favor the N-EMT. Thirty-four are either bridges or favor English markedly. Only six aim eventually to provide bilingual schooling at all grade levels, 1-12.

One project seems to have scheduled only 10-15 minutes' work daily in the other language. Another aims "to provide an opportunity for any student to become truly bilingual," yet it schedules only 25 minutes daily for the mother tongue as a medium.

The adverse criticism explicit and implied in much of the foregoing is not the whole story. Many strong, promising features are to be found among the 76 projects.

Both Albuquerque and Grants, New Mexico, see clearly that mere bilingualism does not prepare a teacher for this work.

Brentwood, California makes a point of the need for full literacy in both languages for teachers and aides.

Chicago makes two important points: (1) that the "bilingual" is not necessarily "bicultural" and may not be able to interpret fairly the other culture; for this purpose they want foreign exchange teachers, and (2) they clearly separate the languages, one in the morning, the other in the afternoon. New Haven also stresses the importance of not mixing the languages during a single class period.

One of the Del Rio, Texas projects has called on experienced teachers from Mexico for help with Spanish-medium tests, and has planned one three-day in-service training session in Acuña, Mexico. Edinburg, Texas arranged for its teacher trainers and the teacher in charge of Spanish language literacy to come from Mexico.

Gonzalez, California sees the importance of employing teachers who are "conversant with Spanish language approaches to the subjects taught," and declares that its staff "will make an effort to avoid producing materials in areas where specialized professional competence is of prime importance." The Naples, Florida project also stresses the employment of teachers able to give training through Spanish in all subject areas.

The Lansing project expects its other-medium teachers to have the baccalaureate and both bilingual and bicultural skills: ". . . ability to discuss in Spanish some of the major language learning problems of the bilingual child and the history and culture of the Spanish-speaking American."

Laredo, Texas (Laredo Independent School District) seemingly alone among the projects, recognizes the extra burdens of dual-medium teachers and has budgeted an annual bonus of 300 dollars for each one. Its plan also calls for bringing from Mexico a special teacher to be in charge of staff and materials development. The Laredo project's bilingual teachers are required to take the Modern Language Association Proficiency Test (in Spanish) for teachers and advanced students.

The Laredo, Texas (United Consolidated Independent School District) bilingual teachers all have earned at least 21 college semester hours in Spanish.

The New York Bronx project includes a six-week summer extension, three hours daily, alternating the languages, in language, reading, and mathematics. The New York Two Bridges project plan offers half of each day for native tongue subject matter classes, and views itself as building a bridge not to English, but on which the children can move easily back and forth.

The Providence, Rhode Island plan seeking to assure that the N-EMT children develop full capacity for conceptualization through the mother tongue, gives less than equal time to English until the participants are in their fourth year of school. English as a second language study begins, nevertheless, in grade one, and they expect to achieve beginning literacy in

English in grade two. They employ different teachers for each medium and secure educated, experienced trainers from abroad for the N-EMT work.

Milwaukee sees the importance of uniting its bilingual schooling project with the efforts of its regular foreign language teachers at the high school level and will offer a history and culture course for both groups of students together.

The Rochester project provides different teachers for each of the mediums, insists on high literacy of all teachers and aides, plus demonstrated ability to teach school subjects through Spanish, and keeps the languages separated in time and place.

Whatever the strengths, whatever the weaknesses of the 76 bilingual schooling projects (and this essay gleaned from written accounts rather than direct observation cannot describe them with complete certainty), they need help. If bilingual schooling, the noblest innovation in American education, is to succeed, it must have close, objective, encouraging attention from all sides. The projects need, above all else, formative evaluation by knowledgeable outside observers who—with the gentle pressure of the Office of Education's authority and responsibility to continue each grant only so long as the work is performed satisfactorily—can help each project to become a model of its kind. Without radical strengthening some could probably never become models. They should either be strengthened or abandoned.

Bilingual schooling needs assistance from research-oriented scholars and other investigators who will answer some of the questions which project directors and teachers are asking:

1. How can project directors ascertain quickly and fairly the degree of scholarly competence of persons who might be employed as teachers or aides in the non-English medium?

2. How can the difference between requiring teachers to work through two languages and having separate teachers for each of the languages be made plain? (The cost is not a serious factor, for the length of the school day is fixed and each teacher usually works alone with a class at any given time.)

3. Bearing in mind the plague of constant borrowing and interference between the tongues in bilinguals who do not maintain separate domains in their lives for each tongue, how can the relative merit of keeping them separate (or mixing them) in respect to time, place, and teacher in the school be determined?

4. What are the administrative and legal impediments to bringing able, experienced teachers and other personnel from abroad, and how can they be overcome?

5. How can school materials of all kinds be produced for teaching American Indian children their own languages and through those languages as mediums of instruction?

6. There is need for a means of measuring the extent to which N-EMT children—even very young children—possess and control that tongue.

7. There is a great need for a search abroad for teaching materials written originally in the other language, both corresponding to the regular school curriculum in the project schools, and dealing with the "history and culture" of the N-EMT child's people and their forbears as viewed by themselves through their own language.

There are questions of methodology. Millions of young children three to eight or thereabouts have learned a second language in a complete, effortless, largely mysterious way, but the literature contains no record of anyone having "taught" one to a child.

8. The main problem is to maintain at maximum effectiveness the circumstances which are known to facilitate natural learning by children when the new language is the necessary, unavoidable means to their involvement in pleasant, significant situations far beyond language itself, and still permit experimentation with highly structured lessons (drill, etc.) designed to increase the speed of learning.

9. Should parents whose English (or any other language) is heavily flawed be asked to speak English to their small children as a means of helping them learn that language? Their efforts will tend to offset those of the child's English teacher, and their failure to stress the mother tongue will offset the efforts of the mother tongue teacher.

10. What is the minimum amount of language contact time short of which children's ability to learn naturally a second language becomes ineffective? (One of the 76 bilingual schooling projects schedules only a 10-15-minute period daily for the second language.)

Beyond the concern for developing and refining the 76 projects and others like them and realizing, *in school,* the full potential of bilingual education, there are broader concerns yet unvoiced for the role of the non-English tongues—certainly this is applicable to Spanish—in the streets, the shops, the offices, the homes. Put otherwise, is it really possible to make a child vigorously literate in his mother tongue if that vigor and literacy are not somehow matched in public places and in the homes? Do children really read eagerly and widely if their parents read reluctantly and seldom? If there are very few books, few newspapers and almost no magazines? Can two languages coexist stably in the same speakers and be expected to serve exactly the same purposes? Will not bilingual schooling, if it succeeds in raising the educational level of the bilinguals, thereby increase their control of English, their social and geographical mobility and so hasten the disappearance of the other tongue?

These are concerns for the adults, the parents, the intellectuals and, yes, for teachers of these tongues as "foreign" languages. "Bilingual education," we saw earlier, can serve the ends of either ethnocentrism or cultural pluralism.

NOTE

1. The author gratefully acknowledges much help and cooperation from the Office of Education staff which administers the Bilingual Education Act. Since their inception the projects have undergone constant modification to improve their effectiveness.

5

TEACHING SPANISH IN SCHOOL AND COLLEGE TO NATIVE SPEAKERS OF SPANISH

ABSTRACT   *This essay shows how teachers of Spanish can respond to the special needs of learners who are native speakers of Spanish, by adopting the more powerful mode of Spanish-medium instruction to reinforce other areas of the curriculum instead of—as is the present practice—teaching it as a* foreign *language. The essay also deals with the question of so-called "standard Spanish" in relation to variant forms of the language. There are suggestions of ways to meet the Spanish-speaking learner's need irrespective of whether the teacher has fluent, authentic command of Spanish.*

It is notoriously difficult to distinguish between dialect and language on either a purely linguistic or even a sociolinguistic basis.
              —Joseph Greenberg

This report,[1] with its detailed recommendations for teaching Spanish in American schools and colleges to mother tongue speakers of that language, had its origin in the confluence of two very similar focuses: the growing acceptance by the Spanish teaching profession of responsibility for maintaining and developing the Spanish that is spoken natively in the United States, and the struggle of the nation's native Spanish speakers for a greater measure of cultural self-determination, including a

61

greater role for Spanish in their lives. Stated in other terms, this report is an effort to close the gap which has so long separated the academic or elitist bilingualism in our schools and colleges from the real world of bilingual people in the nation's streets, shops, and homes.

Thus, the rationale of the report is a simple one: the American Association of Teachers of Spanish and Portuguese will no longer accept the embarrassing anomaly of a language policy for American education which on the one hand seeks to encourage and develop competence in Spanish among those for whom it is a second language, and on the other hand, by open discouragement, neglect, and condescension, destroys it for those who speak it as a mother tongue. The report is explicit on many points concerning teaching methods and materials and the qualifications of participating students and teachers. Its two most significant points are only implicit, but they are basic to the report and the effectiveness of its recommendations. The first of these two basic points is recognition that continental United States includes one major Spanish-speaking region of the world and several minor ones, and that the Spanish spoken in those regions, irrespective of the extent of its equivalence to or variance from "world standard" Spanish, is in every linguistic sense as worthy of study and—in the cultural sense—as worthy of use and development as the Spanish of any other region of the world. The second basic point here implied is that the profession of Spanish teachers will from now on seek to join hands with the nearly ten million native speakers of Spanish in the United States in our common cause.

The more specific objectives of the program are three:

1.   To deepen the learner's sense of his own identity as a member of his cultural-ethnic group, and through him to contribute to that group's effort to achieve cultural self-determination.

2.   To give the learner full command of and literacy in world standard Spanish and thus enable him to realize his full potential as a bilingual person.

3.   To reinforce selectively through Spanish any or all of the other areas of the curriculum and thus increase the learner's understanding and perspective in those areas. This third objective also determines the organization and basic methodology of the program.

The basic recommendation of the report is that wherever in the United States there are pupils or students for whom Spanish is the mother tongue, at whatever grade level from kindergarten to the baccalaureate, there be established in the schools and colleges special sections for developing literacy in Spanish and using it to reinforce or complement other areas of the curriculum, with correspondingly specialized materials, methods, and teachers. What is recommended is essentially a Spanish-S program (Spanish for Spanish speakers) similar to the one in Dade County, Miami, Florida, where in 1961 such a program was begun for Cuban immigrants. Spanish-S in Dade County now (1972) operates in 101 different elementary, junior high, and senior high schools, involves approximately 120 native Spanish speakers as teachers, and serves an estimated total of 15,600 Spanish-speaking children and youths. A Spanish-S program is offered in any public school in Dade County which enrolls 100 or more Spanish speakers.[2]

Ideally, Spanish-S begins in grade one and continues through the four college years. A Spanish-S program can be started at any grade level. It is not a "bridge to English," but even one year of good Spanish-S instruction is better than none at all. Since Spanish is taught most widely at the secondary school level, many of the recommendations which follow are addressed to teachers at that level.

MINIMAL QUALIFICATIONS OF LEARNER PARTICIPANTS

Spanish-S is designed for the "native" or "mother tongue" speaker of Spanish in schools and colleges. Since the actual competence of pupils of whatever age whose first home language is or was Spanish may vary from complete oral command and literacy to the inability to comprehend the simplest expression, a minimal qualification for participation must be set. This is the ability to understand ordinary conversation in Spanish with their parents and their peers plus the ability to follow simple instructions given in Spanish. Students with less than this minimal competence should be advised to study Spanish as a foreign language.

ROLE OF THE LOCAL DIALECT
AND ITS RELATIONSHIP TO WORLD STANDARD

Nothing is more crucial to the success of a Spanish-S program—particularly during the learners' first year of such study—than the attitude of the teacher toward the variant of Spanish spoken by those learners and their parents. (The parents' dialect may differ markedly from the speech used—often adopted voluntarily for effect—by the children. Spanish-S teachers from outside the community may be relieved to note how much closer the parents' speech is to world standard Spanish.) Although one of the objectives of Spanish-S is to give the learner full command of and literacy in the world standard and thus enable him to realize his full potential as a bilingual person, today's children and youth will be unreceptive—even hostile—to the program unless it supports their self-concept and has obvious relevance to their world as seen and foreseen by themselves. Especially in the case of learners whose dialect differs markedly from world standard, the first weeks, months—in some cases, the entire first year—should focus patiently on developing their self-confidence as speakers and writers and readers of their *own kind* of Spanish.

The speaker of a nonstandard dialect must be accepted wholeheartedly as and where he is and must never be censured or subjected to pressure simply because he speaks the dialect. The position to be taken is that each style of speaking, each dialect, is appropriate to certain situations, and that the pupil, eventually, is to learn a world standard in order to increase his repertory of speech styles and so increase his versatility and power.

Although the teacher's basic classroom language will be world standard Spanish, instruction must focus at first and at many other points on the local dialect. He will constantly be talking about the local dialect and using examples from it. Optimally the teacher will have full command in every sense of both world standard and the dialect. If he knows only the former he should adopt an attitude of sincere, enthusiastic interest in the local dialect (for both psychological effect and because of its intrinsic worth as an object of study) and should try to master it.

RELATIONSHIP OF SPANISH-S
TO OTHER SPANISH TEACHING

If we were dealing with an ideal world it would clearly be desirable to link the Spanish-S work at every point with all other formal efforts to teach Spanish in the schools and colleges. Each such possible linkage will be discussed in turn to judge its feasibility. Since we have already seen that Spanish-S is a limited form of bilingual instruction (the use of the mother tongue for at least one full period each day as a medium to teach and reinforce all of the regular areas of the school curriculum), the first question to be decided is whether or not to include when-ever possible learners at the same grade levels who have not acquired the minimal qualifications noted above. The answer is NO. A good case can, of course, be made for including them: every child should have the opportunity to become bilingual; unless the non-Spanish speakers are included, they and their parents might be resentful of the special attention given to the Spanish speakers; above all, the latter and their parents might not accept the necessary separation (or "segregation") of the Spanish speakers into Spanish-S sections. However, the counter arguments are overwhelming:

1.   The minimum amount of time required for an effective Spanish-S program (at least one full period daily) is *not* sufficient to give a non-Spanish speaker control of the language. In order to have effective two-way bilingual educa-tion—i.e., for native and non-native speakers as well—at least half of the day would have to be devoted to Spanish-medium instruction. This, to be sure, is highly desirable and might indeed be feasible in a few buildings, but in each such case the entire community must be oriented and convinced to accept two-language instruction, and the basic school policy must be changed and at least half of the teaching staff must be changed and trained accordingly. Spanish-S is meant to apply to all Spanish speakers in all schools, and this would be impossible if every such school had to become bilingual for all its children.

2.   It is true that Mexican-Americans—and Puerto Ricans, too—have in the past had much reason to be suspicious of any attempt to place their children in separate classes, because this has commonly been done with evil, racist intent. Separate classes for the right reason, as a way of achieving homogen-eous grouping for instruction, are acceptable—e.g., English as a second language—and Spanish-S is an eminently right reason.

3.   In sum, the present stance of both the Puerto Rican and the Mexican-American or Chicano seems to be—and rightly—that what is most needed is

to reaffirm, for each of the two peoples, its own identity: its historical and cultural roots, its language, its own patterns of belief and behavior. After this has been done there will be time enough (and strength and power enough) to exert influence through example on the now dominant majority. In other words, both peoples want first of all to put their own house strongly in order.

It is not feasible to combine Spanish-S in the elementary school with FLES, foreign language instruction for non-native speakers of Spanish in those grades. This is because Spanish-S is essentially *Spanish-medium instruction,* a kind of teaching-learning which cannot be achieved for non-native speakers in the amount of time that can be alloted to either Spanish-S or to FLES.

Likewise, at the junior high school level, it is not possible for non-native speakers, through regular foreign language instruction, to have acquired enough command of Spanish to enable them to join mother tongue speakers for Spanish-medium instruction. At the senior high school level, however, a strong effective linkage is possible. Sufficiently advanced non-native students of Spanish can and should be encouraged to join the Spanish-S groups as a special honor. Since it is already considered highly desirable to offer at the eleventh- and twelfth-grade levels "use" courses, i.e., Spanish-medium courses to regular students of Spanish, non-native students can profitably be placed in Spanish-S courses if they have reached the fourth, fifth, or sixth level of instruction. Incidentally, a Spanish-medium course in history, for example, should produce credit in both Spanish and history.

Finally, a relationship can easily be seen between the Spanish-S program here advocated and work in English as a second language for the same learners. The effectiveness of the ESL program can be greatly reinforced by a good Spanish-S program, since language skills are transferable. It is far easier for children—especially the very young—to learn to read in Spanish and then transfer those skills to the reading of English, the second language. But Spanish-S is not ESL. Spanish-S is exclusively a Spanish-medium, an all-in-Spanish program. As will be noted later in this report, at many points it is imperative that Spanish-S be coordinated closely with the English language arts program and other areas in the regular school curriculum, but the two cannot be combined in one class period without seriously undermining the effectiveness of the work in both.

The same relationships and reasoning are equally applicable at the college level.

RELATIONSHIP OF SPANISH-S
TO CULTURAL SELF-DETERMINATION

The importance of respecting the language of the learner and of accepting him warmly and without condescension where he is has been stressed in the sections above. Even more important to the success of a Spanish-S program is the relationship between that program and the vigorous movement among American Spanish speakers—and most especially among the Chicanos and Puerto Ricans—to achieve social justice and an increasing measure of cultural self-determination. Invariably, among the many demands voiced by the "Spanish-surnamed" is a demand for maintenance of their language and a more positive role for it in their lives. That Spanish-S program will be most effective which identifies itself most effectively with the struggle for social justice and which draws its strength and motivation from that struggle.

In one of the most heartening and promising reform movements in American education, Mexican-American students—and Puerto Rican students too—are organizing themselves to fight for the chance to be educated.[3] It is not an exaggeration to say that these organizations—in colleges, universities, and high schools—are the most powerful driving force in the entire movement, especially among the Mexican-Americans. Invariably one of their demands is for "bilingual education." It may well be said that they are not always certain what they mean by this term beyond the certainty that they want teachers who speak Spanish and who are free to speak it with their pupils. What is unquestionable is that Spanish-S can draw on the powerful emotional and ideological appeal of that movement for backing and a source of learner motivation if Spanish teachers are wise enough to identify their efforts with the efforts of the student groups. The following points seem most important:

1. The attitude of the teacher to the learner's dialect and the place given to that dialect in the instructional program.

2. The teacher's and the entire institution's willingness to yield to the students, through their organization, a fair share in the power of decision over such matters as who shall teach, what is to be taught, and who are eligible to join the learners.

There are other ways of identifying the Spanish-S effort with the Mexican-American's and the Puerto Rican's struggle for a greater measure of cultural self-determination:

1. Working through the student organization (and if there is none, first creating a chapter of the nearest and strongest one with the help of its college-level members), one can set up a literacy-in-Spanish program for younger children, a youth-tutoring-youth, each-one-teach-one program. It could sometimes be during school hours at the nearest grade school, sometimes after school. There could be prizes and public award ceremonies to recognize each child who is able to read aloud a short selection from a book (carefully selected at the proper linguistic and conceptual levels and previously unknown to the young learner) and explain briefly in Spanish what he has just read. These ceremonies should be attended by parents and other prestigious persons.

2. It is good to have frequent Spanish-speaking visitors to the Spanish-S sessions (or to an extracurricular club of the learners) such as elderly people who can recount from personal experience the trials, tribulations, and

triumphs of the "early days"; lively professors from Mexican-American studies programs in nearby colleges; officers of nearby college-level student organizations; union leaders; Chicano Press Association newspaper editors; etc. Needless to say, all of their presentations must be in Spanish.

3.   It is a good idea to make of each Spanish-S program a Mexican-American (or Chicano or Puerto Rican or Cuban) studies program, at least in miniature and embryonic.

4.   The Spanish-S teacher should give active, earnest support to the Spanish-surnamed peoples' movement for social justice. This, admittedly, is a delicate matter and calls for wisdom. It does not necessarily entail participation in street demonstrations, nor does it preclude such participation.

CURRICULUM AND TEACHING METHODS

In terms of curriculum or content, Spanish-S is three things: (1) selective reinforcement of all other areas of the school curriculum, (2) the story—in every sense—of the learner's people and forebears, and (3) Spanish language development (or language arts). The first of these should—over the years—get the major portion of time given to Spanish-S, for two reasons. This emphasis will forestall criticism of the program that will otherwise come from persons who say that the regular school curriculum is already more than enough to fill the school day and its important content must not be displaced by the extensive study of Spanish, year after year. The answer to such criticism is that Spanish-S does not displace any significant part of the regular curriculum; it *reinforces* that same curriculum. The second reason for emphasizing the regular curriculum is that a language is learned more easily when it is an incidental, unavoidable means to other ends, rather than an end in itself.

No special methods are needed for teaching the other school subjects and the ethnic group's history through Spanish, except to the extent that the learners do not have adequate command (for their age and grade level) of Spanish. If their command is more or less adequate, one teaches as if Spanish were the only language in the world and the learner's total education depended on that class. When the learner's command is not yet "normal" the following suggestions are worth consideration:

1.   The teacher's attitude toward the students' dialect is even more crucial: it must be positive and supportive.

2.   The teacher's use of language (both the dialect and world standard) should be normally paced, never slowed in the hope of making it easier to understand.

3.   Comprehension and use can be facilitated in many ways without slowing the **rate** of speech.
   a. Heightened consciousness in the teacher of the language he is using and the learner's reception of it.

    b. Frequent re-use of new locutions.

    c. Regular use and instruction in the use of paraphrase (saying what it means in other, more common words) by teacher and learners.

    d. Exercises in writing conversions: from standard to dialect and vice versa (which may more advantageously be viewed as "informal" and "formal" styles); from direct discourse (conversation) to indirect discourse (reporting without quoting) and vice versa; from present to past, etc.

    e. Oral practice in making the conversions.

    f. Showing of Spanish-language films from various countries, with attention to regional variants of speech. If possible the film print should be available for repeated showing and listening to the sound track, section by section in class, with discussion of any aspect of the film from "story line" to dialectal variants in the actors' speech.

    g. Aural practice in identifying the country of origin of Spanish speakers through recordings of their speech. This can later be combined with analysis of what the differences are and attempts to imitate them. Any such exercise helps to develop auditory discrimination, hence a sharper perspective on language, hence increased ability to differentiate and control various speech styles.

    h. Memorization and mastery of jokes in the several dialects of Spanish, e.g., the speech style of many people from Yucatan.

One useful technique for developing rapport with the pupils—and an especially useful one if the teacher knows only the world standard—is to begin by a simple comparative study of the two. Comparative listings or glossaries of vocabulary, followed by similar objective comparisons of differing syntactic patterns and variant pronunciations, can be an effective introduction to orthography. These techniques also are the first steps toward building the perspective on language that is so essential to mastery of a new speech style. Another powerful technique for developing the sense of perspective is the memorization and presentation of dramatic skits—however short—in which both the dialect and world standard are used appropriately.

The teaching of Spanish as a mother tongue calls for a language arts approach combined with contrastive analysis. Pupils may require extensive practice in both listening and speaking in order to discriminate between *lodillas* and *rodillas, perna* and *pierna, íbanos* and *íbamos,* etc., with immediate reinforcement by the printed word.

It should all be challenging but enjoyable. Spanish-S should above all increase the learner's self-esteem and his sense of power over language.

There is a propensity among some Spanish speakers in the United States to combine that language and English when addressing persons who speak and understand both of these tongues. In addition, there is the beginning of a distinctive literature among Mexican-Americans, some of which, especially the poetry, includes this feature. Occasional words, phrases, even sentences from the one language are interspersed in conversation or extended oral exposition or writing which consists largely of the other language. Apart from this admixture as a stylistic feature, it is not entirely clear why the languages are so combined. There is some reason to believe that it is not usually haphazard but instead is patterned in direct relationship to the subject discussed, the place and occasion, the interlocutor, and other listeners.[4] In part it is a deliberate attempt to foster a "secret" language accessible to the in-group only.

It is the strong recommendation of this report that every effort be made to avoid this mixing of Spanish and English. There should be times and places for the one language and other times and places for the other. If possible, the Spanish-S teacher should not be asked (or allowed) to give any class or course in English to those particular Spanish-S learners. This follows the principle that there should be separate sources of each language. At any rate the teacher should not mix the languages during a given class period (which does not rule out an occasional word or phrase in English to facilitate immediate comprehension). Pupils, especially very young ones or those in their first year of study, should not be censured for occasional lapses into English, but the teacher should work quietly to reduce the need for and the number of these intrusions. The recommendation against mixing the languages does not mean the teachers should all be monolinguals. On the contrary, they may be either well-trained monolinguals or exemplary bilinguals: strongly and proudly competent in both languages.

SPANISH-S PUPILS COMBINED WITH OTHERS IN THE SAME CLASSROOM

The report has thus far assumed ideal circumstances for Spanish-S: separate Spanish-S sections in each building where there are native speakers of Spanish, and teachers who know the world standard and can use it in all subject areas but who are also prepared to work with the dialect in ways that are rewarding to the pupils. It is not necessary, it should be added, to have a separate Spanish-S section at each grade level. Pupils from three successive levels (1, 2, 3; 2, 3, 4; etc.) or even more can be combined very effectively. However, in some buildings it will not be possible to schedule classes for the Spanish speakers alone, i.e., regular Spanish-S. If there are only a few native speakers in the building—or only one—there are several ways to help them to progress faster than regular students of Spanish as a foreign language. In some cases the teacher will be less than well prepared. Despite either or both of these last weaknesses, good work can be done and to this point the report is now addressed.

The parents and other persons in the community who know Spanish should be taken into the confidence of the teacher and their help and advice frankly sought. If the teacher has little real-life command of Spanish this should be no deterrent. Candid recognition of one's own shortcomings is often a powerful stimulus to help and cooperation from others. Parents and other adults may be glad to work—either inside or outside of school—to direct learning for both the Spanish-S and other pupils. For example, parents of Spanish-S pupils can take turns reading aloud (live or on tape) for "listening time" at school.

THE SEVEN-STEP STRATEGY

In the classroom a good learning strategy to develop literacy and discrimination (even if the teacher has little command of Spanish) is the following. High school students can use it individually and with little guidance.

1. Pupil learns quite easily from the teacher the basic orthography of Spanish by recognition of Spanish words on the board and simple directions. This takes only a few class periods.

2. He tape-records an original statement of any kind (very short at first) then transcribes his own statement. The teacher checks the transcription (and might learn something in the process) but does not criticize either syntax or lexicon. Pupil does it over (listening to his words played back) and learns to do an accurate transcription. All final transcriptions are kept in a bound notebook. Pupil then shows that he can read aloud accurately his transcription.

3. The exercise is repeated many times with longer and more varied original statements. The pupil is learning to read and write.

4. Pupil also learns (without ceasing to work with original statements and accounts) to transcribe and then read aloud short passages recorded by other speakers of Spanish. He is learning to read and write other kinds of Spanish.

5. Pupil later reads short statements, bits of conversation, etc., from books or newspapers, hides the selection from sight and records his own version of it, i.e., "telling what he reads." He then transcribes exactly his version and thus has two perfectly legitimate variant forms of the same thing. This powerful exercise should be used many times to develop a sense of the difference between the two. There is no need for invidious comparisons or value judgments by the teacher. The pupil unaided sees and hears the similarities and differences clearly enough.

6. The two versions of every exercise should be copied on facing pages of the bound notebook: the original on the left, the student's version on the right. The exercise material should be chosen for appropriateness of cognitive and linguistic level and, however short or long, should be interesting.

7. The final step in the process of learning to read and write and perceive differences between two versions of Spanish is for the pupil to read aloud *accurately* the sets of two variant transcriptions and thus demonstrate that he perceives *accurately* the differences between them. This seven-step procedure enables the pupil to learn by himself at his own rate with no expertise required from the teacher except elementary knowledge of sound-letter correspondences in Spanish, plus the time to select appropriate sentences and longer selections for practice material.

Many Spanish-S pupils can easily and profitably read widely in Spanish if the material is carefully chosen. (They should ordinarily not be required to use textbooks prepared for use by Anglo students.) For many beginning readers nothing is better than profusely illustrated "comic" books. Those which employ slang and argot are particularly good. One widely published series, made for sale throughout Latin America, is noteworthy for its careful use of language. There is one series from Mexico which is not only folksy and highly amusing, but is at the same time an acutely perceptive sociopolitical analysis of life in that country. These and other recommended reading materials are listed in the bibliography.

Spanish-S pupils (in mixed classes) can often be used to teach the others. Many can serve as models of individual sounds (*r, rr, ll, j,* the vowels, etc.) and of speaking and reading aloud. They can sometimes be used as tutors of individual students. They should always be asked (even if it has to be done in English) to explain any alternative way, lexical or syntactical, of expressing an idea, and the other pupils should be encouraged to transcribe these alternatives in a notebook to be kept and learned.

Teachers of Spanish-S will tend to be overwhelmed by their pupils' lexical and syntactical deviations from world standard. No one, including teachers, can suddenly change his speech from one dialect to another, and the teacher's earnest attempts to "correct" or point out "errors" is almost always self-defeating. In addition to the "seven-step strategy" described above, here are some tricks:

As the listings of corresponding "regional" and "world" variants are developed—covering lexicon (*groserías - abarrotes*), morphology (*váyasen - váyanse*), syntax (*habían dos - había dos*) and idiom (*me los dieron pa' 'trás - me los devolvieron*)—drills and tests can easily follow, orally and in writing, to help assure mastery of both variants. The test, for example has three elements:

Respuesta:

Me los dió pa' 'trás.
a. ¿Es regional o mundial?   *Regional*
b. ¿Cuál es la otra forma?   *Me los devolvió.*
c. ¿Hay una expresión informal?   *Sí. Pa' 'trás en vez de "para atrás."*

Step five of the seven-step strategy can produce two variant forms of an anecdote. Thereafter Spanish-S pupils can be asked to memorize the two forms and show their mastery by working in pairs, one reciting the regional, sentence by sentence, followed by the corresponding sentence in world standard (or in opposite order).

Too commonly the Spanish-speaking child, whatever his "dialect" and despite the fact that he uses it for the real-life purposes of language, will seem to be least successful in those matters to which schools give most attention: orthography, grammatical analysis and nomenclature, and niceties of usage. These relatively inconsequential matters should not be the principal focus of instruction for Spanish-S pupils, and their slowness or lack of interest in mastering them should not result in low grades. They need all the kinds of *experience* in Spanish that their English-dominated milieu has denied them: non-threatening opportunities to talk with and listen to a variety of Spanish-speaking persons, young and old; beautiful books (including picture books, photographs) and films (even in English) revealing the "glories" of Hispanic and Indo-Hispanic peoples; and at the junior and senior high levels, ready access by Mexican-Americans to the newspapers of the Chicano Press Association, and by Puerto Ricans to periodicals which report on the *"movimiento puertorriqueño."* (These papers, fervently devoted to the struggle for social justice, are essential catalysts in a Spanish-S program. They are published partly in English, partly in Spanish. Some articles appear in a mixture of the two languages.)

TEACHER TRAINING FOR SPANISH-S

The attitude of empathy and respect that the Spanish-S teacher must demonstrate toward his pupils, their parents, and their language is plain from the preceding sections, as is the importance of full competence—including a high degree of literacy—in world standard Spanish and knowledge of the local dialect of Spanish. In addition, the ideal teacher has the following qualifications:

1. He is bicultural. It helps, but is neither necessary nor sufficient, to be born into biculturalism. Feelings are fine, but a teacher needs some facts too about the history, sociology, folkways, values, aspirations, and the immediate environment of his pupils and their families.

2. He has some knowledge (or at least has shed his myths) about the nature of language and language learning. This could well include the theory and application of contrastive linguistics.

3. *He has knowledge of the content and methods of teaching through Spanish in all areas of the school curriculum. This ordinarily cannot be acquired except by studying in those areas through the medium of Spanish, using Spanish-language materials. This competence in content and methods cannot effectively be acquired by translation from English.*

There will come a time when former Spanish-S students can themselves fill Spanish-S teaching positions. Until then, there will be much need for intensive study and practice in Puerto Rico and Mexico and much recourse to specialists from these and other Spanish-speaking places to reinforce the Spanish-S program in the United States.

WHO SHOULD TEACH IN SPANISH-S PROGRAMS

There is a place in Spanish-S for any effective teacher—"Anglo," Cuban, Mexican-American, Puerto Rican, Chilean, Spaniard, etc.—who meets the criteria. It simply is not true that "it takes one to teach one." Nevertheless, when one bears in mind the great disparity between the very large numbers of Spanish-speaking children and the very small number of teachers and professors drawn from the same ethnic groups, it seems that every effort should be made to give both the Puerto Ricans and the Mexican-Americans more teachers of their own ethnic background. Having truly competent, proficient native and non-native speakers as teachers of Spanish-

S can help to reduce polarization in school and community. Together, they become living evidence of the cultural egalitarianism basic to Spanish-S.

NOTES

1. The essay was commissioned in 1970 by the Executive Council of the American Association of Teachers of Spanish and Portuguese. It was prepared by a committee of nine members of the profession: Marie Esman Barker (University of Texas, El Paso), Herminia Cantero (Department of Bilingual Education, Dade County (Florida) Public Schools), A. Bruce Gaarder (U.S. Office of Education, Washington, D.C.), Adalberto Guerrero (University of Arizona, Tucson), Hernan LaFontaine (The Bilingual School, 811 East 149th Street, New York City), Maria Olivia Munoz (Houston (Texas) Public Schools), Charles F. Olstad (University of Arizona, Tucson), Alonso M. Perales (Bilingual Center, 623 South Pecos, San Antonio, Texas), and Donald D. Walsh (Northeast Conference on the Teaching of Foreign Languages, P.O. Box 881, Madison, Ct.). Donald Walsh was the project manager, Bruce Gaarder was the committee chairman and drafted the report. Before its publication the manuscript was examined and criticized by 53 other persons.

2. The Dade County Spanish-S program and one of the County's two-way bilingual elementary schools are described in Chapter 3.

3. Among Puerto Ricans in New York the Young Lords; in New York and Chicago the ASPIRA clubs and federation. Among the Mexican-Americans some leading groups are MECHA (Movimiento Estudiantil Chicano de Aztlán), MAYO (Mexican American Youth Organization), UMAS (United Mexican American Students), and others. The best position paper on education for the Spanish speaking is *El Plan de Santa Bárbara,* for which see Chapter 12.

4. The following books together provide an overview of this matter: Joshua A. Fishman, ed., *Readings in the Sociology of Language.* The Hague: Mouton (1970); Einar Haugen, *The Norwegian Language in America.* Bloomington, Indiana: Indiana University Press (1969); L. G. Kelly, ed., *Description and Measurement of Bilingualism: An International Seminar.* Toronto: University of Toronto Press (1969); Uriel Weinreich, *Languages in Contact.* The Hague: Mouton (1963).

BIBLIOGRAPHY

Reading

Torres Quintero, Gregorio. *El método onomatopéyico.* México: D. F.: Editorial Patria. System widely used in Mexico. Phonic approach. Detailed instructions to teachers. Grade level: 1

Reading and Writing

Pastor, Angeles, et al. *Por el Mundo del Cuento y la Aventura.* River Forest, Ill.: Laidlaw Brothers (1962). Used for Spanish-S in Dade County, Fla. and used in Puerto Rican schools. Grade level: K-6. Book 6 in the high school.

Spanish Language

Almendros-Alvero. *Lengua Española.* Guatemala: Cultura Centroamericana. Used for Spanish-S in Dade County, Fla. Book 6 in the high school. Grade level: 1-6

Arce, Eugene, Anita García, and Dora Sáenz. *Español para alumnos hispanohablantes.* Austin, Texas: Texas Education Agency (1970). First two levels of instruction. Prepared by a committee of teachers of Spanish under the supervision of the Foreign Language Section of the Texas Education Agency. Includes treatment of the problem of "dialect" versus "universal Spanish," and appendices on Hispanic culture, pronunciation, grammatical terminology, etc. Grade level: Secondary

Barker, Marie Esman. *Español para el bilingüe.* Skokie, Ill.: National Textbook Co. Author has extensive experience teaching Spanish to Mexican-American children. Grade level: 9-16

Salinas, Pedro. *Aprecio y defensa del lenguaje.* Río Piedras, Puerto Rico: Editorial Universitaria, Universidad de Puerto Rico. Used in Puerto Rican schools. Grade level: 10-16

Social Studies

Marrero, Levi. *Viajemos por América.* Carácas: Cultural Venezolana. Used for Spanish-S in Dade County, Fla. Grade level: 5

Marrero, Levi. *Viajemos por el Mundo.* Carácas: Cultural Venezolana. Used for Spanish-S in Dade County, Fla. Grade level: 6

Geography

Passadori, Josefina. *Elementos de geografía.* Buenos Aires: Editorial Kapelusz. Used for Spanish-S in Dade County, Fla. Grade level: 7-8

Vida en México

Rius (pseudónimo de Eduardo del Río). *Los Supermachos de San Garabato.* México, D. F.: Editorial Meridiano, Tenayuca 55, 6° piso, México 13, D. F. (1967). Se han publicado varios tomos. Análisis agudísimo y de orientación popular de la actualidad socio-política en México. Historietas profusamente ilustradas en la forma de "tiras cómicas." (Desde hace tres años Rius ya no tiene que ver con esta publicación.) Grade level: 6-16

Rius (pseudónimo de Eduardo del Río). *Los Agachados de Rius.* México, D. F.: Editorial Posada, S. A., Yosemite No. 60 (Director: Eduardo del Río; distribución foránea a cargo de Guillermo Mendizabal Lizalde, la misma dirección.) $1.60 moneda mexicana el ejemplar. Por el estilo de *Los Supermachos* (véase). Se han publicado 70 números quincenales. El número 70 lleva índice alfabético de temas. Publicación mensual desde el número 71. Grade level: 6-16

Vida en el "sud-oeste"

Anónimo. *El Chicano.* México, D. F.: EDIPRES, S. A., Sagredo No. 77, México 19. (Distribuidora: Sayrols de Publicaciones, S. A., Mier y Pesado No. 130, México 12, D. F. Director: Carlos Domínguez Oviedo.) Libretas profusamente ilustradas de historietas en las que el Chicano resulta siempre vencedor. El lenguaje que se utiliza es el "español común." Grade level: 6-16

History of Puerto Rico

Morales Carrión, Arturo. *Historia del pueblo de Puerto Rico.* Hato Rey, Puerto Rico: Editorial del Departamento de Instrucción Pública. Used in Puerto Rican schools. Grade level: Junior high

Life in Puerto Rico

Anonymous. *Vida en Puerto Rico–Programa de español, noveno grado.* Originally prepared by the Commonwealth of Puerto Rico, Department of Public Education, Hato Rey, Puerto Rico, for use at the ninth-grade level there. Grade level: Secondary

History, Sociology, etc.

Maldonado-Denis, Manuel. *Puerto Rico: Una Interpretación Histórico-Social.* México, D. F.: Siglo XXI Editores, S. A. 255 pp. Historical development and present problems of Puerto Rico; struggle for national identity and independence; indictment of U.S. policies toward Puerto Rico. Grade level: Secondary

McWilliams, Carey. *Al norte de México.* (traducción de Lya de Cardoza) México, D. F.: Siglo XXI Editores, S. A., Gabriel Mancera 65, México, 12, D. F. (1968). Tells much of the Mexican Americans' side of their history in the American Southwest. Widely praised by Mexican Americans. Grade level: Secondary

Latin American History

Henríquez Ureña, Pedro. *Historia de la cultura en la América Hispana.* México, D. F.: Fondo de Cultural Económica. Grade level: Senior high

Mathematics

Eicholz, Robert E. *Matemática para la educación primaria.* Bogotá, Fondo Educativo Inter-americano. Also: Reading, Mass.: Addison-Wesley (1968). Spanish edition of the Addison-Wesley elementary school mathematics series. The "new" mathematics. Colorfully illustrated. Grade level: 1-6

Science

Schneider, Nina and Herman Schneider. *La ciencia.* Translated by David Cruz Lopez. Boston: D. C. Heath and Co. Used for Spanish-S in Dade County, Fla. Includes laboratory activities. Grade level: 1-6

Biology

Department of Public Instruction, Puerto Rico. *Introducción a la biología,* 5 parts. Hato Rey, Puerto Rico. Used in Puerto Rican schools. Grade level: Junior high

Chemistry

Hered, William. *Introducción a la química,* 2 levels. Hato Rey, Puerto Rico: Editorial del Departamento de Instrucción Publica. Used in Puerto Rican schools. Grade level: Junior high

Physics

Nedelsky, Leo. *Introducción a la física,* 2 levels. Hato Rey, Puerto Rico: Editorial del Departamento de Instrucción Pública. Used in Puerto Rican schools. Grade level: 9

Shorthand

Villaronga, Rosa A. and Amalia Llabrés de Charneco. *Ejercicios de lectura y escritura para la enseñanza de la taquigrafía en español.* Hato Rey, Puerto Rico: Editorial del Departmento de Instrucción Pública. Used in Puerto Rican schools. Grade level: 10

Spanish Literature

Anaya Solorzano, Soledad. *Literatura Española, Tercer Curso de Lengua y Literatura, Manual para uso de los alumnos de segunda enseñanza.* México, D. F.: Editorial Porrúa, S. A. Grade level: 7-16

Gutierrez Eskildsen, Rosario. *Primer Curso de Lengua y Literatura Españolas, Unidades de Trabajo.* México, D. F.: Editorial Tabasco (1961). (Librería Herrero, Avenida Cinco de Mayo 39.) Grade level: 7-16

Health

Gutierrez Eskildsen, Rosario. *El Camino hacia la salud.* River Forest, Ill.: Laidlaw Brothers. Used for Spanish-S, Dade County, Fla. Grade level: 1-6

All Areas

(Teams of authors). Serie *El Arbol Alegre.* Madrid: Santillana (Elfo 32, Madrid 17, 1969), also Santiago de Chile: Ediciones Educativas, Ltda. (Monjitas 580, Santiago, Chile, 1970). Available in the United States from Hispanic American Publications, Inc., 252 East 51st Street, New York, N.Y. 10022. Complete basic series for each of first 8 years: language, social studies, mathematics, art, natural sciences, etc. Includes a "libro guía" for the teacher at each level, and systematic evaluation.

Beautifully illustrated; full color. General focus is universal, more specific focus either on Spain or Chile. Pedagogy modern in all respects. Chilean edition contains following: LIBRO GUIA para el profesor (1° a 8° años); ESPIRAL: Texto de Matemáticas (1° a 8° años); AMANECER: Cuaderno de Escritura para 1° y 2° años; DESPERTAR: Libro de Lectura para el 1er año; LUCERO: Libro de Lectura para 2°, 3° y 4° años. SENDEROS: Texto de Castellano para 5°, 6°, 7° y 8° años; FUTURO: Texto de Ciencias Sociales y Naturales para 1°, 2°, 3° y 4° años; MERIDIANO: Texto de Ciencias Sociales para 5°, 6°, 7° y 8° años; CRISTAL: Texto de Ciencias Naturales para 5°, 6°, 7° y 8° años; VENTANAL: Texto de Educación Técnico–Artística para 1°, 2°, 3° y 4° años; CRISOL: Texto de Educación Técnico-Artistica–Manual para 5°, 6°, 7° y 8° años; MOSAICO: Texto de Artes Plásticas para 5°, 6°, 7° y 8° años.

N. B.: A listing of textbooks used by the Department of Education in Puerto Rico is available upon request to Carlos V. Pérez, Supervisor, Bilingual Education Unit, State Education Department, Albany, N.Y. 12224.

6

THE GOLDEN RULES
OF OTHER LANGUAGE ACQUISITION
BY YOUNG CHILDREN

ABSTRACT   *An attempt to formulate a pedagogy of bilingual schooling in two precepts the observance of which will obviate a number of the most common problems of language teaching.*

During the first ten or twelve years of life young children have the mysterious, miraculous ability to learn languages—in addition to their own mother tongue—completely, effortlessly, and to a large extent unconsciously. Because we understand so little about how this miracle occurs it can fairly be asserted that millions of young children have done this, yet no one can claim to have taught a second language to a little child. Therefore the pedagogy is not at all to analyze the language in order to reveal the items of its phonology, morphology, and syntax—not to mention its semantics—and then devise an optimal order of presentation, practice, etc., of those items; rather, the pedagogy is to place the child in optimal situations for the mystery to occur, in the secure knowledge that it very likely will occur. The focus here is on the "other tongue," a relative term which can mean—depending upon the child's previous experience and education—either its mother tongue or another tongue.

Of course, learning is always a function of the learner, not the teacher, but the essential difference between, on the one hand learning arithmetic or reading or a musical instrument and, on the other hand, learning a new language is not generally understood. For the first three the structured, optimal presentation is essential. For language learning the structured, supposedly optimal presentation is counterproductive, even disastrous. The younger the child, the greater the significance of these statements. (Needless to say, for older learners who have largely lost—it is never lost entirely—the mysterious power to acquire the language "unconsciously," the structured, optimal order of presentation is essential to efficient formal learning.)

The two golden rules of second language pedagogy for teachers of young children are therefore:

Work, speak, and act with complete naturalness, as if the new language were the only language in the world and the children's entire education depended on you, the teacher.

Never try to teach language per se; rather, teach life (joy, sorrow, work, play, relationships, concepts, differentiation, self-awareness of others, etc.) by involving the children in situations and activities which are highly significant to them—although not necessarily and exclusively pleasurable— and with the new language the sole and inescapable, unavoidable means to the children's participation.

There is an instructive—even if limited—analogy between these rules and the golden rule of ethics: Do unto others as you would have them do unto you. The analogy appears when one considers the whole of theology, doctrine, dogma, and ritual that might be said to underlie the rule of ethics; and the sciences of linguistics and sociolinguistics that illuminate the pedagogical rules. These great bodies of knowledge will and must be studied by their specialists. For the more common purposes of human interaction—including linguistic interaction with young children—simple, comprehensive precepts have always been more useful, less subject to misinterpretation.

The first of the pedagogical rules, if followed, will have these effects:

1. The two languages will be kept separate, which is fundamental to the child's later control and conception of them as separate systems representing distinct cultures. This is particularly crucial in bilingual (dual-medium) education if the objective is to maintain both languages rather than simply to transfer the child away from its mother tongue to another language.

2. The teacher will not attempt to teach one language in terms of the other. This practice takes many forms: translation, explanations in one language of the supposed "peculiarities" of the other, mixing elements of one language with elements of the other, etc. It is counterproductive because it tends to prevent the miracle of natural learning from taking place. For example, when the teacher alternates constantly, sentence by sentence (and they will do this!) between the two languages, expressing each thought first in the one then in the other, the miracle cannot take place, for the child then has no compelling reason to acquire the new tongue. He can wait at most a few seconds and comprehend in his own first tongue.

3.   The required "complete naturalness" will prevent the common, unnecessary practice of habitually addressing the learners in an unnaturally slow, syllable-by-syllable fashion, on the mistaken assumption that a child cannot grasp normally rapid speech. This practice is commonly observed in persons who conceive of the new tongue as a "foreign" language and who themselves have difficulty understanding it, but it is also a practice among educated, native speakers.

The second of the pedagogical rules, if followed, will have these effects:

1.   It will largely prevent the teacher from making the almost universal common mistake of assuming that the learning of a new language is essentially and principally the learning of lists of words—new "names" for things. It should be needless to reiterate here that learning a new language is essentially the acquisition of easy, native-like control of the extremely complex, interrelated systems of morphology (form) and syntax (order). Vocabulary expansion becomes, much later, a major problem, and the semantic problems of differing fields of denotation and connotation of seeming cognates are never entirely solved. In both cases, help and strength come only from wide reading and wide discourse. These are not concerns of young children or their teachers.

2.   It will prevent the even more wasteful practice of structuring the supposed language learning process into a supposed optimal order of learning based on phonological analysis, or on contrastive analysis of the two tongues. All such misguided efforts sound reasonable at the level of theory. They are counterproductive for two interlocking reasons: (a) Emphasis and presentation of the new language in terms of the supposed hierarchy of its difficulties (in relation to the first language, e.g., "this week we'll emphasize the ch/sh contrast, next week the ship/sheep contrast," etc.) has the effect of inhibiting, even destroying, the teacher's main source of power: the full flow of completely authentic speech dealing fully with "life" as the child is able to perceive and grasp it, and (b) there is no evidence anywhere that the involvement and participation referred to in the second pedagogical rule are not the *sine qua non* of second language acquisition by young children. Stated otherwise, language per se as an end, rather than a means, is not significant to young children, and the inhibited, constrained speech of the teacher who must focus on the ship/sheep or any other contrast is not the context in which *natural* language learning—i.e., the miracle—occurs.

The constrained contrastive analysis approach overlooks two other facts of linguistic reality: (a) children not uncommonly show aberrant pronunciation of some sounds of their mother tongue even as late as ten years, but these almost always disappear and without recourse to or need for contrastively analytical drill; and (b) in the case of bilingual children who have a marked accent in the other tongue, the explanation can better be sought, not in the supposedly ineffective efforts of the accent-free teachers, but in the much greater influence of the parents and other persons in the child's out-of-school environment whose speech in the other tongue is often heavily accented and who unwittingly insist on or cannot avoid serving as models for the child.

Both rules together carry an unmistakable implication: the kind of teacher needed to follow them is not only well prepared in the theory and techniques for dealing with and instructing children; she (or he) must also have complete, effortless mastery of the new language, the kind of mastery that can come only with extensive education through the medium of that language, wide reading in it, and intensive, direct experience with the culture which it reflects. It has been the observation of the writer of these lines that the propensity of teachers of second language and their supervisors and course designers to do the kinds of things that our two rules are meant to avoid is directly proportional to their lack of the kind of strong background and professional preparation called for in the preceding sentence.

7

TEACHER TRAINING FOR SPANISH-MEDIUM WORK IN UNITED STATES SCHOOLS

ABSTRACT   *This piece identifies four different groups of Spanish speakers in the United States and discusses the correspondingly different kinds of special preparation they need for Spanish-medium teaching in the schools. It also analyzes the role of the three components of a teacher training program: the university or college, the bilingual school used as the training site, and the all-important community of Spanish speakers. A curriculum outline for master's and doctoral level programs is given.*

INTRODUCTORY REMINDERS

The teacher-pupil (master-disciple) relationship is essential at all levels of schooling and no less for doctoral studies than in the first grade of elementary school. The teacher must know that which the learner needs to know and must know more of it. If research is called for to increase the body of pertinent knowledge, the teacher must know its techniques and must also be able to guide and judge the research of the learner. The teacher and the learner are not peers.

It can be expected that in an organized group of scholars there will have developed the bureaucratic propensity to aggrandize the group's prestige and role by increasing the barriers to entry in the group, even to the extent of creating irrelevant requirements. This propensity at its worst can mean that the learner is

81

denied the experiences that he needs and must submit instead to those which the teacher is prepared to give him.

Educators (teachers, their teachers, and the mentors of these latter) are in a never-ending quandary, for while teaching is indeed a noble calling and essential—and in our times increasingly difficult—we have yet to identify a set of teacher behaviors which consistently and unambiguously are related positively to learning. In this respect teacher education resembles the common cold: physicians admit freely that they cannot cure it, but nonetheless—since the patients demand it—they will prescribe endless expensive remedies. This can lead to charlatanism.

Unlike musicology and violin playing, where a master of either need have no competence in the other, the discipline of education subsumes the art of teaching. One can teach in masterful fashion and know nothing of "education," but the position taken here is that the doctor of education who does not know how to teach and how to teach teachers is a fraud.

By way of further orientation, it seems useful to say that in any other country where the decision has been made—for whatever reasons—that a minority people is to use its own language as a medium of instruction for its children, the first step would be to provide for training the teachers by establishing a "normal school" staffed exclusively by that people and conducted exclusively in its own language. Although at the present time this might be impossible—not to say unthinkable—in the United States, it should be borne in mind.

"Bilingual education" is not an academic discipline. The term is an unfortunate misnomer for something old and well known and much simpler. It cannot be too often reiterated that although the goals of "bilingual education" may vary legitimately among educators, there can be no doubt about its immediate essential reality: the addition of another language (besides English) as a medium of instruction at whatever levels—kindergarten through Ph.D—that are involved. There will always be serious questions and problems of the relationship of that other language to English, but the new concern is not for English. English was already there. The institution's budget and staff were already devoted almost entirely to English-medium work. Presumably that staff was competent and was already doing its best. This means that irrespective of other criteria of organization, substance, experience, and method to be met in a teacher training program for bilingual education, it is essentially that old, well-known and simple thing, a little normal school or teachers college in a non-English language (for convenience, let us say Spanish), conducted by and for speakers of Spanish who will be working in turn with children who speak Spanish and want to learn through Spanish. All that is new and different about such a normal school is that

it is embedded in and dependent upon a larger institution which uses English for the same purposes;

it is likewise in a society where English is overwhelmingly dominant;

its teachers and students must have, in addition to their usual baggage of knowledge and skills, extraordinary awareness of the dynamics of bilingualism as a social, political, and economic phenomenon.

The specialist in bilingual education must be prepared to contend with these realities.

The legitimate variation in goals mentioned above was a reference to the view of some educators (and the laymen whose views they reflect) that bilingual education should be a transitional process, a more humane road to the mastery of English by native speakers of Spanish, and to the opposing view of other educators that their mastery of English is important but that the program should also aim at developing and maintaining high competence in the other tongue, the mother tongue. (A third goal, combined often with either of the two above, is that the program should also teach that other language to children who are monolingual speakers of English. Reference will be made later to this notion.)

It would be unwise and unnecessary to choose between the goals of transition and maintenance in designing a program of teacher training. The nature of language use and language learning is such that for the teacher or the teacher trainer there is no such thing as "transitional knowledge" or "transitional skill." The knowledge of language and the language skills needed to work effectively with first, second, and third graders and train their teachers cannot be conceived as transitional. Goal-setting, it might be added, is a prerogative of the local school, its pupils and their parents.

All of the above is but preliminary to the most serious problem in designing an undergraduate program, a master's program, or a doctoral program of teacher training for bilingual education. That problem is the need to start virtually on a *tabula rasa,* for only by chance will there be anyone already on the university faculty who has any competence in these matters. There has been in the past no need for such persons. Therefore the identification, recruitment and budgeting of the new staff will be unusually burdensome and must recognize the need to consider seeking help abroad.

KINDS OF TRAINING NEEDED BY
ELEMENTARY AND SECONDARY SCHOOL TEACHERS

The design and content of master's level and doctoral level programs for preparing teachers and the trainers of teachers for bilingual education can be determined only by examining the needs of those persons who will actually teach in the schools. The kinds of training needed and the extent of the need can be shown by an analysis of the case of the Spanish speakers. The example is illustrative only, but it applies in appropriate degree to all of the other language groups. There are four different groups of Spanish speakers in the United States who might be trained as bilingual education teachers or supervisors or trainers of teachers, and their needs are—in general—correspondingly different.

Puerto Ricans. Middle and economically depressed classes. A strong tradition of education through Spanish. Two kinds of potential teachers:

Many with school (and even university) training in Puerto Rico who are teachers or could quickly be converted. Principal need: the extra education courses needed for them to achieve certification in the United States.

Those born and reared in continental U. S. A., native Spanish speakers but no *education* through Spanish. Principal needs: *b* through *f* below, plus certification. (They also often need help to get into and through college.)

Cubans. Both the immigrants and those born here are largely middle class. They have a strong tradition of education, and among them are many persons already educated and experienced as teachers or capable of being converted quickly to teaching. The basic need is to orient them to American schools and give them the extra courses required if they are to be certified in the United States. Those reared here are similar to the Puerto Ricans in the last paragraph above.

Mexican-Americans (Chicanos). Of all classes, but commonly of economically depressed origins. Have not had a tradition of education through Spanish, hence are commonly victims of the kind of education that bilingual-bicultural schools are designed to correct. For this reason, few Mexican-Americans, even though they may already be certified teachers, are prepared to work effectively as Spanish-medium teachers. Principal needs: *b* through *f* below, plus correspondingly greater need to know Mexico, study in Mexico, and through intensive study of Mexican schools *see how easily Mexican children learn and develop in a truly supportive environment.*

Others. There are probably close to one million "Latin Americans" and Spanish persons in the United States, i.e., Spanish speakers other than those listed above. Their situation most closely approximates that of the Cubans.

Among all of the Spanish-surnamed persons now teaching in the schools there are probably not over 3,000 who could be converted to become Spanish-medium teachers, either because they do not know Spanish, or because they do not want to leave what they are now doing. Therefore, most bilingual education teachers, except those already educated abroad, should get their training at the pre-service, undergraduate level.

Teachers and other educational personnel who are expected to work through the non-English language must have the following qualifications if they are to be maximally effective:

a.   They must be native speakers of the other language or have acquired equivalent competence *as a prerequisite to entering a training program.* (Not all "native speakers" are suitable, because their language may have been overly modified and weakened by contact and confusion with English. Experience has demonstrated that it is exceedingly difficult to remedy this weakness in adults. Non-native Spanish speakers with complete fluency are rare, but their participation should be encouraged.)

b.   They must be literate—able to read and write—in Spanish at least as well as average American school teachers can do these in English.

c.   They should have a superior knowledge of the history and cultures of the children they will be teaching and of those children's forebears. This knowledge should include a sympathetic understanding of the aspirations, problems, life-style, etc., of the group, gained from direct sharing of that group's life.

d.   They should acquire the insights and skills needed for working effectively with children.

e.   They need a more than average knowledge of the phenomenon of bilingualism and of the nature of language and language learning, including the teaching of English as a second language (although this does not mean that they will or should necessarily teach English too).

f.   Ideally, they should have had at least a considerable portion of their own education through the medium of the other language—or must have considerable *special training* to compensate for a lack of this experience. (Knowledge of modern mathematics learned through English, plus ability to "talk Spanish" *does not* enable one to teach modern mathematics through Spanish.) The *special training* referred to is best imparted by giving the trainees a complete course in, for example, mathematics, by beginning with first-grade books and progressing as rapidly as possible through the sixth- (or higher) grade level, using Spanish-language texts and a trained Spanish-language teacher and working out all the problems and explanations *aloud*. It does not suffice—or even help—merely to talk about mathematics in Spanish, or give a methods course in Spanish or merely learn the Spanish terminology. Without considerable additional training of this kind in the major school subjects, no one can be expected to be responsible for the portion of the pupils' education that is to be presented through the non-English medium.

LEVELS OF TRAINING

There is need for four levels of training: career ladder for para-professionals, pre-service (or undergraduate), in-service, and graduate level. (Bilingual schooling should start as early as possible in a child's life, but, as circumstances warrant, projects can be started and be effective at any grade level from pre-K to Ph.D.)

Career-ladder type training (combining college work and service in schools) for teaching aides and aides who seek certification as teachers.

Pre-service, undergraduate training as non-English-medium teachers for persons having native competence or the equivalent.

In-service training for capable persons who are already certified as teachers, either intensive summer institutes, academic year fellowships or part-time during the academic year.

Masters and doctoral level studies for especially promising persons who aspire to become program directors, supervisors, or trainers of teachers.

It is evident from all of the above that

persons already educated through the non-English medium and experienced as teachers through that medium *can be prepared for bilingual education work through part-time in-service training conducted either by a school (LEA) or a college or university*; but

persons lacking that education and experience require intensive full-time training of such duration and intensity that it can reasonably be provided by only a college or university. (Persons already employed in bilingual schooling projects should not be removed from their positions, but should get full-time, intensive summer session training, plus in-service work.)

It should also be evident that much of the success of bilingual education at any level will depend upon the recruitment of faculty and admission to programs of persons whose linguistic skills and literacy are already—happily—close to excellent. Happily, too, there are many such persons.

ESSENTIAL FEATURES OF
A UNIVERSITY TRAINING CENTER

Bilingual education is a pedagogical innovation, but to a much greater extent its significance is sociological and goes far beyond the walls of the school. In truth, if it is not supported vigorously outside of the school among the people, the adults who speak that other language, what happens inside the school will be meaningless. (The truth of this statement becomes apparent when one considers the extent to which children take their cues from society's unvoiced signals. Of 500 children playing together daily on an American school ground, half of them Spanish-speaking, half English-speaking, it is certain that after a year the former would know a great deal of English and the latter would know very little or no Spanish. Yet all have equal ability to learn another language.) There are, therefore, three essential components to the program: the community, the schools, and the university itself. What this implies is that the university training center cannot be confined to the university's cloistered halls: it must concern itself powerfully, taking the role of leadership, with the other two components.

The Role of the Community

This means much more than that of advising on a governing board and winning its share of the controversies. The community should be democratically represented on any such board, but its function (with whatever help is required from the other two component agencies) is to provide the indispensable, highly visible support for bilingual education beyond the school walls, without which bilingual education cannot succeed. That support includes such activities as the following, all in the other language, the non-English language:

Enthusiastic approval in homes, churches, clubs, etc.

Entertainment and pleasure, all in the other language, for children and teachers:

> festivals, suppers, picnics, movies, easy reading—easily obtained—including comics, of which there are, amazingly, excellent ones (at least in Spanish) with rewarding themes and good language; also a world of junk;

folk dance clubs, poetry clubs, singing clubs, story telling, newspaper publicity, trips (to San Juan, to El Paso, to Los Angeles, to Mexico, etc.);

speakers, singers, dancers (brought to entertain)

Community people (parents, businessmen, etc.) should be asked to appear often at the schools, at assemblies and other meetings, to reinforce repeatedly to the children *in the non-English language* the importance of what they are doing. Unless the community itself can act on the conviction that language, literacy, and the other culture really matter, bilingual education will be nothing but another innovative gimmick. Teachers, and their teachers, must learn how to work with the community to encourage such activity.

The Role of the Schools

In a training project the role of the school (and the teacher trainer's role in those schools) is no less essential. Since few of those involved in a school project could be expected to have significant experience in bilingual education, they would all have to learn by doing. As a component of the university training center there would be need for at least one strong bilingual school in the city or very nearby to be used as a training and demonstration site. It would be the task of the teacher trainers and trainees, working cooperatively with the school's faculty, to develop that school into a model (i.e., exemplar of excellence). Ideally, demonstration schools of two kinds are needed:

a one-way—Spanish-S—school (providing Spanish-medium instruction for Hispanics only, in schools where they are only a minority);

a two-way school (both English mother tongue and non-English mother tongue pupils, each group learning through both languages).

These schools would be important sites of pre-service, in-service, and teacher-trainer training. Whenever possible, already existing Title VII schools should be given preference in the selection of participants in training projects.

The Role of the University

The university (or college) must, first of all, openly and forthrightly espouse bilingual-bicultural education and the measure of cultural pluralism that this entails. This means that it must begin to conceive of itself and proclaim itself as, at least in part, a bilingual, dual-medium (two-language) institution, and this would be reflected by printing a portion of the university catalog of courses, and the pertinent announcements, forms, etc., in the non-English tongue.

The university's bilingual education training component may be a single, separate "school," "department," or "center," with all of its faculty and activities exclusive to itself, or it may draw on resources from several established components of the university. In either case, the bilingual education training component should have its own organizational structure and its own director and supporting staff.

On the director and faculty depends the success of the enterprise. The director—whether a woman or a man—must be highly literate and educated in both languages, which means having received a significant portion of his or her education through the medium of each of the languages.

Members of the teaching staff (except, for example, persons whose function is to explain the teaching of English as a second language) must also be highly literate in the non-English language and fully capable of using it as the exclusive medium of instruction in their classes. They must be able to function at the professional level in that language, both orally and in writing. They need not be "native" speakers of the language but must have equivalent command of it. These competencies, especially the ability to write acceptably, must be supported by examples of what they have written.

All members of the supporting staff (secretaries, clerks, etc.) should be speakers (preferably educated!) of the non-English tongue.

In order to meet the above criteria it will probably be necessary, and will in all cases be wise, to include on the faculty of the center either as regular or as visiting professors some individuals who have received all or most of their education in a country where the non-English tongue is the main cultural medium. Understandably, bilingual education for American Indian children is a special case. Because of the delicacy and extreme importance of selecting competent professors, the task of selection should be backed by a screening committee of especially able, disinterested individuals who are themselves highly educated and literate in the language. (See especially the treatment of this topic in the section below devoted to the Puerto Rican or Mexican-American studies program.)

PSYCHOSOCIOLOGICAL CONSIDERATIONS

The above emphasis on reasonable education and literacy in the non-English tongue will astonish those who would find it inconceivable that a university professor—or a school teacher—should not be educated and literate in a tongue which is to be her or his medium of instruction. The same emphasis will anger those who are near-illiterate and totally unprepared in that tongue (their mother tongue) but who see such an emphasis as an irrelevant barrier set up to exclude them. Both points of view have merit. The university cannot condone intellectual fraud (although many do and in this same field), and the Chicanos and Puerto Ricans know that improved education for their peoples can come only through and from themselves.

The point of view taken here is that education through the non-English tongue and literacy in that tongue are *not* the most important qualifications of these persons. *They are merely the minimal, first or lowest level requisite, without which the other more important ones have no meaning whatsoever in terms of bilingual education.* The reason this must be stressed as a *sine qua non* is that most American speakers of Spanish are victims of the kind of educational policy that bilingual education seeks to correct. All over the country, in the bilingual schooling projects, there is frantic emphasis on "learning styles," "criterion-referenced tests," "language dominance," "English as a second language," "bilingual teaching methods," "reading disabilities," etc., and constant complaints that the 10,000 and more separate teaching materials in Spanish already available to them are not adequate and all this in large measure because the teachers' level of literacy is so low that they cannot read and use those materials and teach simply and powerfully in Spanish and must therefore find something else to do.[1]

One more observation about language is in order. It is quite likely that the pupils (mother tongue speakers of a non-English tongue) will use a variant form of that tongue. It should go without too much saying that the child, and therefore the child's and its parents' language, must be respected. Preferably the teachers will know that variant. At least they must understand it and use it as a point of departure for their instruction, which will for the most part be in and should aim toward mastery of a standard form of the language.[2]

To all of the above must be added the reminder that although no one finds ignorance of electronics or algebra or geography an intolerable reflection on her or his worthiness as a person, any hint that one's language is inadequate is intolerable.

How the university which is planning a master's or doctoral program in bilingual education is to deal with this matter is for it to say. Some suggestions are:

> Conditional faculty appointments, plus subsidized preliminary study abroad in the fields of greatest need. (The Spanish-speaking educational psychologist or historian, etc., trained exclusively through English, spends a year in Mexico working closely in Spanish with a counterpart in his field. The "methods" person spends a year abroad teaching mathematics or social studies in a Mexican public school and attending a Mexican normal college.)

> Recruitment of Puerto Rican or Mexican (or Chilean or Argentine, etc.) specialists on two- or three-year appointments to make up most of the first faculty.

> Establishment of a major portion of the graduate program (and undergraduate too) in Mexico or another Spanish-speaking country with American oversight and foreign faculty.

> Organization of a post-B.A. teacher exchange program with Puerto Rico, Spain, etc., by which American native speakers of Spanish aspiring to take an M.A. in bilingual education would have a preliminary, non-credit year teaching regular school subjects through Spanish in a public school. (This has been done in Colombia and elsewhere.)

SUGGESTED CURRICULA

The content of undergraduate training to prepare for Spanish-medium teaching is suggested by lettered items *a-f* above. Apart from those suggestions one has but to bear in mind the UNESCO stress on the importance of giving teachers in these cases "much of their theoretical training and all their practice teaching in the mother tongue." (That is to say, through Spanish, using college-level materials published in Spanish.)

The general outline of the graduate-level curriculum, all presented through Spanish unless otherwise indicated, follows:

Tentative Course of Study

Courses	Language of instruction	Level	Amount
Language Study			
0. (Language proficiency develops from listening to and dialogue with proficient speakers, from wide reading, from disciplined writing, and from the prospect of material or other gain if proficiency is achieved. Therefore, much assigned reading, class discussion, and disciplined writing of précis.)	Spanish.	All levels. This is not a course. All professors must require it constantly.	Frequently
0. (Writing of essays, reports)	Spanish	All levels	
1. Something like "Spanish grammar for teachers"	Spanish	Masters	3 hrs. weekly 2 semesters
2. Contrastive analysis of Spanish and English	Spanish	Masters	3 hrs. weekly 1 semester
3. Teaching English as a second language	English	Masters	3 hrs. weekly 1 semester
Sociolinguistics/Ethnopoltics			
1. Readings and discussion dealing with dual- and multi-language states and bi- and multi-lingualism: Canada, South Africa, the rest of Africa, the Arabic world, India, Switzerland, Ireland, the USSR, Puerto Rico, etc.	Readings in English, Spanish, French, etc., with all discussion in Spanish	Masters	3 hrs. weekly 2 semesters
		Doctoral	3 hrs. weekly 4 semesters
2. Readings in language and language learning	Same as above	Masters	3 hrs. weekly 1 semester
		Doctoral	3 hrs. weekly 2 semesters

History, Anthropology, Sociology, etc.

1. History, political and cultural, Puerto Rico	Spanish, English, with all discussion in Spanish	Masters	5 hrs. weekly 2 semesters
2. Same as above, Mexican Americans	Same as above	Masters	5 hrs. weekly 2 semesters
3. Same as above for Cubans, if their children are substantially involved.	Same as above	Masters	5 hrs. weekly 2 semesters

Methods and Materials of Instruction

1. Intensive review and experience courses (not in methods and materials per se) as described in the text above dealing with special training for mathematics, social studies, and science.	Spanish	Masters	2 hrs. weekly 1 semester in each of the three fields
2. Introduction to evaluation of achievement	Spanish	Masters	3 hrs. weekly 2 semesters
3. Advanced studies in evaluation	Spanish	Doctoral	3 hrs. weekly 4 semesters
4. Extensive readings in pedagogy	Spanish	Masters Doctoral	3 hrs. weekly

School-based Work

(Ideally, the university will be the guide and sponsor of at least one bilingual school in which the teacher trainees, supervised directly by their own professors, will be the teachers. All together they will be developing a model of bilingual education.)	Spanish	Masters / Doctoral	As school schedule requires, 2 semesters / Same as above, but no credit

Community-based Work

(See section in text above, "Role of the Community." Those activities will not happen without leadership, and the masters and doctoral candidates must supply it.)	Spanish	Masters / Doctoral	Continuously, unendingly / Continuously, unendingly

In addition to the curriculum noted, the master's candidate should be asked to do an original essay, in Spanish, on a topic pertinent to bilingualism, sociolinguistics, ethnopolitics, or pedagogy.

The tentative course of study does not provide adequately for the doctoral program. Further guidelines or suggestions are these:

Since bilingual education is not in itself a discipline, the areas of scholarly specialization are *bilingualism* as a linguistic and social phenomenon (see the work of Haugen, Fishman, Weinreich, Ervin-Tripp), *sociolinguistics* (Fishman, Gumperz, Malherbe, Mackey, Kloss, etc.), *ethnopolitics* (Lieberson, Touret, Falch, etc.), and possibly *language* (Lambert, Labov, Ferguson).

It should be required in any case that the doctoral candidate have all the knowledge and skill required of the master, and of course, complete respectability in Spanish.

I would advise requiring a working knowledge of French or German, because much of what is most significant in these fields appears in these languages.

SUPPLEMENTARY TRAINING ABROAD

Even as it is virtually impossible to produce a first-class foreign language teacher in the United States without supplementary training abroad in a country where the language is spoken natively, teachers in bilingual schools who have not already had considerable training abroad need the experience of a sojourn of intensive study abroad. The number of supportive experiences available abroad for such a teacher— experiences which cannot be provided yet in this country—is so obvious as to make this point self-evident. Above all, there is need for the first-hand experience of observing with what grace and ease the non-English-speaking child can learn anything and everything *if he is in a truly supportive environment.* The center should provide such supplementary experience for its trainees.

THE MEXICAN-AMERICAN OR PUERTO RICAN STUDIES PROGRAM

These ethnic studies programs represent one of the most promising reform movements in American education: a vigorous effort on the part of the students themselves to expand, enrich, and ennoble their own learning.[3] The programs' main features and goals overlap considerably with those of a bilingual teacher training center, and the two enterprises can be mutually reinforcing in a powerful way. The features in common are these:

Improvement of the education of their children and youth. (It is not uncommon for Puerto Rican or Mexican-American studies programs to sponsor after-school learning centers for elementary and secondary school youngsters, devoted to tutoring and morale-building activities.)

A strong, participatory relationship by college students in the affairs of the community, especially at its lowest socioeconomic level.

Emphasis on the history and culture of the group.

A desire for education through their own language. (This is usually no more than an aspiration unfulfilled because of the difficulty of finding competent professors. It could be met fully by the training center described here.)

The point is that a university training center for English-Spanish bilingual education would be strengthened greatly by the inclusion of or close collaboration with a corresponding ethnic studies program. In any case, these two should not be separate enterprises on the campus.

RELATIONSHIP TO THE REGULAR DEPARTMENT OF SPANISH LANGUAGE AND LITERATURE

It seems fair to say that on most campuses with Puerto Rican or Mexican-American studies programs, the students and faculty of these programs perceive the institution's department of Spanish language and literature as hostile and uncooperative. To the extent that there is hostility and unwillingness to cooperate, these probably stem from two points:

The department's reluctance to enlarge its concern for literacy, scholarship, and elitist bilingualism in order to embrace the concerns of folk bilingualism with its sociological overtones.

The inability of both groups—the non-English language department and the ethnic studies department—to adopt a reconciling attitude toward the differences between the world standard language and the language spoken by most participants in the ethnic studies program.

These two points of contention can be resolved. A university in which the training program for—as an example—English-Spanish bilingual education did not have the strong support of its professors of Spanish language and literature would be a house too badly divided within itself to stand.

NOTA BENE

1.   In all of the above there is no provision for trainees to work in a language other than Spanish. In truth, unless the professors happen to be fully prepared in another non-English language too, no such other work is possible without compromising unacceptably the scholarly integrity of the program. Any attempt to work simultaneously with two or more language groups of trainees forces the entire operation into English. See Introductory Reminders, above, second paragraph.

2.   There is no mention of "bilingual methods" or "bilingual approaches," for these terms suggest the use of two languages by the teacher during a single class session. This is pedagogically counterproductive, since, as Haugen has said, the bilingual's main problem is to keep the languages apart.

3.   There is no suggestion that a given teacher should be prepared to teach through English as well as a non-English tongue. For many reasons, political,

economic, and pedagogical, to require such dual-language work is unfair and counterproductive.

4. Reference was made above to the possible inclusion of monolingual, English-speaking children in a school program of bilingual education. To do so seems to require completely separate tracks, one for the Anglos, one for the Hispanos, during the first three years of elementary school before the Anglos can learn enough Spanish to be combined in the same classes with Hispanos. To do otherwise, i.e., to combine Anglos and Hispanos from the beginning, requires foreign language teaching methods for the Anglos and this makes unfeasible a program of strong Spanish-medium work with the Hispanos. Stated otherwise, the complications of two-way schools are so great that it is far better to limit the bilingual program to Hispanos. (This subject has been treated at length in other papers—A.B.G.)

NOTES

1. For discussion of the best evaluation to date of bilingual schooling, see B. Gaarder, "Bilingual Education: Central Questions and Concerns," *New York University Education Quarterly*, VI, 4 (Summer, 1975), p. 2-6.

2. See Chapters 5 and 11.

3. See Chapter 10 for *El Plan de Santa Bárbara*.

8

POLITICAL PERSPECTIVE ON BILINGUALISM AND BILINGUAL EDUCATION

INTRODUCTION: EVERYTHING IS POLITICS

Georg Lukacs' aphorism that "everything is politics" is not so true as to obviate all effort to delimit the scope of this inquiry. Drawing selectively on Webster for help, our interest lies in the art or science of government . . . the regulation and control of men . . . adjusting and ordering relationships between individuals and groups . . . concern for the state as a whole rather than for the individual person . . . competition for power. . . . It does not exclude the artful, expedient, dishonest practices that give to politics a sometimes pejorative connotation.

Even so, it will not always be possible within the limits of this essay to sort out from the political those strands that are better labelled psychological or philosophical or economic or sociological, or to assign the proper weight to each of these when they seem to be the very stuff of each other.

Another source of confusion is the need to separate bilingual education from bilingualism itself. In an earlier essay (Gaarder 1969, p. 149) I accepted the definition of Macnamara (1967, p. 60), who used the term bilingual for "persons who possess at least one of the language skills even to a minimal degree in their second language." He considered bilingualism to be "a continuum, or rather a whose series of continua, which vary amongst individuals along a whole variety of dimensions." In that essay I hoped to dispose of the notion of "balanced bilingualism," except as a purely theoretical construct, by pointing out that each successive bit of experience in life comes through one language alone, and since nothing can be relived, equal bilingualism is impossible. A consideration of the domains and times of language usage makes it apparent immediately that no mother could know two diaper languages and use them in a balanced way with each of her babies. No couple could use two languages in a balanced way for love-making. No boy will know equally well two special lexicons used in playing marbles. In short, since nothing in nature has its equal, the only sense in which "balanced bilingualism" could properly be used is to say that quantitatively (or by some other criterion) what the speaker can do in some domains in one language is sufficient to balance what he can do in other domains in the other one. This obviously equates balance with difference.

This broad view of bilingualism omits a differentiation that is crucial to the present inquiry: the distinction between academic (or elitist) bilingualism acquired and developed by choice and that societal or folk bilingualism which is produced not from choice but because two language groups are juxtaposed or intermingled and circumstances—primarily the need to go on eating—dictate the need on the part of some of the people to use both tongues. Here too the distinction is not always perfectly clear. Elitist bilingualism—a hallmark of intellectuals and the learned in most societies—may come from tutoring, from foreign residence, from servants in the home, from foreign language study in schools or even from foreign-medium schooling, i.e., a form of bilingual education. What characterizes it is the element of choice: it was not imposed by economic necessity, by colonial status, or other unavoidable forces. Folk or societal bilingualism does not depend at all on schooling or choice, although it may be either reinforced or weakened by school practices.

A second crucial distinction must be made between bilingualism involving only one people within a state and the same phenomenon where two or more peoples are in unavoidable contact within a single state.

Thus, the rather widespread elitist use of French in Russia at the turn of the 1800's involved only one people: the Russians. The fairly common practice in Latin America of sending one's children to English-language schools involves only one people. In neither case is there aggressive competition of one people against another. Likewise in the Arabic states: only Arabs are involved in their diglossic bilingualism. The attempt in Ireland to reestablish widespread use of Irish is another case in point. On the other hand, French-English societal bilingualism in Quebec, Spanish-English societal bilingualism in the United States, and Marathi-Hindi-English trilingualism in India arise because two peoples (or three) are in contact and competition within a single state. They are not matters of individual choice. The fact that the acquisition of English in India has always led to the development of an English-speaking elite does not override the compelling socioeconomic need for English and the fact that its study is imposed by law.

The essential point of the two distinctions is that at the individual (or group) level of elitist choice within a single society politics plays no role or a very minor one either in bilingualism or in bilingual education. (It is not easy to deny any political implications whatsoever in the Brahmins' exclusionistic addiction to Sanskrit or in Catherine's French-speaking Russians or in an individual priest's use of Latin.) At the other extreme of two peoples in competition within a single state where one of the peoples tends to become bilingual involuntarily in order to survive, political considerations predominate in decisions about bilingual education, and Georg Lukacs' aphorism is quite in order.

Some of these distinctions have been further clarified in terms of the presence or absence of "diglossia," but the introduction of that term would not be helpful at this point.

A further brief digression is in order to make clear what is meant by bilingual education. It is education in which the learner receives significant amounts of formal instruction[1] (schooling) through two languages used as mediums of that instruction. The two kinds of learning experience may be simultaneous, or sequential, or widely separated in time and place. The mere inclusion in the school curriculum of foreign language instruction by itself does not justify the label bilingual instruction, since it is the medium, at most, for teaching itself. Nor is it necessary that the mother tongue be one of the two mediums of instruction, although this is unquestionably desirable and is predominantly the case everywhere. In the nineteenth century in India the Muslims, who spoke Urdu, did not employ their mother tongue as the medium of instruction. Rather they used Persian at the lower level of schooling and Persian and Arabic at the upper. Both were "foreign" languages to them (Kanungo 1962, p. 6). Similarly—although with a totally different rationale—a child in Kenya might not receive his primary instruction in the mother tongue (although nineteen different languages are so used) but might begin directly with the common regional tongue, Swahili, and then go on with the official language, English.

William Mackey has devised a typology which describes 250 essentially different combinations of the key components of a program of two-language education (Mackey 1970, pp. 63-82). (The fact that the above definition and Mackey's typology account for all possible patterns does not at all mean that the patterns are equally effective pedagogically or even that every pattern has been somewhere utilized.)

Not everything, of course, is politics where bilingual education is concerned, but a few examples will serve to hint at the preponderance of political considerations where such education—and societal bilingualism itself—are in play. Samarin has noted that in Africa Europeans have opposed the learning and use of European languages by Africans, because it raises the African's status. He points out similar "discouragement of learning of German and Dutch in the former colonies of the Cameroon and Indonesia" (Samarin 1962, p. 62).

Language planning in "developing" states calls for the best insights of the sociolinguist, but in the end the decisions are political. Ruth Sutherlin offers an example: "The Nandi and Kipsigis of Kenya who speak mutually intelligible languages refused to accept literature written in each other's languages on grounds of unintelligibility. A Nandi-Kipsigis language committee, aware of the similarity of the languages and guessing the political reasons for the claim of unintelligibility, solved the problem by giving the languages equal prominence with the cover term 'Kalenjin' " (Sutherlin 1962, p. 69).

The fact that Dutch and Danish scientists—for example—are most likely to publish their research in English (and to have learned English) is more than a matter of efficiency or convenience. It is an example of the politics of science.

That language classification—and the corresponding educational decisions—is commonly based on socio-political grounds is amply demonstrated. Ferguson and Gumperz (1960, pp. 4-13) discuss this phenomenon as it applies to Hindi, with a learned vocabulary from Sanskrit and using Devanagari script (is it one language or several?) and Urdu, the (same?) language drawing on Persian and using Perso-Arabic script; and to Konkani and Marathi. They see "certain sociological conditions (e.g., use of a standard, speakers' feeling of belonging to a speech community)" as determinants of whether there is in a given case one language or two or several.

Heinz Kloss notes that "the Czarist government in the nineteenth century tried to persuade the Ukrainians that [their language] was . . . a Russian dialect . . . and that the natural thing was that they be educated and governed in Russian" (Kloss 1967, p. 45). In brief, peoples are as prone to attempt to establish the separate autonomy and uniqueness of languages which are all but identical in linguistic terms and have almost total mutual intelligibility (e.g., Serbian and Croatian, Hindi and Urdu) as they are to assert the oneness of languages which by the linguist's criteria are different and which have little mutual intelligibility (e.g., classical Arabic and all its vernaculars).

Another example of the socio-politics of bilingualism—and thus of bilingual education—is the fact that ". . . nearly all speakers of Low Saxon (Low German) and the overwhelming majority of Occitan (Provencal) speakers have lost consciousness of their linguistic identity and consider their folk speech as naturally subordinated to German and French respectively, though linguists continue to group these folk languages with other Gothic and Romance languages" (Kloss 1967, p. 46). These views of Provencal and Low Saxon as nothing but dialects of the "real" languages, arise from school policies (school politics) which show "concern for the state as a whole [and the state language] rather than for the individual person" and his language.

A few more examples of what appear to be decisions taken on preponderant-ly political grounds should suffice to make the case: the low place of German in United States schools after 1918 . . . the spread of French as a language of wider communication (LWC) after 1945 . . . the generous attitude in the USSR toward other languages than Russian . . . the repressive measures in Spain against the Catalan and Basque languages . . . the choice of French or English as official and school languages in some African states.

Nationalism, chauvinism, ethnocentricity, missionary zeal, are emotional correlates of political judgments. Or is it the other way around?

The statements which follow are tentative attempts to reduce the welter of data to useful generalizations.

First Generalization. Bilingual education stemming from societal or folk bilingualism (as differentiated from individual or academic bilingualism by choice) is always the reflection of a political stance. The main burden of this essay is to demonstrate the validity and the implications of this generalization.

Corollary. Since bilingual education seldom represents the original school policy in a two- or more language state, it might more accurately and usefully be defined as the choice and addition of another tongue as a school medium.

Second Generalization. Societal bilingual education or its omission or prohibition may be either an instrument for the destruction of a culture or an instrument for the preservation and maintenance of a culture.

The clearest examples that come to mind are Puerto Rico and the Republic of South Africa. In poor, benighted, beautiful Puerto Rico "political circumstances," as Pedro Cebollero has put it, "springing mainly from the results of a war in which Puerto Rico did not participate, have forced upon the schools the task of trying to give to all pupils a mastery of English, in addition to the normal educational equipment generally accepted as the objective of educational systems everywhere" (Cebollero 1945, p. 1). From Cebollero's account we learn that "the question of the language of instruction . . . became a bone of contention and a source of almost constant debate. The issue was taken over by local politicians and considerable emotion was injected into its discussion. Finally, it became identified with the political question of the attitude of the Puerto Ricans toward the United States, and with the issue of the final determination of the political status of the Island."

From Cebollero's well-documented study, all of the elements typical of such a case are revealed: the usurper's disdain for the Spanish spoken there, "a patois" (Tomás Navarro Tomás thought it as good as that spoken in most of Spain) . . . "the Puerto Rican leaders were very much interested in learning the language of the new rulers" . . . the American who organized the new system of bilingual education after 1898 evidently foresaw or hoped for an eventual shift to English for he justified the continued study of Spanish on grounds that it "is doubtless destined to be the household tongue of the people for many years to come."

Dr. Victor S. Clark wrote that in 1900. Seventy-four years later the possibility of eventual massive shift to English and corresponding abandonment of Spanish is an increasing concern. Meanwhile, official educational policy imposed by the United States went through several stages: (1) 1900-1905—Spanish as the elementary school medium, English as a subject; English as the medium in secondary schools, Spanish as a subject; most of the early supervisors and teachers of English "ex-soldiers, ex-teamsters, ex-packers, and other such men very largely" (quoting Commissioner Brumbaugh); (2) 1905-1916—English as the medium in all grades of the school system; in 1909 the policy excluded the teaching of reading in Spanish in the first grade even as a subject; (3) 1916-1934—Spanish the medium in grades 1-4, Spanish and English in grade 5, and English in grades 6-8; English the medium in secondary schools.

That there are purely pedagogical considerations related to bilingual education is plain. That they may be subordinated to political considerations is no less evident. In 1925 the Legislature of Puerto Rico provided for an extensive survey of the nation's educational system by the International Institute of Teachers College, Columbia University (New York City). The recommendations of the survey (which would have postponed instruction in English until the fourth grade and the use of English as the medium of school instruction until grade seven) were entirely disregarded (Cebollero, p. 17).[2]

The fourth language policy (1934-1937) made Spanish the medium in grades 1-8, with English to be studied as a special subject sometimes receiving double time. After 1937, although there has been a relaxation in fact of policies which imposed English as a language of instruction, official United States policy, enunciated by President Franklin D. Roosevelt, declared that one of the main objectives was to give the Puerto Ricans a mastery of English and develop them into a bilingual population (Cebollero, p. 27). Since 1945 there has been further relaxation of policies which forced the use of English in education, but there is nevertheless evidence of increasing societal bilingualism (Leibowitz 1969, p. 47).

A major source of confusion throughout the seventy-four years of Puerto Rico's colonial relationship to the United States has been the exclusively political question of whether or not, for monolingual Spanish-speaking children in Puerto Rico, English could rightfully be considered a "foreign" language. Throughout those years "the nationalists . . . embraced the cause of Spanish as the language of instruction, and branded the use of English for that purpose as a symptom of American imperialism and as a menace to the personality of the Puerto Rican. The champions of political association with the United States embraced the cause of English as the language of instruction . . . and the issue became definitely identified with local party politics" (Cebollero, p. 13).

The tragic irony of politics applied to decisions about language stands out in a statement by United States Senator Henry M. Jackson, a member of the United States-Puerto Rico Commission on the Status of Puerto Rico, who, speaking of the possibility of Puerto Rico's becoming one of the United States, extolled the "old and rich culture" of Puerto Rico and welcomed "diversity," but pointed out that "the unity of our Federal-State structure . . . requires a common tongue." "Surely," the Senator said, "at a time when we are trying to eliminate ghettos of all kinds, we should not establish within our Federal-State system a 'language ghetto.' A condition precedent to Statehood must be the recognition and acceptance of English as the *official* language" (Jackson 1966). The Senator seemingly did not know that "language ghettos" are caused by the enforcement of political decisions to replace one language by another.

The situation in the Republic of South Africa illustrates the other kind of political decision about bilingual education: placing limitations on it in order to protect a language and culture. E. G. Malherbe, reporting on English-Afrikaans bilingualism and bilingual schooling in South Africa, has pointed out that "the percentage of people speaking both English and Afrikaans dropped from 73% in 1951 to 66% in 1960 as a result of separating Afrikaans and English-speaking children at school and students at universities in separate institutions" (Malherbe 1969, p. 326; 1946). This separatist policy, which reduced the amount of bilingual education in order to reduce the extent of Afrikaans-English bilingualism, reflects the dominant Afrikaners' understanding of our second and fourth "generalizations."

Sociocultural pressures had always caused more Afrikaans speakers to learn English than they caused English speakers to learn Afrikaans. If the entire population became bilingual there would be no reason for two languages of supposedly equal status, Afrikaans would be widely abandoned in favor of the more useful world language, and the Afrikaners' identity as a people would be severely threatened, perhaps even destroyed. Thus the Afrikaans-speakers have sought to defend their language by reducing the number of bilingual individuals in their country.

It was the gradual shift toward linguistic fusion to the profit of French that provoked the reaction on the part of the Dutch-speakers in Belgium and the present linguistic boundaries of 1962 to guarantee the end of that aggression (Touret 1973, pp. 43-69).

Corollary. The use of a language as a medium of formal schooling is a far more powerful way of teaching it and of developing effective bilingualism in its learners than is study of the language as a school subject.

Third Generalization. Societal bilingual education (even as societal bilingualism itself) takes its dynamics from the relative socio-political status of the two peoples in contact. That status might be seen as having two components: prestige of the language and culture, and power (economic, political, military) of the people.

Corollary. It is commonly—at times exclusively—the weaker people that become bilingual. One might be tempted to postulate that at the societal level and where two peoples are in contact bilingualism is a mark of the poor and weak— even as academic bilingualism by individual choice is a mark of the elite. In Canada it is the French who become bilingual; in Louisiana the Cajuns (Acadiens) and speakers of *le français nègre*; in Mexico the indigenes, and so on. But the postulate would not hold; it would have to yield to too many exceptions: in Brussels both the Flemish and the Walloons become bilingual (although not at all in equal degree) and neither is clearly weaker than the other, since the former's numerical and economic weight is offset by the latter's more prestigious culture and language. In the Republic of South Africa a similar situation obtains between native speakers of Afrikaans and native speakers of English and for much the same reasons. Among Jewish males elitist (Yiddish-Hebrew) bilingualism has been common, and in the same individuals, forced by the need to survive, command of the language of the larger society (societal bilingualism). It should be noted that in the German parts of Switzerland, speakers of German and Schwyzertutsch would not be an exception to our suggested postulate, because they constitute but one people. Paraguay would not present an exception either, because the Paraguayans' attitude is that the European and indigenous components of their nationality have been fused into one people.

Fourth Generalization. Societal bilingualism (apart from diglossic situations) is an unstable linguistic and social phenomenon tending toward language shift and abandonment of the socio-economico-politically weaker language when that language no longer has a substantial body of monolingual speakers. No people, Fishman has put it, needs two languages for the same set of purposes. Therefore bilingual education for the weaker people, since it increases the number of bilinguals and decreases the number of monolinguals is potentially destructive of the weaker language.[3]

Apart from this consideration, there is another reason why addition of the mother tongue as a school medium for children of a linguistic minority does not necessarily contribute to strengthening of the minority language and culture. The program may be conceived, designed, and operated solely as a quicker, less painful bridge to the other language and culture, the official ones.[4]

These are only two of the politico-social dilemmas faced by Chicanos (Mexican-Americans), Puerto Ricans, and native American Indians in the United States. They are caught in the destructive position (particularly the Spanish-speakers) of Fishman's *bilingualism without diglossia* (Fishman 1967).

Diglossia means the relatively stabilized situation of two languages or dialects in contact within a single society, with each of them used only for compartment-alized, complementary functions and therefore not in competition with each other. The classic examples are Spanish and Guaraní, peacefully non-competitive in Paraguay and likely to continue so; and classical Arabic and the Arabic vernaculars, each assigned, as it were, to separate, complementary domains of their speakers' lives. The twelve million or so Spanish-speakers in the United States have not established diglossia for their language vis-à-vis English. Rather, in their intra-group speech the two languages alternate constantly, switching and macarronic writing are objects of pride (Chacón 1969, Palomares 1972), and the overall situation is that of "replacive bilingualism . . . during which the yielding language becomes laden with loanwords and loanshifts from the overcoming language" Kloss 1967, p. 44).

The dilemma here is that bilingual education, instituted for them in the United States on a very modest scale in 1969, can be expected to give superior competency in English to children who might otherwise have become discouraged, dropped out of school, and lapsed into virtual Spanish monolingualism, and thus bilingual education can be expected to increase their number who know English well and increase the likelihood of shift. Nevertheless, the present status of the Spanish language, due to school policies (political decisions) which have led to widespread illiteracy in Spanish and the rise of variant regional dialects, makes something like bilingual education mandatory if Spanish is not to be allowed to evolve into a welter of non-standard variants. In either direction lies the prospect of widespread shift, for the stronghold pockets of Spanish monolingualism are ever smaller and fewer. In sum, the problem (for the Spanish-speakers who wish to maintain their language) is to devise a political strategy which will secure for them the benefits and avoid the dangers of bilingual education. An attempt to devise such a politics will be the object of a case study later in this essay.

Corollary. Societal bilingual education in situations where children learn both languages—one relatively strong, one relatively weak—at home and in the home neighborhood (i.e., in the absence of diglossia) can be the surest, swiftest, most generous road to shift away from the weak language.

If peoples such as the Chicanos and Puerto Ricans in the United States should seek to establish a defensive diglossic relationship between their use of English and their use of Spanish it would, it appears, require "assigning" each of the languages to distinct, complementary, non-competitive roles or domains of their life. Such a "solution" would mean relegating their mother tongue to the subordinate, largely unwritten status of use mainly in the home, for "intimate," "folksy," informal purposes only. The case study referred to will return to this topic.

ETHNOPOLITICS AND LAWS
RELATED TO BILINGUAL EDUCATION

Ethnopolitics, says Guy Héraud, is concerned with the phenomenon of domination of one community by another within the borders of a single state.[5] We are concerned in this essay with but a single facet of that science: the use and abuse of bilingual education or the denial of bilingual education as components in the "solution" of ethnopolitical problems, whether protecting the asserted linguistic rights of dominated or threatened peoples or to protect the asserted greater interest of the state and deny those rights. Again an attempt will be made to arrive at useful generalizations, this time concerned with constitutional provisions and other laws. The illustrative material will draw heavily on two of the books cited, those by Bernard Touret and Jean Falch.

Fifth Generalization. It is a fundamental human right for a people to rear and educate its children in its own image, including—centrally—its own language.

The fact that the papal encyclical of 1963, *Pacem in Terris,* affirms this right and the United Nations-inspired Universal Declaration of Human Rights, 1948, denies it by omission are testimonials to the conflict of values suggested in parts of Webster's definition of politics: "concern for the state as a whole rather than for the individual person . . . competition for power." The encyclical puts it thus:

> We must declare most explicitly that any policy which tends to weaken the vitality and development of the minorities constitutes a serious assault (*faute*) on justice, even more serious when such manoeuvers seek to make them disappear. By contrast, nothing accords better with justice than action on the part of governing bodies to improve the conditions of life of the ethnic minorities, particularly in respect to their language, culture, customs, resources and economic endeavors.
>
> It will be noted, however, that the minorities, whether in reaction to the dire (*pénible*) situation imposed upon them or because of the vicissitudes of their past, are quite often inclined to exaggerate the importance of their particularities, even to the extent of giving them precedence over universal human values.[6]

Corollary. Societal bilingualism in two-people states is a major move toward assimilation of the weaker people.

Corollary. During the period of assimilation and language shift of a dominated other-language group to the state or official language and culture, that group will be at a disadvantage with respect to the dominant group. Stated otherwise, the group subjected to assimilation is being sacrificed to the "greater good" of the state as a whole and its dominant people.

A sweeping glance around the world reveals that there are nations which exert pressures toward assimilation and nations that either do not exert such pressures or do so to a much lesser extent. The choice is cultural autonomy for linguistic minorities within the bilingual or multilingual state, or assimilation of minorities to the dominant language and culture. A few examples will suffice to make the point. *Assimilative policies*: the Latin American nations; Canada (with some lessening since the Quebec separatist movement); France; Spain; Great Britain; the United States. *Pluralistic policies*: Belgium; Yugoslavia; Czechoslovakia; the USSR; Switzerland; the "developing" African nations; India; Hungary; Roumania; Democratic Republic of Germany.

The distinction is not so clear as the lists suggest. The multilingual developing African nations, concerned more with the structure, strength and viability of their states as organizations than with cultural unity (Fishman 1968) use as many as nineteen vernaculars (Kenya) in primary education, plus regional languages and LWCs (languages of wider communication). However, it is easy to demonstrate that their leaders look forward to eventual assimilation of all the vernacular groups to the regional tongue or to the LWC. Policies vis-à-vis education through non-Russian languages in the USSR are notably generous, but, as in gambling casinos, the odds always favor the house. Kloss has observed that Latvian or Ukrainian families that move to Siberia have no choice but to send their children to Russian-language schools. Russians who move to Riga or Odessa do not have to send theirs to non-Russian-language schools (Kloss 1967, p. 43). Furthermore, Russian is the language of relationship among the republics and nationalities of the USSR.

The United States has been notable for its "melting pot" policy, including school policies designed to discourage and even punish the use of Spanish by school children, and school policies designed to wipe out American Indian languages by combining children from several tribes in the same school and appointing teachers unable to speak any of their mother tongues. However, the policy of combining attrition of the non-English languages with full social and cultural assimilation of such minorities as the Poles, the Norwegians and the Germans, has not operated the same way with the "visible" linguistic minorities, the indigenes and those marked by admixture of indigenous or negroid stock. Of these it might be said that the dominant cultural group has wanted them to want to assimilate and give up their languages but in the end they have commonly found the door to assimilation closed.

The federal legislation, the Bilingual Education Act, 1968, which supports such schooling in the United States contains no suggestion of cultural autonomy or the preservation of the minority languages. Rather, it is educational assistance for "children of limited English-speaking ability" written ambiguously to give comfort to both assimilationists and cultural pluralists.[7] The Indian Education Act permits and supports ($40 million appropriated in fiscal year 1974) any emphasis whatsoever on developing the American Indian languages and cultures, but in the knowledge that the total effect—as the tiny Indian groups unite supposedly to gain political advantage—will be a reluctant pan-Indianism, perhaps even an avowed pan-Indianism (always and unavoidably in English), and thus a powerful stimulus to assimilation. A complete analysis of laws in the United States bearing upon the language of education is found in Leibowitz (1969 and 1971) and Kloss (1971).

Even the Catholic Church has leaned more to the second paragraph of the above quotation from *Pacem in Terris* than to the first. The devoutly Catholic and fervently French-speaking Franco-Americans in northeastern United States protested long and vainly decisions by their English-speaking (commonly, Irish) bishops, who gave more importance to removing from American Catholicism the "stigma" of foreignness than they did to preserving French as the language of ritual and schooling for Franco-Americans (Lemaire 1964, pp. 9-13).

Sixth Generalization. In those states which have (for whatever reason) attempted to assure for their separate linguistic groups social justice and peaceful co-existence, the goal of legislation dealing with education has been to avoid aggression or encroachment of one language upon another, by defining their domains and keeping them apart.

Corollary. The ideal seems to be unilingual education in the mother tongue, preferably on a territorial basis, and if this is impossible, on the personal basis. In these cases the rival language is preferably studied as a subject, not used as a medium of instruction. A case in point illustrating the territorial unilingual principle is Belgium. There, a single state was formed of two peoples who, says the Belgian historian H. Pirenne, ". . . if they had been consulted, would both have refused the political marriage which was imposed upon them" (Touret, p. 44). In keeping with the territorial principle, Belgium is divided by legal lines of demarcation into four sections: the two major language areas, one for the Flemish, speakers of a variant of Dutch, one for the Walloons, speakers of French; one tiny area where speakers of German predominate; and Brussels, the capital, many of whose inhabitants are unavoidably bilingual. After a conflict-wracked century and a half[8] during which most of the classic aspects of dual language educational politics were manifest; easy domination for many years by French, the more prestigious tongue; deprecation of Dutch by the Walloons and by its own speakers; slow awakening of linguistic consciousness and pride in the Flemish, together with increased economic and political strength; a period of "official bilingualism" which encouraged linguistic aggression rather than checking it; finally the unilingual, territorial solution for all activities, including business and education, was adopted for the two major territories. Governmental services provided at the national level are bilingual, i.e., available to serve every citizen in the language of his choice.

The gradual shift in Belgium toward French, the more widely useful language, had to be stopped. Along with that continuous shift to French there had even arisen a French-Flemish pidgin in the Enghien region (Flemish syntax, French vocabulary) (Touret, p. 27). By 1963 educational policy in Belgium mandated unilingual instruction at all levels. With minor exceptions, all instruction in the Flemish area must be in that language. Diplomas gained from schooling in another language would have no legal standing (Touret, p. 55).

In Brussels, where the two peoples are mixed and commonly bilingual and the territorial principle could not be applied, the law aims at maintaining equilibrium and avoiding shift from Dutch to French. The language of instruction is the child's mother tongue. (During a brief period in the 1960's language inspectors had the right to check on the veracity of the parents' declaration of that mother tongue.) German-speaking minorities are similarly protected. The size of Brussels is rigidly limited (Touret, pp. 56-57). It is important to note that many people in Brussels are bilingual because the conditions of work, business and social relationships and close juxtaposition favor it. Their bilingualism does not come from bilingual schooling. They commonly live in one language and (some of them) use the other language for certain limited purposes. There are dual-language signs and official notices in Brussels, but the "bilingualism of Brussels" does not refer to the use of two languages by large sections of the populace for all purposes. Rather, it refers to the fact that public and official services are available in either of the two languages, with the choice determined by a complex set of laws and regulations.

The point of this sketch is that when two peoples with two languages co-exist in one state the solution to the unavoidable aggression of one language against the other is not increased societal bilingualism and widespread bilingual education, but the adoption of measures to protect the cultural and linguistic autonomy of both groups.

Switzerland, Czechoslovakia, and Yugoslavia make similar applications of the territorial principle to protect all their languages and peoples from this kind of aggression.

A kind of cultural autonomy based on the personal principle has been exemplified in several small states where two or more peoples with different languages are so dispersed as to rule out application of the territorial principle. Lithuania in 1919 recognized the existence of a "Jewish nation" dispersed within the Lithuanian state but without reference to a specific territorial base. Esthonia (1925) granted cultural autonomy to any national group in excess of 3000 persons. Each such group was encouraged to have its own "cultural council" (Touret, p. 209).

Cyprus (448,000 Greeks, 104,300 Turks) was organized in 1960 as a kind of "duoarchy" in order to give maximum cultural autonomy—linguistic, religious, educational, budgetary, legislative, executive—to each people despite their dispersal over the island in mixed fashion. The scheme was interrupted in 1963. At the national level a unitary system prevailed, but each of the two peoples had its own political organization and legislative chamber for ethnic group affairs. The national legislative body had Greek (70%) and Turkish (30%) members elected separately. Legislation of certain kinds required majority approval of each group voting separately. The point in the context of this essay is that in this "bilingual" nation of two peoples, each with a different language, education is by no means bilingual in Turkish and Greek, and language-related laws—as in Belgium—have been designed to protect against rather than encourage the inevitable societal bilingualism. Since neither Turkish nor Greek is an LWC the teaching of an LWC in the schools or its use as an additional medium there (unless such use were imposed from without) does not pose a problem. Any bilingualism thus created is academic or elitist rather than societal.

SCHEMA OF POLITICO-SOCIAL FACTORS

The schema on pp. 108-111 is designed to show the principal factors which combine to determine the socio-political dynamics of bilingual education. In keeping with the thesis of this paper, i.e., that the main decisions about bilingual education are political decisions, based on political factors, it is necessary to lay out those factors and bear them in mind.

Application of the Schema

In the following tentative, illustrative applications of the schema, the first language mentioned is the mother tongue, unless otherwise noted. The available data do not permit unequivocal classification between "widespread bilingualism; few monolinguals" and "not widespread bilingualism; many monolinguals," although this is a key factor for determining the likelihood or danger of language shift.

Type 1   Swiss speakers of Schwyzertutsch plus German. Greek speakers of Dimotiki plus Katherevusa in Greece. Egyptian speakers of Egyptian Arabic plus classical Arabic in Egypt. Norwegian speakers of landsmaal plus riksmaal. In Luxembourg, speakers of Letzeburgish plus German.

Type 2   Paraguayan speakers of Guaraní plus Spanish. Israeli speakers of a vernacular plus Hebrew (see also No. 5). Irish speakers of Irish plus English (see also No. 6). In Luxembourg, speakers of Letzeburgish (or German) plus French.

Type 3   Corsican speakers of Corsican plus French.

Type 4

Type 5   Israeli speakers of (a vernacular) Hebrew, plus English (see also No. 2).

Type 6   Russian speakers of Russian plus French in the Napoleonic era. Uruguayan speakers of Spanish plus English. Mexican speakers of Spanish plus English. Irish speakers of English plus Irish (see also No. 2). Russian speakers of Russian plus English (the latter acquired in the special all-English-medium schools).

Schema of Principal Factors which Combine to Determine the Socio-Political Dynamics of Bilingualism and Bilingual Education

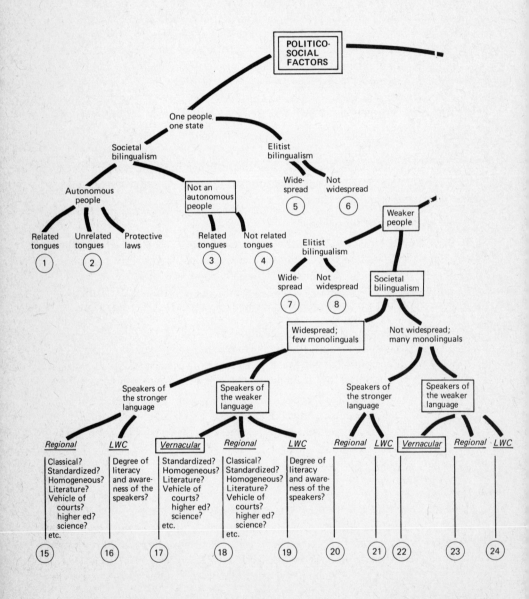

continued . . .

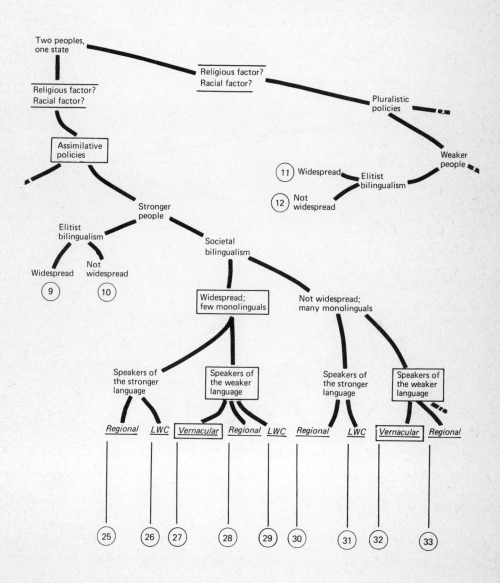

Types 1-14 include the mother tongue; types 15-54 refer to the mother tongue. Factors printed in boxes tend to weaken the position of the weaker people and the weaker language.

continued . . .

Schema of Principal Factors which Combine to Determine the Socio-Political Dynamics of Bilingualism and Bilingual Education (continued)

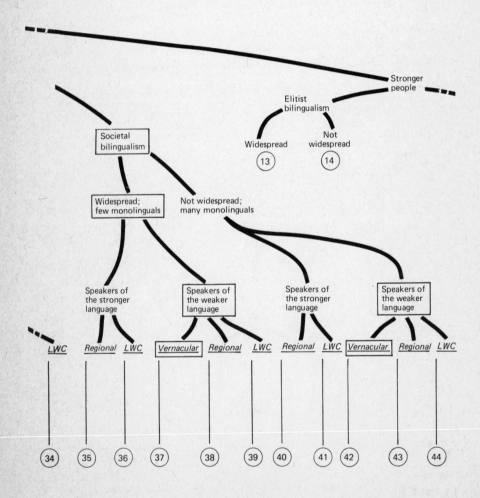

continued . . .

Types 1-14 include the mother tongue; types 15-54 refer to the mother tongue. Factors printed in boxes tend to weaken the position of the weaker people and the weaker language.

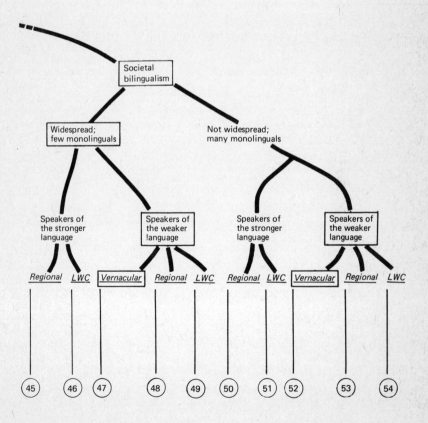

Type 7

Type 8   Catalan speakers of Catalan (and Spanish) plus English or French in Cataluna.

Type 9

Type 10   Canadian speakers of English plus French in Anglo-Canada.

Type 11

Type 12

Type 13

Type 14   Hindi speakers of Hindi plus English in India. (Would be No. 50 if English-medium schooling is imposed by law.)

Type 15

Type 16

Type 17   Navajo speakers of Navajo plus English in U.S.A. All speakers of indigenous languages plus English, U.S.A. Kenya speakers of a vernacular plus Swahili (see also No. 18). French speakers of Occitan (or Basque) plus French. Spanish speakers of Basque (or Catalan) plus Spanish.

Type 18   Kenya speakers of (a vernacular) Swahili plus English (see also No. 17).

Type 19   Chicano and Puerto Rican and Cuban speakers of Spanish plus English in U.S.A. French speakers of French plus English in Anglo-Canada.

Type 20

Type 21

Type 22   Guatemalan indigenes, speakers of an indigenous tongue plus Spanish (Caal, 1967).

Type 23

Type 24   Puerto Rican speakers of Spanish plus English in Puerto Rico (see also No. 31).

Types 25-30   No example.

Type 31   Puerto Rican speakers of English plus Spanish in Puerto Rico (see also No. 24).

Types 32-35   No example.

Type 36   Danish speakers of German and Danish in Denmark.

Type 37   Marathi speakers of Marathi plus Hindi in India. Frisian speakers of Frisian plus Dutch in Holland. Austrian speakers of Slovenian plus German in Carinthia. Greenland speakers of the native tongue and Danish.

Type 38   Turkish speakers of Turkish plus Greek in Cyprus.

Type 39

Type 40   Finnish speakers of Swedish plus Finnish.

Type 41   Belgian speakers of French plus Dutch. Republic of South African speakers of English plus Afrikaans.

Type 42

Type 43

Type 44   Quebec speakers of French plus English.

Type 45   Greek speakers of Greek plus Turkish in Cyprus.

Type 46   Luxembourg speakers of French plus German. (Note that the schema breaks down because French and German are of equal prestige—see also No. 49).

Type 47

Type 48   In the Philippines, speakers of Pilipino plus English (assuming them, as native speakers of the favored national language, to be the "stronger" people).

Type 49   Luxembourg speakers of German plus French. (Note that the schema breaks down because the languages are of equal prestige (see No. 46).

Type 50   Hindi speakers of Hindi plus English in India. (Would be No. 14 if English-medium schooling were not imposed by law.)

Type 51   Quebec speakers of English plus French in Quebec (see No. 44).

Type 52   Belgian speakers of Dutch plus French. Republic of South African speakers of Afrikaans plus English. Finnish speakers of Finnish plus Swedish.

Type 53

Type 54

(See index of peoples classified, page 125.)

The schema is meant to demonstrate that "bilingualism" and "bilingual education" mean many essentially different things. If it were extended to show all combinations of the attributes listed for each language, there would be several times the (theoretical) types noted. A further extension to include the pedagogical components of the bilingual school itself would produce thousands of types.[9]

The purpose of the tentative schematic typology [10] is to show how widely varying are "bilingualism" and "bilingual education" and to show that the controlling factors are essentially political. The schema should be read downward, following the proper line, and each classification ends with consideration of the list of prestige factors as they apply to each separate language. Each of the fifty-four types represents a single people, and the language referred to is its mother tongue. In Types 1-14, one of the two languages is the mother tongue. The LWC is assumed to be standardized, the vehicle of an extensive, important literature, a medium of scientific investigation and dissemination, etc. In the case of an LWC, consideration should be given each time to the degree of a people's literacy in and awareness of the highly prestigious position of their language, because this prestige factor has no effect if it is not reflected in the people's attitude toward their language. This is the widespread case among Chicano speakers of Spanish in the United States.

The schema could have been made in several other ways. It does not pretend to present all of the factors which determine the dynamics of bilingual education and bilingualism in a given state, or more especially, in a given school. For example, recognition as a national or official language can be an important variable, but it can be insignificant too, as in Canada, where the supposed official equality of French and English has never checked the aggression against French. A more important factor is monolinguality or bilinguality in infancy and early childhood, since the former strengthens the position of the language and favors diglossia, while the latter facilitates shift. The data available for this study did not permit inclusion of this factor in the schema. Still another factor is the sheer numerical strength of the subordinate people, although this is partially accounted for as a component of political power. Charles Ferguson has noted two situations where a vernacular and French are juxtaposed with the signal difference that in France two per cent are Bretons and ninety-seven per cent French-speaking, whereas in Malagasy the percentages are reversed: the ninety-seven per cent are speakers of Malagasy, the two per cent a French-speaking elite (Ferguson 1962, pp. 2-3).

Nor does the schema present all possible types of bilingualism. At the border between France and Germany, for example, the bilingualism which develops (whether or not the other language is studied in school) has no place in the schema, but neither does it involve bilingual schooling.

Notably, the psychological or attitudinal factors do not fall within the scope of this essay. The following three examples of such factors show how nearly impossible it is to separate what is political from what is something else.

1.   A school which claims to give exactly equal time and treatment to all of its curriculum through each of the two languages will be favoring one language and culture enormously if the school is *administered* in that one language.

2.   No amount of effort to give equal time and treatment to the two languages in school—or simply to teach one of them and use it as a medium—could compensate totally for the parents' attitude that the language—irrespective of whether it is their own or the other one—is unworthy of study in school.

3.   It makes a great deal of difference whether the dominated people (minority or majority) was overrun or conquered in war by the dominating people, or whether it was merely included arbitrarily within a nation's boundaries.

IMPLICATIONS FOR EDUCATORS

For educators the most useful perspective of the politics of bilingual education can be gained by making the assumption here that an educator is part of a "language planning" team charged with bringing about certain results by means of the schools. How then would that educator design bilingual education in order to protect a given language or in order to encourage its disappearance?

First, it will help to examine what we will call the three major components of such education. The components are the same whether the aim is in some measure protection of the rights of the linguistic and cultural minority, including effective education for its children and preservation of that language and culture, or whether the use of the minorities' mother tongues as mediums of instruction is to be nothing more than a quicker, one-way bridge to the dominant official language. The three components are:

1.   The linguistico-substantive or pedagogical component. It embraces the school curriculum, preparation of the minority-language teachers, methods of instruction, etc. This component is played out in the classrooms. It is of major importance, but in relation to the following two is only third in importance. It is only marginally the concern of this essay.

2.   The psychological or spiritual component. It embraces those activities, attitudes, and circumstances within the school which combine to make the child feel that his people and their culture and language are preeminently worthy and should be nurtured and protected, or that their ways and tongue should be abandoned. Of the three, this component is second in importance. It too is only marginally touched in this essay.

3.   The politico-economic component. This one, the most powerful of the three, has its locus far outside of the school and the school grounds. It is the force which signals to the student and everybody else in a hundred silent ways either that the language and culture are worth his effort or that they are not. Number three underlies number two. This component can be subdivided into two parts: the prestige of the language and the power of the minority people.[11]

Prestige of the language, power (politico-economic power) of the people, and perhaps a third, the concept of social justice, are the three forces which underlie decisions about bilingual education. The third of these will be left for the concluding paragraphs of the essay.

Some of the elements of linguistic prestige were mentioned above as parts of the tentative typology. William Stewart's typology (1962, pp. 17-22) lists four *elements* (historicity, standardization, vitality, and homogenicity) and seven *functions* (official use, group use, wider communication, educational use, literature, religious, and technical) which can be applied to language *types* (standard, classical, vernacular, creole, pidgin, artificial, marginal) ranked in descending order of prestige to obtain a kind of index of prestige. William Mackey (1970, pp. 77-78) lists five indices of the status of a language: degree of standardization, demographic index (number of speakers), economic index (population/gross national product), distributional index (areas and nations), and cultural index.

Two key points concerning language prestige emerge from the data of this survey. First, language prestige may at times be a more powerful force than politico-economic power. This is shown in Belgium and the Republic of South Africa, where in both cases the Dutch-origin people, speakers of Dutch and Afrikaans, have unquestioned political, numerical and economic superiority, yet find that they must take legal measures to avoid the shift of their bilingual citizens to the more prestigious French and English languages. The second point is that the prestige of a language is of little avail if that prestige is not reflected in the attitudes and activities of its own speakers. This is exemplified in the United States, where Spanish is spoken by perhaps twelve million persons, yet in terms of attitudes and activity seems to matter very little *as a language of the people,* even to those who profess it as a discipline in the universities. To be sure, although it is an LWC, Spanish is less prestigious than English.

The power factor is first of all economic: the amount of capital controlled by speakers of that language and the status levels at which work is performed in that language. Quebec is a prime example. Lieberson has shown the extent to which French there is preponderantly the language of menial, lower- and middle-class jobs, of small shopkeepers and the service fields, while in large business and industry, above the level of the supervisor or shop steward and at the highest levels of decision-making English tends to take over (Lieberson 1970).

Power is also manifest by the use of a language in public administration at all levels, in the courts, church administration and rites, and in the military services. Power or its absence can be seen in the extent to which constitutional or other legal protection is provided to safeguard the rights of the weaker group and its language.

"Cultural pluralism," without the prestige and power—and corresponding laws—needed to safeguard it, is another name for the melting pot. Quebec's proudly-maintained policy of strict equality for the two languages, French and English, has never been able to assure that equality—given the political dynamics of bilingualism there. It is like being proud of a slow leak in the dike.

The language planning exercise for educators continues with an examination of the kinds of bilingual schooling that would correspond to and be conducive to Joshua Fishman's four types of societal bilingualism: both diglossia and bilingualism, bilingualism without diglossia, diglossia without bilingualism, and neither diglossia nor bilingualism (Fishman 1967, pp. 29-38). In this analytical model bilingualism is individual; diglossia is societal and denotes a societal allocation of roles to each of the languages.

In Fishman's analysis, *diglossia and widespread bilingualism* is the aim in some of the "old developing nations" where the sense of nationalism based on traditions associated with the vernacular is very strong and irreplaceable. There, Fishman says, "successful language policy . . . need aim at nothing more than rendering bilingual each successive monolingual generation. . . as each generation arrives at the modern school and in the modern work-arena with its home and neighborhood language variety . . . its language repertoire is expanded by the addition of the modernized variety without any intended displacement." The same would be equally true of expansion by the addition of an LWC.

Since the aim in these cases is not transitional, replacive bilingualism but rather stable, diglossic role differentiation for each language, bilingual education will seek to differentiate in every way between the languages and keep them separate:

> By presenting the modernized variety or the LWC late in the primary school after literacy in the home tongue is firmly established.

> By use of different teachers (sources) for each language and discouraging mixing or switching. Implied here is the establishment of separate teacher training institutions, each in its own language.

> By using completely different materials for each language and using each exclusively for teaching certain subjects.

> By discouraging use of the modernized variety or LWC in the homes and for children's play.

> By establishing cultural relationships—student and teacher exchange, cultural centers, etc., with nations where the home tongue is spoken natively.

Bilingualism Without Diglossia. Transitional, replacive "bilingualism en route to monolingualism" seems to be the aim of some of the "new developing nations" in Africa where the large number of vernaculars and the lack of a sense of nationalism based on the traditions associated with those languages dictate the adoption and widespread use of an LWC, usually French or English.

The aim of bilingual education in these cases is to develop minimal literacy in the mother tongue, using it as a medium only during the early primary school years as the pedagogically most effective bridge to the LWC. Since the purpose is to shift swiftly as possible from the vernacular(s) to the LWC, bilingual education and language policy will seek to associate the two tongues in every way for the same purposes:

> By teaching the LWC (at least as a subject) from the beginning of primary school, and its use as the principal medium as soon as feasible.

> By use of the same teachers for both languages and encouragement of their switching from one to the other.

> By use of teaching materials translated from the LWC for teaching through the home language.

> By encouragement of the use of the LWC in the homes so that children will learn it there and at play with other children.

> Enhancing by every means the prestige of the LWC. (This can be easy, because it is the language of government, of the cities, and of the elite.)

The fact that merging of the two languages facilitates transitional, replacive bilingualism is not widely understood. This is indicated in a typical statement by a Mexican-American writer on the subject: ". . . the Mexican-American teacher himself [in a bilingual school] may not teach effectively Mexican-American children without some type of introduction into . . . the general problem of *merging together two different cultures.*" (Italics added.) (Sánchez, p. 158). Similarly, the changing situation of French for Franco-Americans in the United States is instructive. In 1949 they had 249 *"mi-anglais, mi-français, à parts égales"* French-medium schools with 88,097 pupils. By 1965 French-medium instruction had almost disappeared and they were struggling to assure that French would at least be taught one full period each day as a subject. This change represents a shift from Type 24 to Type 19 and then a major shift to English in keeping with the fact that the Franco-American children were learning English from their own bilingual parents and, at play, from other children. Yet in 1965 the parents—and grandparents—were seeking the cause for their youngsters' decreased command of French and lack of enthusiasm for French in the teaching methods of the schools (Comité. . . 1965).

Assimilation and disappearance of the mother tongue may be seen as a two-step process. First, the parents, monolinguals during their childhood, become coordinate bilinguals in school or at work; thereafter, yielding to the prestige of the second language, they speak both languages at home. Second, their children become compound bilinguals at home; their second language is greatly reinforced at school and work, and they rear their own children in the second language. The two steps may be compressed or they may take longer. The key to language shift is the use and transmittal in the home of both languages for all purposes, to the children. The key to diglossic stability is avoidance of this practice. Stanley Lieberson's research in Canada bears this out (Lieberson 1970).

It appears that the way to forestall (for example in the new African states) the later emergence in disruptive ways of latent loyalty to one or more of the vernaculars is to use them minimally as mediums of instruction for the children who speak them and encourage each people to undertake any further language development that it desires. There is small likelihood that any people will attempt such development before it is too late. This politics takes into account the propensity of some peoples to disparage their languages as unworthy of use in schools. It takes into account the possible eventual reaction against the elitist LWC and in favor of the group's own tongue. It is also the soundest pedagogy.

Diglossia Without Widespread Bilingualism. This is most typically the situation in countries where an upper class indulges itself in elitist bilingualism, using the national language, plus a second language widely used for its own special intra-group purposes, while the lower classes, using only the national language, have so little interaction with the upper class that they develop no societal bilingualism in that second language. Danish in Norway, French in Catherine's Russia are examples of second languages that have been so used.

Bilingual education in these cases is elitist, Type 5 of the schema. It is heavily favored in terms of prestige and power and is burdened by none of the problems discussed in this essay. Unlike Types 17-19 and 22-24 of the schema, where society's covert signals to the child motivate him not to cherish and learn that language, in Type 5 those signals convince him that learning it is exactly the right thing to do. Typical features of such schools:

> Use of the elite tongue as the medium at all levels. (Commonly, such schools in Latin America made it the exclusive medium; lately, the national language and its literature are mandated, and through Spanish.)

> Use of teachers, preferably, who are educated natives of the country where the elite language is dominant.

"Neither Diglossia nor Bilingualism." This is postulated by Fishman to complete his analytical model. Since no bilingual education is involved, the situation does not concern us here.

HYPOTHETICAL CASE STUDY

The utility of the tentative generalizations about bilingualism and bilingual education and of the schema setting forth their political dynamics can be tested by applying them to a specific situation, that of the twelve million Spanish speakers in the continental United States. For this illustrative purpose the assumption will be made that a large majority of this group desires to defend and maintain Spanish as a necessary correlate to affirming and maintaining their cultural identity. (It is not at all certain that a poll would show the assumption to be warranted.) The further assumption of the exercise is that use of Spanish as a medium in school for instructing their children—bilingual education—is a key to the defense of the culture and language.

The schema places the Chicanos (Mexican-Americans), the Cubans, and the Puerto Ricans as Type 19. We find (leaving aside momentarily the significant differences among the three) that they are one of a number of subordinated linguistic minorities in a country noted for strongly assimilative policies. There is compulsory societal bilingualism among the Spanish speakers almost exclusively, a bilingualism so widespread that monolingualism is virtually limited to the very old, the very young, and recent immigrants and in-migrants, as Puerto Ricans who emigrate to continental United States are called. Although there is a general tendency to prefer Spanish for the home and intimacy, there is not the kind of non-competitive, complementary, compartmentalization of domains of usage of Spanish and English that would be called diglossia. Rather, children commonly learn both languages in the homes and at play from the same speakers, and both serve most ordinary purposes.

The mother tongue is Spanish, one of the great world languages of wider communication, but its prestige as a language-of-the-people is notably low. Apart from its being the medium of a few newspapers and a fair number of radio stations, there is virtually no prestigious use of Spanish. A schizoid irony is that in the nation's other-worldly academic circles, including its secondary schools, Spanish is the most widely studied language.

The Chicanos and Puerto Ricans are deeply engaged in an ever more success-ful struggle for social justice in all spheres of life, but they are unquestionably weak in terms of political and economic power. It will be noted from the schema that all of the factors examined thus far are negative ones that can be expected to favor assimilation and therefore widespread shift from Spanish to English and disappearance of the distinctive Hispanic culture.

On the positive side there are at least six factors. It can be hypothesized that their predominant Catholicism tends both to unify them and to differentiate them to some degree from the predominantly Protestant majority. To whatever degree this is true, religion is a protective force. Likewise, the racial factor, with the discrimination it produces, is a strongly unifying and protective force. Their self-identification with pre-hispanic indigenous peoples and consequent historical primacy may eventually be a factor of great significance. The strongest positive factors at present are their numerical strength (twelve million), the continuous arrival of newcomers from Puerto Rico and Mexico, and the proximity of those protective hinterlands.

As for bilingual education in service to the Spanish speakers, it is officially conceived as assimilative, a surer, more generously constructed bridge to English (see above, page 00), it is grossly inadequate in terms of numbers of pupils served (in federally-supported programs, 91,138 children enrolled out of 4,280,000 (Swanson 1974), and it is the kind of bilingual education described above as characteristic of and conducive to Fishman's "bilingualism without diglossia."

As a final exercise in application of the schema and generalizations an answer will be proposed to the question: What would be the political dynamics of a program of bilingual education designed to support maximally and maintain the Hispanic (or Indohispanic) culture and the Spanish language in the United States? Bearing in mind the three components of any such program (see page 115) and the essentially political nature of decisions concerned with bilingual education, the elements would be these:

1. Recognition of the weaknesses of the present situation (based on further studies and analysis to confirm, modify, or negate the formulations of the present study).

2. A politics designed to legitimize the concept of cultural autonomy as a right. Recent decisions of the U.S. Supreme Court have indicated the direction of that politics. *Cisneros v. Corpus Christi Independent School District* (S.D. Texas 1970) affirmed and established the separate ethnic identity of Mexican-Americans. *Wisconsin v. Yoder* (1972) held that the Amish (a distinctive group of farming folk in several parts of the United States, inclined to strict separatism on religious and other grounds) could not be compelled to send their children to secondary schools which teach attitudes, goals and values which are markedly at variance with those held by the Amish, and which therefore carry "a very real threat of undermining

the Amish community and religious practice as it exists today . . ." and which force the choice either to "abandon belief and be assimilated into society at large or be forced to migrate to some other and more tolerant region" (92 Supreme Court Reporter June 1, 1972). *Lau v. Nichols* (1974) requires affirmative action in the schools to meet the special language needs of non-English mother tongue children.[12]

3.   Determination of the extent to which that autonomy might be based on the territorial principle, the personal principle, or a combination of these (given the fact of both wide dispersal of the Spanish speakers throughout continental United States and their heavy concentration in certain areas).

4.   A long-range campaign to re-establish the prestige of Spanish in the United States. This calls for development, first among the group's leaders and then widespread as possible, of symbolic (attitudinal) *reintegration* of Spanish in the United States to "world standard Spanish," the prestigious LWC. This is to cultivate the concept of Spanish as the precious symbol of peoplehood and to combat the destructive notion that Spanish in the United States has disintegrated into a set of regional variants. All languages show regional variation. What matters most (in terms of prestige) is the people's attitude toward their language. Fishman has noted that the "lower the status of the native speakers of a variety, the more it is reacted to as if it were somehow a defective or contaminated instrument, unworthy of serious efforts or functions, and lacking in proper parentage or uniqueness" (Fishman 1970, p. 27).

   The key to that symbolic reintegration is recognition of the importance of standardization, "the codification and acceptance, within a community of users, of a formal set of norms defining 'correct' usage" (Stewart 1968, pp. 531-545). *The acceptance of standardization means that the speakers of a language consider it worthy of cultivation, protection, and symbolic elaboration.* Rejection of standardization means the opposite.[13] A major purpose of efforts to standardize a people's language, establish its autonomy, and glorify its literature is to defend that people's political autonomy.

   The second requirement is public use of Spanish for prestigious purposes: cultivation of an intellectual elite . . . literary and journalistic production and publication . . . television, radio . . . theater . . . the professions . . . association with religious ritual . . . use as medium of instruction and administration in education . . . the right to use Spanish in any process or contact with the federal and state governments, in the courts, for paying taxes, in the legislatures, etc.

5.   Consideration of the power factor. This is essentially the struggle for social justice referred to elsewhere. Insofar as language is concerned (and the effectiveness of bilingual schooling) the crucial points are two:
   the existence of as many as possible work situations (roles) at all learning levels which require the regular, professional use of Spanish;

accessibility (as perceived by Spanish-speaking children and youth) of those roles.

The old saw, "money talks," is particularly true in situations of two-people societal bilingualism: if the means of production—and therefore the language of work—is controlled by one language community and manpower is drawn from another language community, the children of this latter group will not be inclined to learn their parents' language in school.

6.   Bilingual education of the kind noted above (page 117) as conducive to Spanish-English diglossia and stable bilingualism. If there is a key to bringing about the change from the present transitional, replacive bilingualism to a stable (perhaps diglossic) bilingualism it seems to be that each generation must begin monolingually and later become bilingual (but not in the homes or at child's play or in the earliest years of school). The literature dealing with experience in other countries gives no precedent for doing this.

In the case of the Chicanos a likely dilemma unresolvable at this point becomes apparent. It is widely conceded that their Spanish has evolved into a number of regional variants. Apart from these regional variations, individual members of the group have varying degrees of control of the language, corresponding to the extent of their exposure to and use of Spanish as compared to English. The question: Is the extent of dialectalization of Mexican-American Spanish in the United States such that a strong effort toward standardization in their bilingual schooling would cause (and require) a significantly divisive shift away from the language of the home and community? In such a case bilingual education might be conceived as transitional from a dialect of Spanish to Spanish, the LWC. On the other hand, if dialectalization is sufficiently advanced and the decision were made to avoid that divisive shift, what would be the role—if any—of Spanish, the LWC? A limited model of bilingual schooling to resolve this dilemma has been proposed (see Chapter 5).

CONCLUSION

Three forces were postulated above as those which underlie decisions about bilingual education: prestige of the language, power of its speakers, and the concept of social justice. The first two are the main resources of peoples struggling either to impose or to escape from policies of repression and assimilation. Belgium and the Republic of South Africa and Quebec are examples of such conflict. Other examples—the relatively protected cultural and linguistic status of the Slovenes in Carinthia; the Germans in Denmark; the Swabians in East Germany; the Danes of Schleswig, West Germany; the Frisians in Holland; the Swedes in Finland; the Serbs, Montenegrins, Macedonians, Croates, Slovenes, etc., in Yugoslavia; the varied peoples of Czechoslovakia; the many nationalities of the USSR—these are harder to categorize.

Jean Falch has seen a pattern and stated it thus: "All the constitutions of socialist countries protect their linguistic minorities, in contrast to our 'liberal' countries where the constitutions are generally mute on the subject." His compendium and analysis of pertinent laws supports the statement (Falch, p. 3).

Yet the matter is not so simple. In certain European nations the minorities are protected not so much by their national "majorities" as by international treaty under the aegis of the Council of Europe: Austria, Italy, Denmark, the Federal German Republic . . . (Falch, pp. 72-85). Touret quotes significantly from the "Programme du Parti Communiste" at the time of the XXII Congress (1961) to show that the *effacement* of class distinctions in the USSR is no more a goal than is the *effacement* of the differences of nationality and those of language. The latter will simply take much longer (Touret, p. 153).

What weight, in all of this, can be assigned to the concept of social justice? The data available for this study are of little help in answering the question. On the side of the weaker and dominated people it is doubtless part of the moral force that makes the pen sometimes stronger than the sword. Not, of course, if they do not take up that pen forcefully. As for the dominating peoples, "social justice" for linguistic minorities is often either compelled by circumstances, i.e., unavoidable if the state is to exist at all, or is simply a more clever politics. Until evidence to the contrary is displayed, the conclusion must be that it is illusory to suppose that the language(s) of dominated people(s) can be protected without legal recognition and protection of some form of cultural—including linguistic— autonomy. Anything short of such autonomy means assimilation of the weak to the strong.

NOTES

1. In Spanish a useful distinction is commonly made between *instrucción* (imparted formally by tutors or in schools) and *educación* (all of the other learning about morals, manners, and the practicalities and subtleties of social interaction. The distinction is useful but was not observed in this essay.

2. The Columbia University group undertook a testing program to measure pupil achievement in all grades and particularly to explore the relative effectiveness of learning through each of the two language mediums. To test reading, arithmetic, information, language, and spelling they used the Stanford Achievement Test in its regular English version and in a Spanish version modified to fit Puerto Rican conditions. Over 69,000 tests were given.

The results were displayed on charts so as to reveal graphically any significant difference between achievement through English and achievement through Spanish. Both of these could be compared on the same charts with the average achievement of children in schools in the continental United States. The findings can be summarized in two sentences:

a. In comparison with children in the continental United States, the Puerto Ricans' achievement through English showed them to be markedly retarded.

b. The Puerto Rican children's achievement through Spanish was, by and large, markedly superior to that of continental United States children, who were using their own mother tongue, English.

The Columbia University researchers, explaining the astonishing fact that those elementary school children in Puerto Rico achieved more through Spanish than continental United States children did through English, came to the following conclusion, one with extraordinary implications: Spanish is much more easily learned as a native language than is English; the facility with which Spanish is learned makes possible the early introduction of content into the primary curriculum; every effort should be made to maintain it and to take the fullest advantage of it as a medium of school instruction.

What they were saying is that because Spanish has a much better writing system than English (i.e., the writing system more nearly matches the sound system) speakers of Spanish can master reading and writing very quickly and can begin to acquire information from the printed page more easily and at an earlier age. (Adapted from Gaarder 1969, pp. 162-163.)

3. Lieberson's statistical study of this matter in Canada led him to this conclusion: "Some exceptions are found in specific provinces, but overall there is little doubt that a French Canadian who becomes bilingual is increasingly likely to raise his children in English" (Lieberson 1970, p. 222).

4. In the U.S. Office of Education (1974) an official planning document at the highest level of policy-making for bilingual education states that "The fundamental goal of a federally-supported bilingual education program is to enable children whose dominant language is other than English to develop competitive proficiency in English so that they can function successfully in the educational and occupational institutions of the larger society. Bilingual/bicultural education is seen as a necessary and appropriate means of achieving this end." And later: "The point to underscore is that this view of the federal goal regards use of the home language and reinforcement of its culture and heritage as a necessary and appropriate means of reaching the desired end of giving the children from various language groups proficiency in the dominant language, and not as ends in themselves." (Document dated March 13, 1974, prepared for the Secretary of Health, Education, and Welfare, by the HEW Assistant Secretary for Planning and Evaluation, the Office of General Counsel, the Director, Office of Civil Rights, and the United States Commissioner of Education.)

5. In the preface to Bernard Touret, *L'aménagement constitutionelle des Etats de peuplement composite.* Québec: Les Presses de l'Université Laval, 1973. On ethnopolitics see also Jean Falch, *Contribution à l'étude du statut des langues en Europe.* Québec: Les Presses de l'Université Laval, 1973; Heinz Kloss, *Les droits linguistiques des Franco-Américains aux Etats-Unis.* Québec: Les Presses de l'université Laval, 1970; François Fontan, *Ethnisme, vers un nationalisme humaniste.* Nice: 1961; and Heinz Kloss, *Grundfragen der Ethnopolitik im 20. Jahrhundert.*

6. Translated from Touret, op. cit., p. 31-32, from *Pacem in Terris,* "dans *Trois Encycliques sociales,* présentées par R. de Montvalon, 1967, p. 163."

7. In private conversations one of the administrators of the Bilingual Education Act in the U.S. Office of Education told this writer, "We are not interested in Spanish. We're interested in the education of these children." Another said, "This is not a language program. We don't have language experts; we have psychologists and experts in tests and measurements." See also Gaarder, 1970.

8. Touret, op. cit., pp. 43-69 and Falch, op. cit., pp. 11-30 give accounts of the evolution of law bearing on language and education in Belgium.

9. For a typology of bilingual school curriculum and school organization, see William F. Mackey, op. cit., pp. 63-82. A typology of languages in multilingual polities has been devised by William Stewart (1962 and 1968).

10. The schema itself was suggested by William Mackey's diagram of the school curriculum.

11. Despite the common applicability of the term minority, the concept might better be expressed, at times, by "dominated people." Non-Spanish-speaking Americans dominate in Puerto Rico, but they are a minority. The British dominated in India during their long rule

there as a minority. The Afrikaners and the English combined in the Republic of South Africa are but a small minority of the total population there.

12. A rationale for attempting through legal action to establish educational policy maximally supportive of educational pluralism and cultural autonomy appears in Chapter 11, The Dilemmas of Cultural Pluralism.

13. This writer listened to a young woman in Edinburg, Texas, who, speaking in Spanish, deprecated her tongue embarrassedly, as "Tex-Mex." In fact, however, she spoke beautiful, standard Spanish but had no formal education through Spanish and thus lacked the criteria for judging and defending its excellence. This is common in the American southwest among Mexican-Americans.

INDEX OF TENTATIVE CLASSIFICATIONS (See listing of types, pp. 107-113.)

	Type No.		Type No.
Belgium	41, 53	Israel	2, 5
Canada	10, 19	Kenya	17, 18
Carinthia	37	Luxembourg	1, 2, 49
Cataluna	8	Mexico	6
Chicanos	19	Navajos	17
Corsica	3	Norway	1
Cyprus	38, 45	Paraguay	2
Denmark	36	Puerto Ricans (USA)	19
Egypt	1	Puerto Rico	24, 31
Finland	40, 52	Quebec	44, 51
France	17	Rep. of S. Africa	41, 52
Greece	1	Russia	6
Greenland	37	Spain	17
Guatemala	22	Switzerland	1
Holland	37	Uruguay	6
India	14, 50	USA	17, 19
Ireland	2, 6		

REFERENCES

Caal, Esteban Pop. "Los Centros de Castellanización en Guatemala y algunos datos estadísticos," *Addresses and Reports Presented at the Conference on Development of Bilingualism in Children of Varying Linguistic and Cultural Heritages.* Austin, Texas: Texas Education Agency (1967), p. 44-52.

Cebollero, Pedro A. *A School Language Policy for Puerto Rico.* San Juan, Puerto Rico: Educational Publications, series II, no. 1 (1945).

Chacón, Estelle. "Pochismos," *El Grito,* vol. III, no. 1 (1969), p. 34-35.

Comité de Vie Franco-Américaine. *La Crise de l'enseignment du français dans nos écoles paroissiales.* Manchester, New Hampshire: Comité de Vie Franco-Américaine (1965).

Falch, Jean. *Contribution à l'étude du statut des langues en Europe.* Québec: Les Presses de l'Université Laval (1973).

Ferguson, Charles A. "Background to Second Language Problems," *Study of the Role of Second Languages,* ed. by Frank A. Rice. Washington: Center for Applied Linguistics (1962), p. 1-7.

Ferguson, Charles A. and John Gumperz. "Introduction," *Linguistic Diversity in South Asia.* Bloomington: Indiana University Publications in Anthropology, Folklore and Linguistics, Publication 13 (1960).

Fishman, Joshua A. "Bilingualism With and Without Diglossia; Diglossia With and Without Bilingualism," *The Journal of Social Issues* 23, no. 2 (1967), p. 29-38.

———. "Nationality-Nationalism and Nation-Nationism," *Language Problems of Developing Countries,* ed. by Joshua A. Fishman, Charles A. Ferguson and Jyotirindra Das Gupta. New York: John Wiley (1968).

———. *Sociolinguistics—A Brief Introduction.* Rowley, Massachusetts: Newbury House (1970).

———. "Language Problems and Types of Political and Sociocultural Integration: A Conceptual Postscript," *Language Problems of Developing Countries,* ed. by Joshua A. Fishman, Charles A. Ferguson and Jyotirindra Das Gupta. New York: John Wiley (1968), p. 491-498.

Gaarder, A. Bruce. "Bilingualism," *A Handbook for Teachers of Spanish and Portuguese,* ed. by Donald D. Walsh. Lexington, Massachusetts: D. C. Heath (1969), p. 149-172.

Héraud, Guy. "Préface," *L'aménagement constitutionelle des Etats de peuplement composite,* by Bernard Touret. Québec: Les Presses de l'Université Laval (1973).

Jackson, Henry M. "Supplemental Views of Senator Henry M. Jackson," *United States-Puerto Rico Commission on the Status of Puerto Rico.* Washington: U.S. Government Printing Office, 21 (1966).

Kanungo, Gostha Behari. *The Language Controversy in Indian Education.* Chicago: The University of Chicago (1962).

Kelly, L. G., ed. *Description and Measurement of Bilingualism: an International Seminar.* Toronto: University of Toronto Press (1969).

Kloss, Heinz. "Types of Multilingual Communities: A Discussion of Ten Variables," *Sociological Inquiry* 36, no. 2 (1966), p. 135-145.

———. "Bilingualism and Nationalism," *The Journal of Social Issues,* 23, no. 2 (1967), p. 39-47.

———. *Les droits linguistiques des Franco-Américains aux Etats-Unis.* Québec: Les Presses de l'Université Laval (1970).

———. *Laws and Legal Documents Relating to Problems of Bilingual Education in the United States.* Washington: Center for Applied Linguistics, Clearinghouse for Linguistics (1971).

Leibowitz, Arnold H. "English Literacy: Legal Sanction for Discrimination," *Notre Dame Lawyer,* 45, no. 1 (1969), p. 7-67.

———. *Educational Policy and Political Acceptance: The Imposition of English as the*

Language of Instruction in American Schools. Washington: Center for Applied Linguistics, Clearinghouse for Linguistics (1971).

Lemaire, Herve-B. "Franco-American Efforts on Behalf of the French Language in New England," *Language Loyalty in the United States,* by Joshua A. Fishman et al., prepublication edition. New York: Yeshiva University. II, chapter 14 (1964), p. 9-13.

Lieberson, Stanley. *Language and Ethnic Relations in Canada.* New York: John Wiley (1970).

Mackey, William F. "A Typology of Bilingual Education," *Bilingual Schooling in the United States,* ed. by Theodore Andersson and Mildred Boyer. Washington: U.S. Government Printing Office. II (1970), p. 63-82.

Macnamara, John. "The Bilingual's Linguistic Performance—A Psychological Overview," *The Journal of Social Issues,* 23, no. 2 (1967), p. 58-77.

Malherbe, E. G. *The Bilingual School.* London: Longmans, Green (1946).

–––. "Commentaries," *Description and Measurement of Bilingualism: an International Seminar,* ed. by L. G. Kelly. Toronto: University of Toronto Press (1969), p. 325-327.

Palomares, Uvaldo. "Psychological Factors Teachers Must Recognize in the Bicultural Child," *Proceedings—National Conference on Bilingual Education—April 14-15, 1972.* Austin, Texas: Dissemination Center for Bilingual Bicultural Education (1972), p. 210-220.

Samarin, William J. "Lingua Francas, with Special Reference to Africa," *Study of the Role of Second Languages.* Washington: Center for Applied Linguistics (1962), p. 54-64.

Sanchez, Gilbert. *An Analysis of the Bilingual Education Act,* dissertation presented to University of Massachusetts, Amherst, Massachusetts (1973).

Stewart, William. "An Outline of Linguistic Typology for Describing Multilingualism," *Study of the Role of Second Languages,* ed. by Frank A. Rice. Washington: Center for Applied Linguistics (1962), p. 15-25.

–––. "A Sociolinguistic Typology for Describing National Multilingualism," *Readings in the Sociology of Language,* ed. by Joshua A. Fishman. The Hague: Mouton (1968), p. 531-545.

Sutherlin, Ruth E. "Language Situation in East Africa," *Study of the Role of Second Languages,* ed. by Frank A. Rice. Washington: Center for Applied Linguistics (1962), p. 65-78.

Swanson, María Medina. "Bilingual Education: The National Perspective," *ACTFL Review, V, Responding to New Realities,* ed. by Gilbert A. Jarvis. Skokie, Illinois: National Textbook Company (1974).

Touret, Bernard. *L'aménagement constitutionelle des Etats de peuplement composite.* Québec: Les Presses de l'Université Laval (1973).

9

LANGUAGE MAINTENANCE
OR LANGUAGE SHIFT: THE PROSPECT
FOR SPANISH IN THE UNITED STATES

ABSTRACT   This study deals with the factors which will determine whether Spanish will be maintained as a language of the people in the United States or will be subjected to a massive shift and tend to disappear. Conceived as the best available substitute for a conference of experts on the subject, it calls on experience in South Africa, Belgium, Switzerland, Paraguay, and the United States to reveal the dynamics of bilingualism. The study focuses on the socio-cultural and psychological factors in play, particularly as these affect the Chicano or Mexican-American. Twenty-two such factors are identified and discussed. It shows why and under what conditions societal bilingualism tends to destroy itself.

*One might be tempted to define
bilingualism as divided linguistic
allegiance.*
　　　　　—André Martinet[1]

What is the likelihood that Spanish will endure as a language of the people in the United States with increased prestige and usefulness, or that its uses, users, and importance will quickly decrease in extent and number? Can it be maintained or will there be a widespread shift to English? This essay will not answer the question, but it will examine many of the factors which are even now determining the answer. Beginning with its title, which follows U. Weinreich and J. Fishman, the essay is conceived as the best available substitute for a conference of experts on the subject. The role of the author is to keep the world-ranging discussion focused on Spanish in the United States.

SOCIAL JUSTICE AND CULTURAL PLURALISM[2]

The difference between these two is essential to the discussion, because it is at the base of the ambivalence among the Spanish speakers themselves regarding their language and culture. The two main groups of Spanish speakers in the United States—the Mexican-Americans and the Puerto Ricans—are engaged in an increasingly intense and successful struggle for social justice. In a score and more of different ways they are pressing for an end to discriminatory practices which have given them much less than the full rights and privileges of citizenship. But social justice can be achieved most easily within a context of social, cultural, and ethnic assimilation to the dominant culture of the majority. Cultural pluralism, quite a different thing, implies social justice, but it is a negation of assimilation. It calls for social justice plus the right not to assimilate. In their thinking about these matters the Spanish speakers are ambivalent and at times seemingly confused.

It is not a simple two-way division, with some favoring assimilation and preferring English while the others reject assimilation and want a continuing and increasing role for Spanish. Rather, even as all clamor for social justice, all want English and few would happily forgo Spanish. The ambivalence lies in seeking the closest possible integration with the "Anglo"[3] majority and at the same time insistently defining themselves as a distinct, identifiable minority group, the "brown" in contrast to the "black" and the "white," with a distinct culture and language which must be preserved. The confusion comes from the same insistence on preservation of that culture and language *without regard for the contradictions implied and without a vision either of the new sociolinguistic pattern that would result or of the means required to secure it.*

Certain lawsuits and court rulings in Texas are revealing in this respect. The specific problem was that although Mexican-Americans had gone to court in 1954 to establish that they are white (to protect themselves from the discriminatory segregation suffered by the blacks), in some Texas cities, notably Houston, the school authorities attempted in 1970 to meet the requirements of the Civil Rights Act for the elimination of segregated schools by "integrating" blacks and Mexican-Americans. Relief from this kind of discrimination was sought and secured in the courts. Mario Obledo, Director and General Counsel of the Mexican-American Legal Defense and Education Fund, remarked in this connection, "To facilitate the enforcement of these remedies, the Mexican American should be classified as a class apart, as a significant identifiable group, as the brown in contrast to the black and white" (MAE, 2524). In the same discussion Mr. Obledo said, "The Mexican American was lost because we are part of the white race, so to speak. That is why it is very important . . . that the brown be classified as a class apart . . ." (MAE, 2533). Regarding a similar case in Austin, Mr. Jesús J. Rubio, Research Director, Mexican American Development Corporation, remarked, "Austin supposedly had a beautiful integration plan, but the whites turned out to be brown. . ." (MAE, 2510). Abraham Ramírez, Jr., one of three lawyers representing the Fund, asked, "For instance, if a school is to have 555 Negroes and 395 Whites, we want to know—whites or Mexican Americans?" (MAE, 2560).

Dr. Hector García, distinguished champion of civil rights and founder of the G. I. Forum, a nationwide veterans' organization for Mexican-Americans, in testimony before a U.S. Senate committee was discussing the history of the conflict between the United States and Mexico and the grievances of Texans and Mexican-Americans against Mexico. Ambivalence is plain in the following paragraph of his text, to which parenthetical explanations have been added.

> They complained [both Texans and Mexicans in what is now Texas] about the Mexican military, they talked about being quartered in their houses and being tyrannical. Then the hate against us [Mexican-Americans] started. By 1845, we [the entire U.S. people or its government] knew we wanted the Northwest Mexican Territory. We had to make a "*cause célèbre.*" We had to have a scapegoat. This is where history was perverted and distorted, by making the Texas revolution completely an English, Anglo fight against Mexicans, when it was never so. We [again the Mexican-Americans] became the scapegoats. We became the "hate symbol." (MAE, 2567)

In the same discussion Dr. García said, "Of course, we were always white, legally we were white, but it didn't make any difference" (MAE, 2567). Later he spoke of the great importance of the Pete Hernández, Petitioner vs. The State of Texas, case in 1954, by which ". . . it was legally established that we were caucasian" (MAE, 2570).

Armando Rodríguez, at that time head of the Mexican American Affairs Unit, U.S. Office of Education, an ardent supporter of bilingual-bicultural education and opponent of segregated schooling, testified against the "mono-cultural and monolingual educational philosophy of the American school that confuses homogeneous learning environments with 'providing for individual differences' which results in ethnic and linguistic isolation." It is not at all clear in what way such a learning environment in unsegregated schools for all children would produce such isolation, nor how ethnic and linguistic isolation would be lessened by recognition of and provision for those ethnic and linguistic differences (MAE, 2595).

While the linguistic position of the Spanish speakers is notably unlike that of any other non-English minority in the United States, and in some ways notably stronger, there are many similarities and no few disadvantages which in the end may be overriding. Briefly, the strength rests on nine points:

1. They were here first. This goes far beyond such facts as colonization in the American Southwest before the landing of the Pilgrims. The brown-white point referred to above is buttressed by a growing inclination among

Mexican-Americans to see their own origins in common with those of the American Indian 20,000 or more years ago in that same Southwest. Dr. George I. Sánchez, illustrious defender of the Mexican-American, has said, "After all, we are not immigrants. As Indians, we have been here since time immemorial and as Spanish speakers, since the sixteenth century" (TNESP, 103). Dr. Sergio D. Elizondo, professor at California State College, San Bernardino, writing on the curriculum of Chicano studies programs, says, "An introductory course in Mexican American history must have its beginnings in Pre-Columbian Mesoamerica" (Elizondo).

In April of 1971 land occupied by a former U.S. army camp near Davis, California, became the site of a new Indian-Chicano institution, Deganawidah-Quetzalcoatl University, a school to be "run from the bottom up instead of from the top down," according to Dr. Jack D. Forbes, a Powhatan Indian and one of the founders, and "expressly designed to meet the unique needs of Indo-Americans."[4] A group of "Indo-Americans" had "occupied" the camp site from November 3, 1970 to January 12, 1971. Most significant is the symbolic linking of these already ethnically linked peoples, particularly the fact that both parts of the name (Deganawidah, known as the founder of the Iroquois six-nation federation, and Quetzalcoatl, a principal deity of the Aztecs) exalt the ancient indigenous origins which they have in common.[5]

2. The proximity and easy accessibility of Mexico and Puerto Rico.

3. The constant in-migrant and immigrant streams from Puerto Rico, Mexico, and other Spanish-speaking countries.

4. The large numbers involved: roughly six million Mexican-Americans, two million Puerto Ricans, one million Cubans, and one million other Latin Americans and Spaniards.

5. The relative isolation—hence linguistic solidarity—of the rural, or segregated, uneducated poor.

6. The similarities of religion and folkways among all the Spanish speakers.

7. The fact of their being, in large measure, a "visible minority."

8. The intergenerational stability of the extended family (Hayden LLUS, 205).

9. The present-day climate in the United States of tolerance—even encouragement—of cultural diversity. For example, Congressman Roman Pucinski, at the hearings on a proposed Ethnic Heritage Studies Act, said, "Experience has taught us that the pressure toward homogeneity has been superficial and counterproductive; that the spirit of ethnicity, now lying dormant in our national soul, begs for reawakening in a time of fundamental national need."

The similarities and contrasts with other ethnic groups in the United States and other tongues are even more instructive. For example—and too briefly to give anything approaching a clear picture—German-Americans at one time, 1910, counted close to nine million who spoke German natively; many lived in "language

islands" or in monolingual urban settings; they published extensively in German,
"books on poetry, local history, theology, philosophy, . . . also some non-narrative
prose covering various branches of the sciences and humanities, such as zoology,
archaeology, medicine, general history, linguistics, etc."[6] There was a steady influx
of immigrants including highly cultured intellectuals. Daily newspapers in German
by 1904 had a circulation of nearly 800,000. German-American clubs once
numbered close to 10,000. Close to four million attended church services in
German. In 1900, 4,127 public and private schools used German as the language of
instruction. Theological and teachers seminaries and colleges were numerous. Yet
despite the immense prestige of German and the vigor of its speakers, their efforts
were largely swept aside. It was only in part because of World War I. And the
Germans were not in any sense disadvantaged.

COMPARISON WITH NORWEGIAN-AMERICANS

Those who know the situation of Spanish and its speakers in the United States
may find several parallels with an experience that they might suppose to be
different in every way: that of Norwegian told by Einar Haugen in his monumental
study, *The Norwegian Language in America* (TNLIA). It took roughly a century
for that people—almost a million immigrants from Norway—to live through it all,
from the early years when the permanence of Norwegian in this country was never
questioned until—somehow by the very nature of things—the shift had taken place
and the few remaining speakers were like museum pieces.

   Bilingualism began as a marginal phenomenon mediating between two
groups of monolinguals . . . most of them could read Norwegian, many could write
but there were few books . . . distance cut them off from renewal from the old
country . . . the bilinguals were almost all of Norwegian mother tongue, for the
English speakers did not learn Norwegian . . . the accomodation was all in one
direction . . . among the bilinguals there was ever more facile switching from
English to address the major society and back to Norwegian and the number of
these borrowings grew constantly . . . borrowing from English while speaking
Norwegian ("mixing") increased: "it is so easy and practical a way of getting
along" . . . all in all, the learning of English had a disastrous effect on their
Norwegian . . . the immigrants were scorned, made fun of, patronized and
exploited . . . their feelings of shame for being Norwegian and their sense of
inferiority are recorded over and over . . . the solid, usually rural enclaves of
Norwegian monolinguals sustained the language; their dispersal hastened its
disappearance . . . educated people from Norway did not understand the "underlying necessity in the process" of "mixing"; they found the Norwegian spoken here
offensive, which created a barrier of misunderstanding and resentment between
them and the immigrants . . . their hyphenated state, says Haugen, played the role
of a "home in passage" . . . in no less measure their "mixed" Norwegian was a
half-way house on the road to English.

   Norwegian-Americans—most of them—cherished their mother tongue, but
Haugen found that they "stoutly resisted those who advocated parochial or other

schools that would have segregated their children from other Americans."

Finally, with the Norwegian Lutheran churches beginning to shift their services to English and the number of newspapers (they too were notably "mixed"—how better could they communicate with their readers?) decreasing, came the anxiety to "preserve" Norwegian. Uncounted organizations were formed with that as a main goal. In 1917 there were supplementary Norwegian schools with 1796 teachers and 41,716 pupils. There was widespread abhorence of the melting pot and impassioned pleas arose to preserve the language or lose the "Norwegian soul." Haugen quotes an eminent Norwegian-American author and editor, Waldemar Ager: ". . . the so-called American does not himself wish to be assimilated with the foreigners; he does not wish either to assimilate or take up in himself the Russian, the Pole, or the Jew: but he wants these to be absorbed in each other" (TNLIA, 251). Meanwhile, teachers in the public schools were threatening the pupils with punishment for speaking Norwegian on the playgrounds; children rebelled against their parents by replying in English when addressed in Norwegian. But the monolingual Norwegian group was no more; the reason for bilingualism had ceased to exist; the shift to English had run its course.[7]

RESTATEMENT OF THE PROBLEM

To equal or excel the German-Americans' language maintenance efforts (if that is indeed required for Spanish to survive) would not be easy. It might be impossible even to reverse and avoid the kind of slow, then ever faster linguistic interference which changed Norwegian in the United States into a pastiche before the shift to English was complete. Yet it may be that neither of these is the most essential factor. Rather, the fundamental issues seem to be: (1) *If all the group becomes bilingual there is no further need for binguality*; and (2) *No people needs two languages for the same set of purposes.*

The first of these propositions recalls the essential marginality of bilingualism. Two human communities come in extended, long-term contact, each speaking a different language. From that contact there develops a marginal group of bilingual persons, intermediaries. As Einar Haugen says, "Those who learn the language of the other group become carriers of intergroup relations, but from the point of view of the group their behavior is *marginal* rather than *central.*" They are not indulging in an activity that all can share (TNLIA, 5). Haugen finds that ". . . it appears to require considerable *social pressure* for such a group to remain bilingual for any length of time. As long as the group is a true link between monolinguals, this pressure exists. But if the monolinguals on the one side disappear, becoming bilinguals or going over to the other language entirely, the reason for bilingualism disappears and its functional importance is reduced" (TNLIA, 7). He is saying in effect that societal bilingualism is inseparable from this marginality and that if all the Spanish speakers become bilingual, one language (Spanish) must go. In this view, it is only to the extent that the monolingual Spanish speakers exist as a group apart from their bilingual element that bilingualism can continue.

William F. Mackey, speaking to the same point, says, "An individual's use of two languages supposes the existence of two different language communities; it does not suppose the existence of a bilingual community. The bilingual community can only be regarded as a dependent collection of individuals who have reasons for being bilingual. A self-sufficient bilingual community has no reason to remain bilingual, since a closed community in which everyone is fluent in two languages could get along just as well with one language" (RITSOL, 554-55).

E. G. Malherbe (TBS; DMB, 46, 326), reporting on English-Afrikaans bilingualism and bilingual schooling in South Africa notes that "the percentage of people speaking both English and Afrikaans dropped from 73% in 1951 to 66% in 1960 as a result of separating Afrikaans and English-speaking children at school and students at universities in separate institutions." This policy of segregation imposed by the Nationalist (Afrikaans) regime reflects the proposition of marginality. Sociocultural pressures had always caused more Afrikaans speakers to learn English than they caused English speakers to learn Afrikaans. If the entire population became bilingual there would be no reason for two languages, Afrikaans would be abandoned in favor of the more useful world language, and the Afrikaners' identity as a group would be severely threatened, perhaps even destroyed. Thus the Afrikaans speakers seek to defend their language by reducing the number of bilingual individuals in their country.

It should be noted that many countries popularly believed to be bilingual are only marginally so. Only 11% of Finns reported a knowledge of both Finnish and Swedish in Finland's 1950 census, and in the 1960 census this percentage dropped to seven. In Belgium only 18% spoke Flemish and French in 1947 (DMB, 318). In Paraguay slightly more than half of the population is bilingual. In all of Canada "only about 12% of the population reported a knowledge of both official languages in 1961; three-quarters of these were of French mother tongue, according to K. D. Macrae (DMB, 318). In the Quebec capital, as Everett Hughes points out (DMB, 322), three-quarters of the people are of French mother tongue and ethnic identity, and of the remainder most are of English mother tongue. Although many of these are bilingual, their bilingualism becomes functional mainly at limited points of contact, e.g., the foreman passing orders from the English monolingual industrialist to his French-speaking workmen, or in large department stores among salespeople, but there are in Montreal completely separate religious and educational systems with one or the other language used exclusively. "From kindergarten," says Hughes, "to the doctorate of law, medicine or philosophy one may be taught in one language [exclusively] or the other, so far as the daily contact of the pupil, and of teacher with teacher are concerned" (ibid.). Again we see that within the totality of the two ethnic groups in contact, bilinguals and their bilingualism are marginal.

The second fundamental proposition is as Joshua Fishman has said, that no people needs two languages for the same set of purposes. It would be difficult to find a case of bilingualism at the societal (as opposed to the individual) level in which both languages serve the same general purposes. Stated otherwise, it is probably true that societal bilingualism is stable to the extent that the purposes served by the two languages are different (distinct, compartmentalized, complementary, in Fishman's terms) and it is instable—hence tending toward or verging on shift—to the extent that they are the same. The term *diglossia* was coined (Ferguson) to specify a situation such as that in Arabic countries, where a H(igh) language (classical, koranic Arabic) and a very divergent L(ow) language (any one of the Arabic vernaculars) stand in a relatively stable relationship to each other, each being used by bilingual persons in distinct domains of their lives. *Diglossia* has since been extended (Fishman) to embrace a relatively stable relationship of distinct, compartmentalized, complementary functions between two or more related languages such as the example above, between unrelated ones such as Spanish and Guaraní in Paraguay, and even between two or more code varieties or registers within a single language, e.g., standard and nonstandard native United States speech in English (Stewart; Labov; Hymes).

The case of Paraguay (Rubin 1962, 1963; Garvin and Mathiot) is particularly illuminating. There in 1951 about 52% of the people, of all social classes, including city dwellers, spoke both Spanish and Guaraní, *but not usually for the same purposes.* The 1951 census also showed for the nation as a whole 4% monolingual in Spanish and 40% monolingual in Guaraní. However, in Asuncion 90% were bilingual; in Luque, a nearby town, 60%; and in all of the interior, 48%.

Rubin's study shows that among bilingual Paraguayans Spanish is used in the domains of public administration, schooling, between doctor and patient, lawyer and client, and in general for most formal, nonintimate functions. Guaraní is associated with the domains of informality, intimacy, jokes, love. Rubin found that the sociolinguistic system which determines the uses of Spanish and Guaraní closely parallels the system found by Brown and Gilman to determine the choice between the formal and informal pronouns of address in certain European languages, e.g., *vous* and *tu* in French (Brown and Gilman).

Bilingualism is increasing in Paraguay and with it, according to Rubin, comes a trend toward greater alternate use of both languages. Garvin and Mathiot, writing almost a decade earlier than Rubin, found a concerted, government-backed effort among Paraguayans to have the two languages coexist as equals. An "Academia de Cultura Guaraní" had been founded for the purpose of codifying Guaraní and was preparing "normative orthographic, grammatical and lexical materials preparatory to an expected and hoped-for introduction of the teaching of Guaraní in the schools" (RITSOL, 367). These two investigators found among Paraguayans an increasing pride in and loyalty to Guaraní. Most significantly, they reported that immigrants, whether or not they knew Spanish, commonly learned Guaraní. Paraguayans make of the language a treasured symbol of their nationality and adopt a puristic, prescriptive attitude toward its use. "Many Paraguayans," say Garvin and Mathiot, "are bilingual and would like to speak both Spanish and Guaraní elegantly; they feel that mixing them, especially introducing unnecessary Spanish loans into Guaraní, is sloppy" (RITSOL, 373).

Robert Di Pietro has gone so far as to propose as a "universal" that "the presence of multilingualism [he includes bilingualism in this term] in a speech community depends on the association of each language involved with specific domains of social interaction." He finds "at the base of the matter . . . a criterion of simplicity, statable as follows: Given two or more codes [i.e., languages] to convey the same set of messages, all but one will be abandoned." In Di Pietro's view "a perfect balance of multilingualism in which, say, English and Spanish would be used equally as well for all domains of interaction is highly transitory and represents the step just before a new stage of monolingualism in one or the other language" (LALS, 18-19).

A quotation from Kroeber used by Weinreich in a discussion of the relative stability of cultural practices (including language) is highly pertinent here:

> That a cultural practice is invested with emotion is an important thing about it, but is not decisive for its stability or lability. What decides between continuance or change seems to be whether or not a practice has become involved in an organized system of ideas and sentiments: how much it is interwoven with other items of culture into a larger pattern. If it is thus connected . . . it has good expectations of persisting, since large systems tend to endure. But a trait that is only loosely connected and essentially free-floating can be superseded very quickly. (Kroeber)

Are the uses made of Spanish in the United States part of an organized system, a larger pattern, or are they loosely connected and essentially free-floating?

Another example of bilingualism elsewhere is instructive. Uriel Weinreich (LC, 84-110 and passim) described in 1959 the relationships of the Raetoroman language, of the Schwyzertutsch German dialect vernacular, and of standard German in the Swiss territory of Romansh. The Raetoromans without a unilingual hinterland (Mexico is the Mexican-Americans' hinterland) were becoming, all of them, bilingual in their mother tongue and Schwyzertutsch, and the functions of the two languages were overlapping. Weinreich found the overlapping aggravated by the fact that many children learned both languages from the same persons, their parents, and thus tended to use both languages with the same interlocutors and the distinction between the two tongues was blurred. This is in contrast to more stable situations, where children learn each language from different speakers, use them with different speakers, and for complementary purposes. Weinreich described the Raetoromans (in the Sutselva area he was studying) as largely a peasant population with little schooling. He found most bilingual speakers to be of Romansh tongue, since few native speakers of Schwyzertutsch would learn the less prestigious tongue.

Needless to say, Weinreich found the Romansh population of the Sutselva was undergoing a language shift. German elements in Romansh speech were tolerated practically without limit. Knowledge of German was considered essential to acculturation and social advance. When speaking German, the bilingual guarded against Romansh borrowings. On the other hand, no value was attached to purity or correctness in Romansh.

FACTORS TENDING TO WEAKEN
SPANISH AND LEAD TO SHIFT

Weinreich (LC-5) distinguishes between: (1) purely structural or linguistic mechanisms which promote or impede interference in the speech of bilinguals and contribute to or impede the abandonment of one of the languages; and (2) the sociocultural, nonstructural factors which have the same effects. The former, which he says are "to a considerable degree independent of non-linguistic experience and behavior," will not be considered in this discussion, which focuses solely on the latter, the sociocultural factors amenable to control.

We saw in the previous section how the relative status of Schwyzertutsch and Romansh worked to encourage interference and borrowings in Romansh and protected the Germanic tongue. A different order of values obtains in western Switzerland, Weinreich points out (LC, 86, 88), where Schwyzertutsch is in contact with French, "a standardized language with zealously guarded norms propagated by the schools." He notes that in that area of Switzerland, "the functional 'inferiority' of Schwyzertutsch (predominantly a spoken language) as against French—a language of unrestricted functions—is so deeply felt by many bilinguals of both mother-tongues that the flow of borrowings from French to Schwyzertutsch in border areas is considered as natural as the inhospitality of French to loanwords from Schwyzertutsch." The difference between the two cases stems primarily from the status ascribed to the languages involved.

Consider a moment some related facts about Spanish in the United States. The Spanish-English bilinguals in this country are virtually all mother tongue speakers of Spanish. Although children are all remarkably facile learners of second languages, contact among mixed groups on the schools' playgrounds in the United States teaches only English as a second language. Very few Anglo children learn Spanish. Although, as we pointed out above, linguistic interference is notable in the English of many Spanish-English bilinguals, the English language itself remains untouched by the seven score years of contact in the Southwest except for a few lexical items. It is notable that although linguistic borrowing and switching commonly go unhampered when Spanish-speaking bilinguals address each other, when addressing monolingual speakers of English they do not borrow from Spanish, and interference is avoided entirely or as much as possible.

One frequently hears the plaint that bilingualism should be reciprocal: "the Anglos—especially schoolchildren—should learn Spanish too." The notion is cruelly illusory because—apart from college and university departments of foreign languages—Spanish in the United States has virtually no prestige, especially among its own native-born speakers.

Since Spanish is one of the great world languages, the reasons for its lack of prestige in the United States must be sought in its cultural setting: the relationships between the two groups in contact, the uses to which Spanish is put, and the attitudes of its speakers toward their language. Notable among those attitudes is a widespread "disdain for correctness," and an even more widespread seeming unawareness that language norms serve any purpose beyond pedantry, or as

Weinreich says, "an intellectualistic affliction" (LC, 102). Spanish speakers as a whole are loyal—often fiercely loyal—to Spanish. Those whose family traditions or personal experience include—even indirectly or vicariously—schooling, high literacy, and professional activity in Spanish probably see it as the symbol of Hispanic culture in the "great tradition." Those whose traditions and experience are largely or exclusively with oral Spanish see it simply as a symbol of *la raza*.

The result—at least among Mexican-Americans—is that neither in their struggle for social justice nor in their yearning for cultural pluralism does one find evidence of regard for Spanish as the ideologized symbol of ethnic group identity replete with esthetic and emotional overtones, to be defended from every encroachment by English, to be cultivated by the poet and the scholar and taught assiduously to the young. Haugen (BLCIL, 94) reported on a reflection of this in a study of Puerto Rican intellectuals in New York by Fishman. When asked, "What makes you a Puerto Rican?" ordinary people simply pointed to the facts of birthplace and parentage, but the intellectuals stressed their attitudes, knowledge, sentiments, and behaviors (Fishman, et al.).

Among the Chicanos, rare is the writer on *Chicanismo,* education, or any other aspect of the *movimiento* who does not extol "bilingual-bicultural education." The Chicano half of the second part of this dichotomy is well and often described. What is to be done about Spanish is not specified. "The educated Spanish-speaking person who has survived the [American] school system is likely to be one who has been stripped of his native language, or, at least, speaks and writes it imperfectly," says Dr. David Ballesteros, Chicano activist and California State University dean (TNESP, 26-27). "We are desperately trying to retain what we have, or regain what we have lost . . . ," says Marcela Trujillo, director of a Chicano studies program at the University of Denver (TNESP, 90).

But in no Chicano publication or public statement known to this writer (e.g., the November 1970 special edition of *The National Elementary Principal* on Education for the Spanish Speaking; *El Plan de Santa Bárbara,* by the Chicano Coordinating Council on Higher Education; the issues to date of the Chicano journals, *El Grito, Aztlán, Con Safos, Regneración*; the volume of proceedings of the first Texas Conference for the Mexican-American, April 1967, *Improving Educational Opportunities of the Mexican-American* (Austin: SEDL 1967); the volume of proceedings at the *National Conference on Educational Opportunities for Mexican Americans* (April 1968); the Congressional testimony in support of the Bilingual Education Act; the dozen scholarly papers in the Chicano Studies Institute series (1970) with support from the National Endowment for the Humanities; those issues which I have seen of the newspapers in the Chicano Press Association; etc.) is there so much as an allusion to the problems of language maintenance or the imminence of language shift. The closest thing to such an allusion that I have found is a statement by Joseph Fitzpatrick, in a study of education for Puerto Ricans in New York commissioned by the Puerto Rican Forum, that the Spanish language might be a rallying point to unite the Puerto Ricans (TNESP, 70-71).

In the published curricula of three score "Chicano studies programs" there are courses in "Barrio Spanish," "Chicano Spanish," "Bilingual Communication Skills" and such Spanish-language requirements as "proficiency equivalent to completion of the fourth semester college course"; and some courses are taught "bilingually." Several programs include Mexican literature in translation and children's literature of Latin America in translation. Among the proposed courses at one college was one on "Chicano Poetry: Creative Writing. Reading and Writing of Spanish/English macaronic verse . . . bilingual poetry. . . ."

The position taken in 1970 by Marcela Trujillo, then an instructor in the Chicano studies program, University of Denver, rejects world standard Spanish but is somewhat stronger and may be widely shared: "For I believe that language is the mirror that reflects the soul of a culture. Language and culture are so interwoven that one cannot exist without the other. Although some of our Chicano students no longer speak Spanish, they have inherited the attributes and characteristics of the ancestors who spoke Spanish. . . . but they are in danger of losing those qualities if the language is not learned. . . . It is necessary for the professor to be bilingual and bicultural. . . . The Chicano professor does not need to be proficient in the standard Spanish of Spain or Latin America."

LINGUISTIC INTERFERENCE

In the speech of bilinguals, deviations from the norms of either language are called linguistic interference (LC, 1). It has not been proved that interference—often loosely referred to as "mixing"—is the cause of language shift, i.e., the final abandonment of one language (Spanish) and its replacement by another (English). Nevertheless, Haugen reports (BLCIL, 53-54) that the research of Morgan E. Jones found borrowing from English to Spanish was an index of acculturation to the dominant English-language culture in Puerto Rico; and that Stanley M. Tsuzaki's study "showed how the acculturation of Puerto Ricans in Detroit was correlated (a) to the incidence of borrowing from English, up to the time when the shift to English occurred and (b) after that time, to the use of English." At the same point Haugen reports John J. Bodine's finding about Taos, New Mexico, Indians that "the adaptation of names was another clue to acculturation."

It is unquestioned that gradual increase of interference phenomena in the recipient language (Spanish) and increase in the *kinds* of stimuli which result in switching (temporary or momentary change from the use of one language to that of another) *are sure indicators of increased distance from the original language and of the likelihood of complete shift.*

Haugen found "an underlying necessity" in the process of interference (TNLIA, 71). As he put it, "To save themselves effort bilinguals in speaking to each other take shortcuts that collapse distinctions which have no communicatory value. The result is a more or less gradual shift from two codes towards one. . ." (BLCIL, 28). Weinreich's explanation is that "a partial identification of the systems is to the bilingual a reduction of his linguistic burden" (LC, 8, 24). He also makes an important distinction between the kinds of interference which are purely linguistic and can be analyzed in terms of descriptive linguistics, and the extralinguistic factors—psychological and sociocultural—which also determine the nature and extent of interference (LC, 3, Chapters 3 and 4).

For the purposes of this essay it will suffice to consider only the extralinguistic factors, which, according to Weinreich, are the ones that determine whether language shift will occur (LC, 107). Leaning further on Weinreich (who does not deal in any way specifically with Spanish) the following table gives the principal sociocultural factors and this writer's best effort to indicate whether each factor contributes to an eventual shift to English or contributes to the resistance of that shift. Each reader is, of course, encouraged to correct these judgments.

Predictability of Language Shift

Extralinguistic Sociocultural Factors	Favors the Shift to English	Resists the Shift to English
1. Size and homogeneity of bilingual group		Powerful resistance
2. Historic priority of bilingual education		Powerful resistance
3. Access and renewal from a hinterland[8]		(Potentially powerful factor of resistance, but is in fact unexploited)
4. Reinforcement by in-migration and immigration		Powerful resistance
5. Relative social isolation, including racist attitudes toward a visible minority	The struggle for integration in schools, in housing, etc., favors shift, as does the assimilative bridge-to-English orientation of bilingual schooling.	Differentiation as a culturally-distinct "brown" people, pluralistic orientation to bilingual education, and resistance to integration also resist shift to English.
6. Stability of the three-generation extended family		Close-knit, extended family, especially grandparents and other elders living with grandchildren.
7. Order and age of learning of the two languages		Spanish mother tongue and language of childhood is powerful psychological factor of resistance.
8. Relative proficiency in both tongues	Education solely through English favors shift; bilingual education is presently too weak to offset this.	(Bilingual education, i.e., the addition of Spanish as a co-equal medium of instruction, could resist shift. This has not been exploited.)

Extralinguistic Sociocultural Factors	Favors the Shift to English	Resists the Shift to English
9. Specialized use by topics, domains, and interlocutors	Use of both languages for the same purposes favors shift. Absence of sociocultural divisions to reinforce the difference in mother tongues facilitates shift. (LC-98)	Use of each language exclusively for certain topics and domains of life resists shift.
10. Manner of learning each language	Learning both from same persons in same situations facilitates switching and shift.	Learning from different persons in different situations resists shift.
11. Status of the bilingual groups	Except to the extent that the bilinguals' status favors Nos. 5 and 9 above, that status at present facilitates shift.	(Improved status, if made congruent with Nos. 3, 8, 9, 17-22, would resist shift.)
12. Disappearance of the Spanish monolingual group	Powerful force toward complete shift	(Establishment of diglossia, No. 9, could forestall shift.)
13. Attitudes toward cultural pluralism	Present absence of appropriate action by Spanish speakers facilitates shift. See Nos. 5, 8, 9, and 12.	Overall national attitude of relative tolerance favors cultural pluralism.
14. Attitudes toward both cultures	Prevailing attitudes of both groups favor shift.	
15. Attitudes toward each language	Most attitudes favor shift. See Nos. 17, 18, 19, 20, and 22.	Emotional attachment to Spanish (language loyalty) resists shift.
16. Attitudes toward bilingualism	Spanish speakers' unawareness that bilingualism normally destroys itself favors complete shift.	Present interest in bilingualism tends to resist shift temporarily.
17. Attitudes toward correctness	Powerfully facilitate shift	(Emphasis on standardization, purism, would resist shift.)
18. Attitudes toward "mixing the languages"	Powerfully facilitate shift[9]	
19. Modes of use of each language	Virtual absence of reading and writing of Spanish by adults powerfully facilitates shift.	
20. Relative usefulness of each language	Limitation of Spanish to oral, intimate, informal uses limits prestige, facilitates "mixing" and shift.	(A state of diglossia would tend to maintain Spanish but would greatly limit its prestige.)

Extralinguistic Sociocultural Factors	Favors the Shift to English	Resists the Shift to English
21. Function of each language in social advancement	Present situation exalts English, degrades Spanish.	
22. Literary-cultural value	Absence of emphasis reduces prestige, facilitates "mixing" and shift.	

FACTORS THAT COULD SUPPORT SPANISH AND RESIST SHIFT

The preceding chart has indicated, if only by implication, some of what would be required to maintain Spanish and forestall a widespread shift to English. The sum of those indications is that *it probably cannot be maintained*—the shift for most speakers would be inevitable—*at its present level of status, function and interference from English.* All of the evidence suggests that the potentially advantageous position of Spanish cannot be realized without certain affirmative actions.

Spanish as a "World Language"

The indigenous languages of the Americas, whatever their equality in purely linguistic terms with all others, are at a severe disadvantage in terms of usefulness and prestige compared to the great "world languages" such as English, Russian, Spanish, and French. The mark of a world language is not simply its extensive spread but also its use in all domains of human activity and the consequent vast body of printed material available to its users. It follows that to the extent that Spanish in the United States is anything but world standard Spanish—*el español común*—it will be unable to benefit from the prestige of Spanish and draw on that vast treasure of writing in every field.

Two typical statements by prominent Chicanos suggest that this judgment about *el español común* is not widely known or shared or is considered of no consequence. Lionel Sánchez, director of "Farm Workers United" in Lupton, Colorado, was writing of the relationship of Chicano studies programs to the Chicano community: "There is no doubt that the Chicano of today must learn Spanish but it must be the word usage that is continued in the Barrios. Too often a Chicano learns the Castillian [sic] Spanish which is of little or no benefit in his work with Chicanos who speak only the barrio Spanish" (L. Sánchez).

René Núñez, of the Centro de Estudios Chicanos at San Diego State College, in a similar formal paper on the qualifications of teachers for such centers had this to say of Chicano studies: "It speaks in a language that is at once English and Spanish—caló . . ." (Núñez).

There is a broader view—that the farm worker, the barrio dweller, and the school child could be met and served at their own language levels while the society as a whole, in its schools and other institutions, in its mass communications, and in its aspirations would see itself as a part of the world community of Spanish speakers. I have not yet found that broader view represented in the literature.

Renewal from the Hinterlands

Unlike all other non-English languages in the United States except French in New England, Spanish could easily draw strength and continuous renewal from Puerto Rico and Mexico. Given the strong and unquestioned tradition of standardization among the *boricuas,* there is virtual unanimity on island and continent alike regarding the Spanish language—hence nothing to impede such cooperation.

Among Chicanos there is a continuum of attitudes ranging from the other-worldly purism of a few university professor-scholars in departments of Romance languages to the *bato loco* in the barrio who may control a dialect marked only slightly by interference but who disdains it and flaunts the *pachuco caló* in contempt for all norms. The continuum is markedly skewed toward disdain for standardization.

Any attitude short of full respect for *el español común,* world standard Spanish, is virtually certain to give rise to disdain and even hostility on the part of Mexicans, even Mexican intellectuals. That attitude is already impeding the use of visiting teachers from Mexico in programs of bilingual education and the establishment in Mexico of centers for training Chicano teachers for employment in the Southwest.

The potential of renewal from the hinterlands is incalculable: teacher and student exchange relationships, dual-campus arrangements between American and Puerto Rican or American and Mexican universities to facilitate work in residence at both sites; establishment by Puerto Rico and Mexico of a system of teaching centers in continental United States on the order of the *Alliance Française*; greater access to the flood of printed matter in Spanish; extended exchange visits by children at the individual home level for language learning, etc.

Difference as a Source of Strength

What was said above about ambivalence relates directly to our subject. The hypothesis is that any factor which serves to differentiate Spanish speakers from non-Spanish speakers is also likely to favor maintenance of the language and to resist the shift to English. A corollary of the hypothesis is that factors which assimilate (cause to resemble or be like) the Spanish speakers to other Spanish speakers in other areas of the world also favor maintenance and resist shift to English.

The propositions can be expressed as three continua, the first poles of which strongly favor maintenance, with the opposites strongly favoring shift:

1. a distinct identifiable, "visible" group ("brown," "bronze," with indigenous roots in the New World)   an undifferentiated group, "the same as everybody else"

2.   settlement, housing, and school-   wide dispersal among the English-only
        ing patterns to form strong   majority
        enclaves[10]

3.   a pluralistic orientation, includ-   an assimilative orientation, including
        ing diglossia (separate language   use of both languages for all purposes
        domains for Spanish)

It is apparent immediately that the choices are at the heart of the ambivalence referred to earlier.

Language Planning

Such planning may be concerned with diverse matters: the choice of one or more languages among many in "developing" countries; choice and standardization of one dialect among many; systematic, intensive expansion of the lexicon of a language to make it more widely useful; relationship and use of two or more languages for school purposes; and above all, manifestations of *language loyalty* and activity of any kind to enhance and use the prestige of a language as symbolic of the integrity and prestige of the people who speak it and thus resist encroachment against the language and the people. Encroach means "to intrude usurpingly, by insidious or gradual advance, on the territory or rights of another."

Peoples under threat of encroachment have very commonly seized upon their language as the precious, ideologized symbol of their people-hood and have fought to defend it.[11] The defense has not always been successful—certainly not when undertaken too late.

In view of the histories of language planning efforts elsewhere, and very briefly, the remainder of the report on this simulated conference of experts will suggest a few limited approaches to language maintenance which are presently most accessible.

Reform of the Teaching of Spanish to Spanish Speakers in Schools, Colleges and Universities

It is widely reported and conceded that the least "successful" students of Spanish in the United States, especially at the secondary school level, are its native speakers. The explanation of this embarrassing incongruity is also widely known: the predominance of "Anglo" teachers with little functional competence in Spanish; use of materials and methods designed to teach English monolinguals; exaggerated-ly prescriptive attitudes toward "correctness"; ignorance and fear of and disdain for the learners' dialect (which may indeed be close to the cultivated standards of Puerto Rico or Mexico); failure to build on the learner's strengths; insistence upon combining native speakers with ordinary foreign language learners on the basis of grade level instead of the basis of proficiency, etc.

The American Association of Teachers of Spanish and Portuguese has commissioned a study of this matter which recommends strategies for correction of the anomalies by institution of a limited form of "bilingual education": special classes or sections for Spanish speakers at all levels, with competent (preferably native-speaking) teachers using the language as an exclusive medium to reinforce all other areas of the curriculum rather than limited to teaching the language per se. The recommendations emphasize and specify ways to build strongly on the learner's dialect and emphasize strong rapport with the struggle of Spanish speakers in the United States for a greater measure of social justice and cultural pluralism.[12]

Strengthening the Effectiveness of Bilingual Education

In a study of the orientation of some bilingual schooling in the Southwest, Rolf Kjolseth, University of Colorado sociologist, used the construct of a continuum running from the most assimilative orientation to the most pluralistic. Both orientations are, of course, equally defensible, but only the latter favors language maintenance. Kjolseth's findings indicated not only that the tendency in the schools he studied was markedly assimilative but that the projects' administrators tended to assume and claim a pluralistic orientation which the analysis showed to be otherwise (Kjolseth).

In a study of the explicit objectives, organization, and curriculum of twenty-three bilingual schools in California, Tay Lesley found that the general objective most supportive of Spanish was "to improve the academic achievement of non-English mother tongue students by using the mother tongue to further concept development." There was a notable absence in the study of an explicit intention to preserve or maintain Spanish or to increase its prestige or to develop in its native speakers a high degree of literacy and other competence. For monolingual speakers of English in the programs, "mastery of Spanish" ranked in importance after "appreciation of the other culture" and "development of an impartial attitude toward one's own and the second language and culture" (Lesley, 55-56). Lesley found little correspondence "between factors in the curriculum and stated objectives" (p. 108) and noted a marked shift during the programs' periods of operation toward the predominant use of English.

Gaarder studied documentation on seventy-six federally supported projects of bilingual schooling in the United States and found a notable absence of regard—especially in those projects serving Mexican-American children—for teacher competence in respect to either speech or literacy in the Spanish language or its use as a medium of instruction.[13]

In 1970 more than thirty teachers regularly employed for Spanish-medium work in public school bilingual schooling projects in New Mexico and Colorado—all of them native speakers of Spanish—were asked what books they had read in Spanish. Only one of them had read such a book. In 1971 most of a similar group of bilingual teachers were found to be unaware that there are differences between the alphabets of English and Spanish. In both cases their bilinguality was largely limited to speech. In respect to reading and writing they were virtually English monolinguals.

Malherbe, in his thorough study of English-Afrikaans bilingual schooling in South Africa (TBS, 19-25) was very specific about the linguistic competence required of the teachers. He distinguished six stages of bilingual competence: (1) ability to follow intelligently an ordinary conversation, speech, or sermon, and read the newspapers; (2) in addition to the above, to converse intelligibly with fair fluency and read "literature"; (3) to write correctly, "free from grammatical and spelling errors and without gross violations of idiom"; (4) "a correct and convincing power of expression both in writing and speaking . . . [serving] as fit models for growing minds to imitate." *This stage, says Malherbe, represents the minimum requirements for being a bilingual teacher or the principal of a bilingual school.*

Malherbe's stage five is attained by only those who command the languages better than 90% of their native speakers. Stage six is the unapproachable ideal: perfection in both tongues. Needless to say, Malherbe found many teachers below stage four.

The specialists meeting under UNESCO sponsorship to discuss the use of vernacular languages in education noted (RITSOL, 696) that:

> Teachers who have themselves received their education and professional training in a second language have real difficulty in learning to teach in the mother tongue. The main reasons for this difficulty are of two kinds. First: they have to teach subjects in a language which is not the language in which they are accustomed to think about them; and some of what they have to teach involves concepts which are alien to their pupils' culture and therefore have to be interpreted in a tongue to which they are alien. Secondly, there is often a lack of suitable books to guide or help them both in teaching and in teaching through their mother tongue; they have to depend, therefore, more on their own initiative and skill than when teaching through the second language in which they themselves have been trained. In those regions where a mother tongue is spoken by a large population, *it should not be difficult to give teachers much of their theoretical training and all their practice teaching in the mother tongue.* (Italics added)

There have been numerous references in the discussion to the effect of associating (or failing to associate) each of the languages with specific domains of usage. The consensus seems to be that bilingualism is stabilized and language shift resisted if the languages are kept apart and not used for the same purposes. Malherbe's research (DBM, 44) convinced him that in the young child becoming bilingual the "differentiation or realization that [the two sets of] symbols constitute different languages is facilitated when these are consistently associated with different persons or sets of persons, for example . . . where the infant hears different members of the family or friends consistently speak different languages . . . in a bilingual country like South Africa a child has no difficulty in operating linguistically in different universes of discourse. It becomes naturally bilingual because it finds out very soon that certain persons are 'persons-to-whom-English-is-spoken,' that other persons are 'persons-to-whom-Afrikaans-is-spoken.'. . ." It follows that if bilingual schooling is not to aggravate what Haugen calls "the basic problem of the bilingual, that of keeping his languages apart" (BLCIL, 70), the times, places, and persons for each language should be kept separate. Indeed Malherbe recommends that bilingual schools have "where possible specialist teachers for the language instruction in the case of both the first and the second languages" (TBS, 24).

Another major factor in the organization of bilingual schooling is whether or not to teach the young Spanish-speaking learners separately when such separation would make their learning more effective or to prefer a policy of combining them when possible with equal numbers of monolingual Anglos. The problem does not arise in two-way bilingual schools when, after the first three or so years of instruction, the Anglos have enough command of Spanish to permit its free use as a medium. It arises seriously in two other situations: (1) during the first years of elementary school instruction, when to combine Spanish speakers with Anglo monolinguals prevents the teacher from working with full force and authenticity in Spanish because the others would be unable to understand; and (2) in those cases where less than half of the day is devoted to Spanish, e.g., a single class period. In these cases, in addition to the weakness just described, the practice of combining the two kinds of learners means that while the Hispanos get watered down Spanish-medium instruction the Anglos get nothing but FLES, *foreign language instruction.* Teaching a language as a subject is entirely different from using it as a medium. The two are strongly incompatible.

Here again the ambivalence described above causes the confusion. Special classes for Spanish speakers in English as a second language are "homogeneous grouping." Special Spanish-medium class work for them is likely to be viewed as "segregation."

Language Maintenance Efforts Elsewhere in Spanish America

For centuries Spanish speakers have cherished their language, and in every country the motto of the Royal Spanish Academy, *limpia, fija, y da esplendor,* has had strong adherents. Guillermo L. Guitarte and Rafael Torres Quintero have summarized formal and official efforts in support of the uniformity of Spanish, and the following account is drawn from that summary (CTL, 562-604). The Royal Spanish Academy and its former corresponding academies were a major force since 1870 in combatting the linguistic nationalism and other centrifugal tendencies that threatened to fragment the Spanish language following the wars of independence in Latin America. They have been organized since 1951 in an *Asociación de Academias de la Lengua Española* "whose purpose is to work assiduously for the defense, unity and integrity of our common language, and to see that its natural growth follows the traditional paths of the Spanish language." Related to that *Asociación,* an *Oficina Internacional de Información and Observación del Español* made up of linguists from the Spanish-speaking countries has been established in Madrid. Guitarte and Torres Quintero report that in its efforts to assure that every region with a large population of Spanish speakers will have a means of working for the control and defense of the language, the Association is considering the establishment of branches in such cities as Los Angeles, San Antonio, Chicago, and New York (CTL, 570).

In a number of Latin American countries the efforts to develop pride and respect for Spanish include holding literary and philological contests, the celebration of an annual "language day," special lectures, and regular newspaper articles dealing with language, and, in some countries, laws which seek to encourage correctness of language in all media of mass communication including public signs (CTL, 586-87).

SUMMATION

The four-hundred year drama of Spanish in the United States is still far from its denouement. The evidence presented and weighed by our "conference of experts" is that there are extraordinary, potential advantages that favor the maintenance of Spanish. They are as yet an almost totally unrealized potential. In the face of this we have found no evidence to contravene one of the overall conclusions from Fishman's study of six separate cultural-linguistic groups in the United States, three of high prestige (French, Spanish, German) and three of low prestige (Ukrainian, Hungarian, Yiddish): that language maintenance and language shift have proceeded along quite similar lines in the six cases despite seemingly essential differences among them (LLUS, 394-95). "The drift has been consistently toward Anglification and has become accelerated in recent years."

The most significant disclosure is the seemingly obvious one (developed in detail by U. Weinreich and others) that language, and languages in contact, are primarily and overwhelmingly social phenomena subject irremissibly to other social phenomena which in some measure can be controlled. A kind of corollary of this is the disclosure that there seems to be something like rules which lend a measure of predictability to the interaction of languages and peoples. The two fundamental issues set forth above as a "restatement of the problem," are unavoidable. The disdain for correctness implies abandonment of the language that Hispanic peoples have in common. The ambivalencies will be resolved.

Spanish speakers in the United States may choose a kind of stable diglossia with English by dividing the domains of usage, and irrespective of the extent to which their mother tongue becomes dialectized. Or they may aspire to be the marginal bilingual group mediating between the Spanish monolinguals of Latin America and the English monolinguals of the United States and Canada. To function on this larger stage would require allegiance and adherence to standard Spanish, *el español común.* There are other choices, including the preference not to choose at all.

Let the conference conclude by noting that in purely linguistic terms the speech habits of all peoples (with whatever repertory of varieties of usage from whatever number of "languages") are equally adequate in service of the purposes for which they were developed. When new purposes are envisaged and factors beyond the purely linguistic must be considered, the matter becomes more complicated.

NOTES

1. Preface to Uriel Weinreich, *Languages in Contact.* The Hague: Mouton, 1968.

2. Treated at greater length in Chapter 11.

3. This term, in the Spanish speakers' vocabulary, designates their fellow-citizens who are not of "la Raza," usually (but not always!) excepting the blacks, American Indians, and those of Oriental ancestry.

4. *El Grito del Norte* (Chicano newspaper), Espanola, New Mexico, April 26, 1971.

5. During the author's boyhood in New Mexico it seemed more common for Indians to be speakers of Spanish in addition to their mother tongue than for them to have a smattering of English.

6. This entire summary account is taken from Heinz Kloss, "German-American Language Maintenance Efforts," in LLUS 206-52.

7. All the above section on Norwegian is from Haugen's two-volume work, *The Norwegian Language in America.* Bloomington, Indiana: Indiana University Press (1969). This comprehensive history and analysis, both sociological and linguistic, is indispensable to an understanding of the immigrant languages in the United States.

8. There is increasing evidence (1973) of a tendency among Chicanos to identify with their Mexican (including the indigenous) origins. A notable example—one of many that could be cited—is an anthology of Chicano literature published in 1972. Of 142 pieces in the anthology, 5 are of aboriginal, pre-Cortesian origin, 64 are by Chicano writers, and of these, 28 are in Spanish, 29 in English, and 7 are macaronic English-Spanish verse. The remainder are by Mexicans, Puerto Ricans, other Latin Americans, and the original *conquistadores.*

9. Dr. Uvaldo Palomares, Chicano psychologist, addressing himself in 1972 to "the problem of the child that mixes the two languages," has proclaimed, typically, "Mixing a language is not a problem, it is a good thing." In *Proceedings—National Conference on Bilingual Education,* April 14-15, 1972. Austin, Texas: Dissemination Center for Bilingual Bicultural Education (1972), p. 214-15.

A notable exception to that attitude is Rafael Jesús González, professor at Laney College, Oakland, California (1972) who has defended the integrity of each of the languages, has demonstrated yet another reason for not "mixing" them, and has found a place for "pachuco" too. See his "Pensamientos sobre la Literatura Chicana," ibid., p. 26-39.

10. Note the paragraph, page 102, in this regard.

11. Fishman's LLUS, Sections VI and VII of RITSOL, and Chapter 10 of TNLIA are concerned with language planning.

12. See Chapter 5.

13. See Chapter 4.

KEY WORKS CONSULTED

BLCIL.   Haugen, Einar. "Bilingualism, Language Contact and Immigrant Languages in the United States: A Research Report 1956-1970," *Current Trends in Linguistics,* vol. 10, ed. Thomas A. Sebeok. The Hague: Mouton (1973).

CTL.   Sebeok, Thomas A., ed. *Current Trends in Linguistics—Ibero-American and Caribbean Linguistics.* The Hague: Mouton (1968).

DMB.   Kelly, L. G., ed. *Description and Measurement of Bilingualism: An International Seminar.* Toronto: University of Toronto Press (1969).

LALS.   Alatis, James, ed. *Linguistics and Language Study* (21st Annual Round Table
           Meeting). Washington, D. C.: Georgetown University Press (1970).
LC.   Weinreich, Uriel. *Languages in Contact.* The Hague: Mouton (1968).
LLUS.   Fishman, Joshua A., et al. *Language Loyalty in the United States.* The Hague:
           Mouton (1966).
MAE.   Anon. *Equal Educational Opportunity, Part 4—Mexican American Education*
           (Hearings Before the Select Committee on Equal Educational Opportunity of the
           United States Senate, Ninety-first Congress, Second session. August 18-21, 1970).
           Washington, D. C.: Government Printing Office (1971).
RITSOL.   Fishman, Joshua A., ed. *Readings in the Sociology of Language.* The Hague:
           Mouton (1970).
TBS.   Malherbe, E. G. *The Bilingual School.* London: Longmans, Green (1946).
TNEP.   *The National Elementary Principal,* I (1970), p. 2.
TNLIA.   Haugen, Einar. *The Norwegian Language in America.* Bloomington, Indiana:
           Indiana University Press (1969).

OTHER AUTHORS AND WORKS CITED

Ballesteros, David. "Toward an Advantaged Society: Bilingual Education in the 70's," TNEP,
     25-28.
Bodine, John J. "Taos Names: A Clue to Linguistic Acculturation," *Anthropological
     Linguistics,* 10.5, p. 23-27. (BLCIL)
Brown, Roger, and Albert Gilman. "The Pronouns of Power and Solidarity," *Style in
     Language,* ed. Thomas A. Sebeok. Cambridge: Technology Press (1969), p. 253-76.
     (RITSOL)
Di Pietro, Robert J. "The Discovery of Universals in Multilingualism," LALS, 13-23.
Elizondo, Sergio D. *Critical Areas of Need for Research and Scholastic Study* (in the series
     Chicano Studies Institutes—Summer 1970). Washington, D.C.: Montal Systems, 600
     Federal Bldg., 1522 K Street, NW (1970).
Ferguson, Charles A. "Diglossia," *Word,* XV (1959), p. 325-40.
Fishman, Joshua A. "Bilingualism With and Without Diglossia; Diglossia With and Without
     Bilingualism," *The Journal of Social Issues,* XXIII (April 1967), No. 2, p. 29-38.
Fishman, Joshua A., Robert L. Cooper, Roxana Ma, et al. *Bilingualism in the Barrio,* 2 vols.
     Final report, U.S. Office of Education. New York: Yeshiva University (1968),
     p. 124-25.
Fitzpatrick, Joseph P. "Educational Experience of the Puerto Rican Community in New York
     City: A Review Paper." Study commissioned by the Puerto Rican Institute for School
     and Community interaction of the Puerto Rican Forum, Inc., p. 67 (cited by Hector I.
     Vasquez).
Garvin, Paul L., and Madeleine Mathiot. "The Urbanization of the Guaraní Language: A
     Problem in Language and Culture," *Men and Cultures: Selected Papers of the Fifth
     International Congress of Anthropological and Ethnological Sciences,* ed. A. F. C.
     Wallace. Philadelphia: University of Pennsylvania Press (1956). (RITSOL)
Guitarte, Guillermo L., and Rafael Torres Quintero, "Linguistic Correctness and the Role of
     the Academies," CTL, 562-604.
Hayden, Robert G. "Some Community Dynamics of Language Maintenance," LLUS, 205.
Hughes, Everett C. Commentary in DMB, 322.
Hymes, Dell. "Models of the Interaction of Language and Social Setting," *The Journal of
     Social Issues,* XXIII (April 1967), No. 2, p. 8-28.
Jones, Morgan Emory. "A Phonological Study of English as Spoken by Puerto Ricans
     Contrasted with Puerto Rican Spanish and American English." Dissertation, University
     of Michigan (1962). (BLCIL)

Kjolseth, Rolf. "Bilingual Education Programs in the United States: For Assimilation or Pluralism?" Paper presented in the section on Sociological Perspectives on Bilingual Education of the Sociolinguistics Program at the 7th World Congress of Sociology held in Varna, Bulgaria, September 14-19, 1970.

Kloss, Heinz. "German-American Language Maintenance Efforts," LLUS, 206-52.

Kroeber, A. L. *Anthropology*. New York: Harcourt, Brace & World (1948), p. 402. (LC, 5-6)

Labov, William. *The Social Stratification of English in New York City*. Washington, D.C.: Center for Applied Linguistics (1966).

Lesley, Tay. "Bilingual Education in California." Master's dissertation, University of California, Los Angeles (1971).

Mackey, William F. "The Description of Bilingualism," RITSOL, 554-84.

Macrae, K. D. Commentary in DMB, 318.

Malherbe, E. G. Commentary in DMB, 46, 326.

Núñez, René. *Criteria for Employment of Chicano Studies Staff* (in the series Chicano Studies Institutes—Summer 1970). Washington, D.C.: Montal Systems, 600 Federal Bldg., 1522 K Street, NW (1970).

Rubin, Joan. "Bilingualism in Paraguay," *Anthropological Linguistics,* IV (January 1962), No. 1, p. 52-58.

———. "National Bilingualism in Paraguay." Doctoral dissertation, Yale University (1963), Chapter 7, p. 200-35. (Chapter 7 appeared in RITSOL, 512-30.)

Sánchez, George I. "An Interview with George I. Sanchez," TNEP, 103.

Sánchez, Lionel. *La Raza Community and Chicano Studies* (in the series Chicano Studies Institutes—Summer 1970). Washington, D.C.: Montal Systems, 600 Federal Bldg., 1522 K Street, NW (1970).

Stewart, William. "Sociolinguistic Factors in the History of American Negro Dialects," *Florida FL Reporter,* V (Spring, 1967), p. 2.

Trujillo, Marcela L. *Guidelines for Employment in Chicano Studies* (in the series Chicano Studies Institutes—Summer 1970). Washington, D.C.: Montal Systems, 600 Federal Bldg., 1522 K Street, NW (1970).

———. Review of *Mexican Americans in School: A History of Educational Neglect.* Thomas P. Carter, New York: College Entrance Examination Board (1970), in TNEP, 88-92.

Tsuzaki, Stanley Mamoru. "English Influences in the Phonology and Morphology of the Spanish Spoken in the Mexican Colony in Detroit, Michigan." Doctoral dissertation, University of Michigan (1963). (BCLIL)

UNESCO. *The Use of Vernacular Languages in Education.* Monographs on Fundamental Education, VIII. Paris: UNESCO (1953).

10

BILINGUAL-BICULTURAL EDUCATION AND CULTURAL PLURALISM: THE SPECIAL CASE OF THE MEXICAN AMERICANS

ABSTRACT   *This piece attempts an overview of the bilingual-bicultural education movement in the United States against a background of the Mexican-Americans' struggle for social justice. It is not meant to be comprehensive, hence the discussion is limited to certain historical, sociological, and linguistic matters which have a bearing on bilingual schooling. It was written at the request of the World Jewish Council for its international symposium on education and cultural pluralism in London in 1969, and is published here in revised form by permission of the World Jewish Council.*

It has become popular to say that the melting pot has been discredited as a model of nationalism in the United States. It is being forcefully repudiated by some of the nation's major ethnic groups, and there are stirrings of demand for something called cultural pluralism. This essay is concerned with the phenomenon in three ways. The first concern is to show the extent and significance of the movement to establish and legitimize bilingual education for the children of non-English mother tongue groups, principally the speakers of Spanish and the American Indian tribes. Closely related to this legitimization of bilingualism, but going beyond it to touch all ethnic groups in the nation, is the effort underway to promote bicultural education and awareness of our diverse ethnic heritage. Neither movement is the same when viewed by the minority groups which demand these changes as when seen by the middle-class majority which permits and even fosters them.

The third concern is the special case of the Spanish speakers in the American Southwest, the second largest minority in the nation and the largest by far in that region. There one finds hints of a demand for cultural self-determination and self-realization in a much broader sense. The clamor for social justice is strident and unanimous, whether in a context of assimilation or not, and what the role of the Spanish language will be when the new order prevails is still an open question.

For the most part the essay focuses on changes in attitude, law, and educational practice during the years since 1967.

PART ONE: BILINGUAL EDUCATION

The Bilingual Education Act,[1] the first Federal legislation in the nation's history to promote the preservation of the non-English languages spoken in the United States by supporting their use as mediums of regular instruction in the public schools, is masterfully ambiguous. Its terms permit both the ethnocentrists and the cultural pluralists to see what they want to see in the Act. It could mean the merest token obeisance to the non-English mother tongue and the culture it represents, or it could—as an example—support for any of the American Indian tribal groups the production of a full panoply of teaching materials in their language in all the school subjects, the complete training of a corps of native speakers of that language, and the installation and operation of the resulting curriculum from kindergarten through the twelfth grade, plus schooling in the native tongue for the parents of the school children. English as a second medium of instruction could, of course, not be excluded from those children's education.

The U.S. Office of Education, which administers the Act, has interpreted bilingual education officially to mean "the use of two languages, one of which is English, as mediums of instruction for the same pupil population in a well-organized program which encompasses part or all of the curriculum and includes the study of the history and culture associated with the mother tongue" (USOE, 1). The Office of Education began by taking a safe, noncommittal position between those who would want to produce full literacy in children by maintaining and developing the mother tongue at least on a par with English throughout the twelve (or at least the first six) school years, and those who would focus hard on English, grudgingly conceding it to be the second language (chronologically) in the child's life and using so-called "second language" methods, thus permitting the use of the mother tongue only as a quick expedient, a temporary bridge to English. Since 1974, the official (but unpublished) policy has favored the quick transition to English.[2] The official guidelines document also encourages the temporary bridge procedure by saying that "children are taught one or more academic subjects in their dominant language [English could be deemed as dominant for many Spanish speakers] at least until they have mastered enough English to enable learning in English" (USOE, 3). As it is presently administered, the strength of the Act in support of serious development of the non-English tongues is further attenuated by the requirement that English mother tongue children be taught the other language. This attempt to make all the children bilingual (and avoid the semblance of segregation of the Spanish speakers) slows the progress in Spanish of the native Spanish-speaking child to match that of the monolingual Anglo. The official guidelines also encourage "the instructional use of both languages for both groups in the same classroom," a practice which weakens the program in other ways. (See Chapter 2.)

A further limitation of the Bilingual Education Act is its poverty criterion, which restricts participation to those schools which have a "high concentration" of children from environments where the dominant language is not English and who are from families with incomes of less than $3,000 per year or from families receiving payments through a program of aid to dependent children. Einar Haugen finds that because of this criterion, "It was a kind of poor relief available to school systems applying for the aid dispensed under the Act, so that once again 'bilingualism' was associated in the popular mind with poverty and alienation, a 'problem' to be 'solved' by its gradual elimination" (Haugen).[3]

Official ambiguity and obeisance to English at the federal level can be offset by local option at the school level. Certainly the enthusiasm of the ethnic groups for bilingual education cannot be doubted. Nevertheless, preliminary analysis of the first seventy-six Bilingual Education Act projects revealed what appeared to be such inadequate attention—time, resources, and understanding—to the other tongue tongue, as compared to the attention paid to English that on the whole bilingual education in those projects was not getting a fair trial. (See Chapter 5.)

[During school year 1975-76 there were 406 school projects of bilingual education supported under the Bilingual Education Act. Each project could expect support for five years. The projects were in 38 states and territories: 88 in California, 60 in Texas, 49 in New York, 1 (with 26 separate schools) in Illinois, 16 in Arizona, 15 in New Mexico, 9 in New Jersey. Spanish and 46 other languages had projects, with as many as five languages per project: 24 for French, 19 Portuguese, 16 Italian, 15 Chinese, 8 each for Greek and Pilipino, 6 Navajo, 5 Vietnamese, 3 each for Japanese, Keres, Korean, Miccosukee, and Samoan, and at least one in Arabic, Chamorro, Hebrew, Ilokano, Kusaiean, Lauwan, Marshallese, Micronesian, Palauan, Ponapean, Russian, Trukese, Ulithian, Woleian, Yapese, Yiddish, Yup'ik, and 15 other American Indian languages. Most of the projects were in Spanish.]

Obstacles to Effective Bilingual Schooling

Effective bilingual education must contend with difficulties of at least seven kinds:

1.   The pervasive ethnocentrism of the English mother tongue majority and the corresponding traditional view among school people that folk bilingualism is a handicap to be overcome, rather than an asset to be encouraged. The fact that the Congress has chosen to stigmatize bilingual-bicultural schooling as a kind of medicine appropriate only for the children of the poor.

2.   The unfortunate linkage of bilingual-bicultural education with integration, which gives unreasonable importance to placing English monolingual and

other-language children together, thus making it impossible to use that other language fully, completely, and exclusively as the medium during those parts of the school day devoted to it.

3.   The high incidence of near-illiteracy in Spanish among its speakers, their consequent inattention and unconcern for the prestigious uses of Spanish. (It does not seem possible to make a child vigorously literate in his mother tongue if that vigor and literacy are not matched in public places and in the homes.)

4.   The widespread notion that bilingual education is *any kind of school activity whatsoever* in which teachers who speak two languages are engaged with pupils who also speak two languages, irrespective of whether the non-English tongue is actually used as a medium of instruction.

5.   The common use of a single "bilingual" person to teach through both languages instead of the more powerful—and no more expensive—model which uses one or more English-medium teachers and one or more Spanish- (or Navajo- or Chinese-, etc.) medium teachers.

6.   The lack of teachers adequately trained to work using Spanish as the medium and of institutions prepared to train such teachers.

7.   Misunderstanding and contention over dialectal differences.

Spanish as spoken in the Southwest varies somewhat by region, by age level of the speaker, by social class, and in relation to distance in space or time from Mexico. Regardless of how close to or far from "world standard" the Mexican-American's Spanish is (and undoubtedly many hundreds of thousands speak "standard" Mexican Spanish, fully as prestigious as American English), the fact of being unlettered in Spanish makes it difficult for him or her to defend that language against the often spurious, often invidious attacks of three groups of critics: (a) Anglo-Americans in general who do not know Spanish, but who derive satisfaction from making slighting remarks about "Tex-Mex," "border Spanish," "Mexican," etc.; (b) Anglo-American teachers of Spanish, who often have little practical command of the language and who protect themselves by saying, "I don't understand their dialect: I studied Castilian"; (c) Mexicans from Mexico and other Latin Americans, who commonly make fun of even inconsequential lexical Anglicisms, thoughtlessly or from pique because the Mexican-Americans emigrated, and who call them, derogatorily, "*pochos*." Another group of unwitting enemies of Spanish is made up of those Mexican-Americans—usually the most militant of the unlettered youth—whose dialect is often closer to "standard" Spanish than they realize, who noisily scorn and reject any move favoring "standard" Spanish and insist that the Chicano must continue to speak and write only his own (as they say) *caló* or *pachuco*.

The Extent of Writing in Spanish
One criterion for gauging the significance of the demand for bilingual-bicultural education is the extent of writing and publication in Spanish by its advocates. By

1969 two score newspapers representing the movement had been started and were
linked in a Chicano Press Association. All were "bilingual," with the Spanish
ranging from the standard *"español común"* through many degrees of doing one's
honest best. Except in a few cases, notably *La Guardia* (Milwaukee, Wisconsin) and
El Grito del Norte (Taos, and later Española, New Mexico), the proportion of
Spanish to English tended to diminish and by 1973 most were no longer being
published. (See list below under "references.")

A few school systems with bilingual education projects have published
newsletters and notices to the parents in Spanish. The extent of their use of
Spanish and its quality have varied, with many articles typified by an official
brochure from the Los Angeles public schools which carried as a headline, *"Las
Escuelas Son Para Ir A."*

In an excited and exciting outburst, Mexican-Americans—Chicanos—are
writing ever more poetry, perhaps half of it in Spanish, a part in a macaronic
Spanish-English. Following tradition in Hispanic countries, much of it is published
in newspapers. Some novels and short stories have appeared as well as extended
sociological and historical studies related to the movement, virtually all in English.
Notable exceptions in Spanish are the collection of short stories . . . *Y no se lo
tragó la tierra,* by Tomás Rivera (Quinto Sol, 1972) and *Peregrinos de Aztlán,* a
1974 novel of great poetic power and promise by Miguel Méndez (Editorial
Peregrinos, 2740 Aurora Drive, Tucson, Arizona 85706). (See Chapter 13.)

Two Mexican-American scholarly journals of admirable quality have been
founded, *Aztlán* (Los Angeles) and *El Grito* (Berkeley); four popular magazines,
Regeneración (East Los Angeles), *La Raza* and *Con Safos* (Los Angeles), and
Magazín (San Antonio); as well as a magazine of creative writing, *Tejidos* (Austin).
Mexican-Americans also now have several publishing houses.

In all cases the editorial information and most of the contents are in English,
but occasionally an article or poem appears in Spanish. *El Espejo,* the first
anthology of Mexican-American writings, includes works in Spanish, in some cases
translations of the original English.

The Chicano (Mexican-American) Studies programs (see Part Two, below)
seem to encourage—and even require for some courses—a limited command of
Spanish and offer courses for the study of Spanish, including "barrio Spanish."
Some courses are given in a now-Spanish, now-English mode, but in no case known
to this writer are students offered full courses such as history, economics, etc.,
through the exclusive medium of Spanish, with the books and other materials also
in that language.

Four major factors have strongly favored wide retention and dominance of
the Spanish language for most Mexican-American intragroup (as opposed to
intergroup) purposes. The factors are: (1) proximity and access to Mexico and
ethnic identity with the Mexican people; (2) constant reinforcement by
immigration; (3) social isolation in enclaves, whether rural or urban; and
(4) traditional discrimination by Anglo-Americans against any visible minority in
respect to educational policy (thus limiting education and upward mobility) and

in respect to social commingling (thus favoring isolation and linguistic solidarity). The first two factors, which can always be expected to favor the retention of Spanish, are far less potent than they might be. The effect of the other two is now being reversed, thanks to the Mexican-American movement for social justice, which leaves Spanish today peculiarly exposed to an accelerated shift to and replacement by English.

The present movement in the United States toward egalitarianism finds the Mexican-Americans with an intelligentsia—developed through English, oriented toward the dominant English community, and increasingly vocal in English— demanding and likely to achieve an end to the discriminatory practices. That intelligentsia speaks Spanish too and is demanding a place and a role for Spanish, but no one has suggested what the place and role are to be. The answer—for the Mexican-Americans and any other enclave of Americans who continue to speak a tongue other than English—might be found in the concept of diglossia. Instead of the prevailing confusion of views which find the two languages competing with each other for the bilingual speaker's loyalty and thus forcing his decision to choose between them, diglossia offers a pattern for coexistence in the two languages within the bilingual individual, for intragroup and international purposes and without competition.

The Case for Diglossia

Diglossia, for the purposes of this essay, is the socially recognized, approved and protected use of two languages at the societal level (rather than the individual level), each for a set of compartmentalized complementary functions or domains of use. This *stable* relationship is in contrast with the *unstable* relationship of bilingualism in which the languages compete with each other because the functions of each are not differentiated, not complementary, not recognized or approved. Without a status approaching diglossia it appears that the use of Spanish in the Southwest except in border cities and towns will diminish constantly and quickly. Enclaves large in numbers, or reinforced by immigration, or isolated by illiteracy and poverty, can be remarkably language-tenacious. But, as Joshua Fishman says, "no society needs two languages for one and the same set of functions."

There has always been diglossia of a sort in the Southwest. The difference between what has been and what must be if Spanish is to survive and flourish is a subtle but all-important one. Although in the past, as now, Spanish has always been used for some things and English for others in fixed and predictable ways, both the past and current view has always been that English will inevitably replace Spanish. Each person must choose, they say, and education forces the choice of English. At best it has been either/or: either remain isolated and continue to speak Spanish, or cut all ties and Anglicize. The key to diglossia, to stable coexistence of languages, has been noted above: the socially recognized and approved (hence supported) use of the two tongues for compartmentalized, complementary (not competing) functions. This means virtual exclusion of the second language from the home so that each new generation of children remains safely monolingual with the parents. The assignment of functions to each language can be made only by the speakers themselves. The fact that such assignments are usually reached by a social process outside of the speaker's awareness does not preclude conscious sociolinguistic planning. *Nor does complementarity preclude a high degree of literacy in both tongues.* Full exploitation of Spanish for intragroup and educational and international purposes demands such literacy. (See also Chapter 8.)

Along with literacy in Spanish—achieved through bilingual schooling in a social context of diglossia—would come an unexpected revelation and reward: a realization of the excellence of much of the Spanish spoken in the Southwest. Millions of Americans in the Southwest speak Spanish which is as good as the English spoken around them, group for group at any level, and most of the children are capable of it.

PART TWO: BICULTURAL EDUCATION

That the melting pot theory is under attack is supposedly made evident by the rise and popularity of ethnic studies in American schools, colleges, and universities. But here no less than in the case of bilingualism there is marked ambivalence. A case in point is the Ethnic Heritage Studies Program (1972) which provides federal funds to support the opportunity of elementary and secondary school children to study the cultural heritages of American ethnic groups and gain greater appreciation of the multiethnic nature of the United States. In the belief that "in a multiethnic society a greater understanding of the contributions of one's own heritage and those of one's fellow citizens can contribute to a more harmonious, patriotic, and committed populace . . ." this legislation supports the development and dissemination of appropriate curriculum materials, teacher training, and cooperation with ethnic organizations.

Congressman Roman Pucinski, sponsor of an early version of the bill, set the theme:

> There is a growing sense of sameness permeating our existence—threatening to quiet the creative outpourings of the human soul and the gentle sensitivity of one man to the uniqueness and humanity of another. Clearly, this sustained melancholia has touched all our lives. Perhaps most seriously afflicted by the deteriorating quality of human life are the young. The Nation's youth are engrossed in a restless, sometimes tumultous, and often threatening search for identity. Our young people want to know who they are, where they belong, how they can remain distinctive, special individuals amidst the pervasive pressure for conformity.
>
> Experience has taught us that the pressure toward homogeneity has been superficial and counterproductive; that the spirit of ethnicity, now lying dormant in our national soul, begs for reawakening in a time of fundamental national need.

The American blacks' powerful drive to establish "Black Studies" or "Afro-American studies" centers in American colleges and universities is well known.

Less known—and largely ignored by the press—is the equally vigorous drive of the Mexican-Americans who have founded about four score such programs of Mexican-American or Chicano studies.

The Chicano Studies Programs

The Chicano studies programs are at the heart of a remarkable reform movement in American education. These programs, linked closely to and supported by the Mexican-American student organizations, are far more than a mere expansion of the college's or university's curriculum, teaching, and research to include at last the history, culture and concerns of a heretofore almost ignored segment of the American people. In a time when institutions of higher education are being attacked from all sides as dehumanized servants of other times and other interests, the Chicano studies programs, plus their student group sponsors, have established a unique mutually supportive relationship between the community of scholars and the folk community.

The beliefs and principles listed below, which guide Chicano studies programs, are summarized from *El Plan de Santa Bárbara,* a book-length statement (1969) by the Chicano Coordinating Council on Higher Education (q.v.), and from thirteen booklets "prepared for the Chicano Studies Summer Institutes to be held in Summer, 1970, in Aztlan" with support from the National Endowment for the Humanities, an agency of the United States government ("Chicano Studies").

In 1909 the widely influential American educator, Ellwood P. Cubberly, boldly stated the function of the nation's schools:

> Our task is to assimilate or amalgamate these people as a part of the American race, and to implant in their children, so far as can be done, the Anglo-Saxon conception of righteousness, law, order, and popular government . . . . (Vecoli)

This policy, as Rudolph Vecoli has said, "not to Americanize but to Anglo-Saxonize," has been perceived as destructive by the Mexican-Americans, and it is to counteract it that Chicano studies programs are established. In this respect, the self-designated Chicano sees that the white Anglo majority wants him to want to assimilate but has little intention of allowing that assimilation to take place (the Anglo could easily have had assimilation any time since 1848 had he desired it) even if he, the Chicano, pays the masochistic price of abjuring and renouncing all that he is: his language, his beliefs, his behavior, his way of being human. On the other hand, if the Chicano (or any other ethnic group) ceases to want annihilation-by-assimilation and turns to cultural self-determination (or "separatism" in any other form) he meets fear and resistance at every hand. The unanswered question: To what extent is the Chicano turning away, turning inward, toward self-determination and self-governance?

Twelve points summarize the philosophy and intent of the Chicano studies programs:

1. The convinction that American education from kindergarten through graduate school has distorted and suppressed Chicano history and culture, has been destroying the Chicano child, and must be changed.

2. "Academic excellence, insofar as that excellence relates to the priorities of the Chicano community, is of greater necessity and more highly cherished than it is to the majoritarian culture because it is the Chicano who needs more Chicano teachers . . . more Chicano lawyers . . . more Chicano organizers—writers and historians" (Núñez, 11).

3. ". . . without a strategic use of education, and education that places value on what we value, we will not realize our destiny" (PSB-E1 Plan de Santa Bárbara, 9).

4. "Chicano students, faculty, administrators, employees and the community must be the central and decisive designers and administrators of those programs" (PSB, 10).

5. A *Junta Directiva* on each campus, with "the widest possible representation of Chicanos, i.e., students, staff, community and employees . . . would oversee all Chicano programs . . . [with] complete autonomy insofar as internal policy, hiring and firing procedures, student admissions and program development are concerned" (Núñez, 13).

6. "It (the Chicano Studies Program) should be provided full resources . . . and must have a direct line of communication to the highest level of authority on the campus . . . a Chicano vice president would be the ideal . . ." (Núñez, 13).

7. Chicano studies staff (preferably limited to persons of Mexican ancestry) must meet four criteria: (a) sensitivity to the values and needs of Chicanos; (b) teaching excellence, including ability to relate to youth from the lowest socioeconomic strata; (c) commitment to the Chicano Movement; and (d) acceptance of the governing role of the Chicano student (adapted from Núñez, 14-20).

8. Chicano studies programs must seek by every means to maintain close ties of service between the movement's intellectuals and the least favored of Chicanos, the field workers, the slum dwellers, the victims of drugs, and those imprisoned. To this end, each program encourages its students to become "involved in the life and policies of their barrio, and demands that upon graduation they return to their home to help develop its resources and help end the exploitation that drains it" (Núñez, 19 passim).

9. The Chicano studies movement recognizes that the Chicano's history begins not in Spain or Mexico, but with that of the aborigines of this continent.

10. Chicano studies are strongly humanistic in orientation. The ideological and philosophical import of Chicano studies is their greatest value (Elizondo, 7).

11. The "cowardice" and unconcern of those Mexican-Americans who have chosen to "cut all ties and Anglicize" is repudiated.

12.   Belief that "the viability . . . of those programs will depend largely on the continuing support of Mexican-American student organizations, for without them academics will tend naturally to gravitate toward scholastic stagnation. . ." (Elizondo, 11).

The most powerful features of the Chicano studies movement are its location of power and control in the students, and its linkage with the Mexican-American community. The driving force, in much of California, for example, is the MECHA organization. MECHA (formerly UMAS, United Mexican-American Students) stands for *Movimiento Estudiantil Chicano de Aztlán*. Convinced that American colleges and universities "are all simple microcosms of this (American) society and . . . feature this society's same interests and rigid structures which have absolutely no thought of sharing power, providing access, or permitting true pluralistic participation," the autonomous MECHA chapters "have to act . . . to seize power on campuses and force the colleges to satisfy some of their obligations to our community." Once a power base has been established on a campus, demands are articulated and subsequent political action dramatizes the cause—for example, the establishment of a Chicano studies program. At least half of the governing body of any Chicano-oriented program must be students, not in an advisory capacity but with full voting rights, and "the student representation on all departmental committees [must] be at all times selected by the Chicano student organization on campus. . . ." MECHA chapters have not avoided head-on confrontation with the college administration and faculty on matters of official policy, especially admissions criteria and academic standards which have the effect of excluding Mexican-Americans.[4]

The significance of these student-initiated reforms can be appreciated only when they are compared with other current programs of educational reform which recognize the importance of "community involvement" if education is to be made more relevant but which merely *permit* a modest measure of such involvement by benevolent dispensation from the top of the hierarchy. The difference becomes clear when one reflects that by its very nature power cannot be given; it must be taken.

In sum, the typical Chicano studies program is a special curriculum—sometimes leading to a degree, sometimes not—of courses and activities designed to explore and explain the Mexican-American experience past and present to himself and others, controlled and taught by Chicanos, initiated, sustained, and guided by the driving force of a sociopolitically-oriented organization of student activists, with three undergirding aims: social justice through cultural self-determination, admission of ever more Chicanos to higher studies, plus programs of financial and tutorial support for them, and close, mutually reinforcing ties to the lowest, most needy stratum of Chicano society.

The limitations of this essay permit no more than a hint of the successes of the Chicano student and studies movement. Let one example suffice:

At the University of California, Santa Barbara, the academic Department of Chicano Studies, born in 1969 out of severe, massive confrontations between students and the university's administration has been supplemented since February 1970 by a separate Center for Chicano Studies, devoted primarily to research, training and public service, including an Educational Opportunity Program focused on recruitment, counseling and financial support for students of that ethnic group. It grew strong under a *Junta Directiva,* a kind of board of overseers, with equal representation from four Chicano sectors: students, faculty, staff, and the community.

The Center, housed in its own building—an old wooden one—also maintains a reference library, sponsors conferences and lectures, and has organized and directed special training sessions, e.g., a six-week intensive institute for forty Mexican-American teachers, counselors, and administrators from elementary and secondary schools. It is the prime mover in the Tiburcio Vasquez community center in Santa Barbara, which offers tutoring and special classes for Chicano school children; it has operated for Chicano children four to ten years old a free community school on the university campus, directed and taught by Chicano college students; it has operated an employment and counseling service for all Chicanos in the Santa Barbara area; has undertaken a research project on the nature of political communication as it relates to Mexican-Americans; and has worked with a university theater group, Teatro MECHA.

The significance of the Santa Barbara situation becomes apparent when it is borne in mind that the university is in an area where although Chicanos constitute about one quarter of the population, there were as recently as 1965 fewer than a score of them in the student body and virtually no recognition of their existence as a people and as a legitimate focus of interdisciplinary study. By 1970-71 some 300 of the 13,000 students on the Santa Barbara campus were Chicanos. In June, 1973, the number had increased to 425. By February of 1976 there were at UCSB approximately 500 Chicano undergraduates and some 50 enrolled in masters and doctoral studies.[5]

The Chicano Theater Movement

Another educational development, the creation of the Chicano theater, must be mentioned, for the players and playwrights are commonly drawn from the Chicano student movement. The first group or company, "El Teatro Campesino," had its start in 1965 out of the grape workers' strike in California. Since 1965 several other groups have been formed:

El Teatro Campesino, P.O. Box 2302, Fresno, CA.
Teatro MECHA, Box 116-USCC, Crown College, Santa Cruz, CA.
Los Reveladores del Tercer Mundo, 233 121 Street
Teatro Venceremos, 2755 El Camino Real, Redwood City, CA.
Teatro Triste, 1389 64th Avenue, Oakland, CA.
Teatro Aztlán, 9500 Zelzah Street, Northridge, CA.
Teatro Popular de la Vida y Muerte, California State College, Long Beach, CA 90801.

Teatro MECHA, P.O. Box 11445, Santa Barbara, CA.

Teatro de los Barrios, 1017 E. Hadley, Phoenix, AZ.

Teatro Urbano, P.O. Box 8052, San José, CA.

Teatro Bilingüe de la Universidad de Texas en El Paso, Dept. of English, U. of Texas, El Paso, TX.

Teatro de los Actos, 653 62nd Street, Oakland, CA.

Teatro Mestizo, 5167 Campanlia, San Diego, CA.

One final example of the movement toward bicultural education—and many more could be cited, for the movement is extending itself, however weakly, into the public schools of the Southwest: Four hundred Chicano convicts in Leavenworth Federal penitentiary in Kansas, inspired by news of the "movimiento de la Raza," began publication of a newspaper, *Aztlán,* in May, 1970 and organized a series of weekly classes on "culture of the Southwest." The first session dealt with ". . . our Spanish heritage and our Indo-American origin."

PART III: THE SPECIAL CASE OF THE MEXICAN-AMERICAN

An estimated ten million Spanish-surnamed persons live in continental United States: roughly two million Puerto Ricans or persons of that origin, some two million Cubans and other Latin Americans, and the large remainder Mexican-Americans, also self-designated as Spanish, Spanish-Americans, Latins, Latin Americans, Hispanos, Mexicans, Chicanos, Indo-Spanish (Indo-hispanos) and Indo-Americans—with corresponding forms in Spanish except for the term "Spanish," which they never call themselves when speaking in that language. The names matter a great deal.

The central fact to bear in mind is the search for and affirmation of identity by a people who, beginning with the loss of the territory itself to a victorious American army in 1848, followed by the loss of the immense Spanish and Mexican land grants and most smaller holdings, were systematically overwhelmed and reduced by the essentially "racist" victor to the status of a quasi-caste of menials and second-class citizens and then derided and blamed for having that status. No one can predict whether most Mexican-Americans will in the future choose assimilation or reject it. In no American ethnic group is the question raised more vigorously.

The Importance of the Name

In California a full generation ago, says the Reverend Rubén Reyes of St. Stevens Methodist Church in San Bernardino, "we, the 'Mexicans' (as we were called by the Anglos) always thought of the Anglos as 'Los Americanos' " (*El Chicano*). When the author of this piece was a boy in New Mexico, Spanish speakers, speaking Spanish, called themselves *mexicanos* with utmost naturalness, but the name "Mexican" had an insulting connotation and was used only with great care in English. There were indeed Spaniards among the earliest pre-Jamestown invaders of the Southwest from Mexico, and some "Spanish-surnamed," notably those in

Colorado, still cling to "Spanish-American." Likewise there are still "Old Californians" (*californios*) in California. The point is that in the lapse of 45 years there has come a surging affirmation of identity, and the self-designation "Mexican," in all its forms now rings proud and clear—but not quite for everyone and not quite everywhere.

But the evolution of the self-designation has passed through still two more stages. First, although there is no repudiation of Mexico (resentment at times, yes, because that nation has been less than vigorous in defense of her *emigré* sons and daughters) or of Mexicans and things Mexican, the question "Who am I?" is being asked by a man who sees himself there in the Southwest before Jamestown and Plymouth Rock, there before General Winfield Scott, a man who in painful coexistence with the "Anglo" has lived his own unique history, different from that of Mexico and from that of all other Americans. The result is the new term "Chicano," once over-familiar, a bit derisive and derogatory, now ennobled, proclaimed, and preferred by the youth, the young intellectuals, and almost all activist and militant groups. The Chicano is the once-Mexican-American who experienced what has happened in the Southwest—and, by extension, wherever he has lived in the United States—and who has had enough. He is the one who has been saying, "*¡Ya basta!*" (We've had enough!). For a few Chicanos "Mexican-American" now means "*tío Taco*" (Uncle Tom) or *vendido* (sold out to the *gabacho,* the *gringo,* the Anglo).[6]

It had been common in the past for upwardly mobile Mexican-Americans to escape from their semi-caste by acculturation and by self-designation as "Spanish." However, a study of social mobility of Mexican-Americans of Pomona, California showed that already in 1961 "upwardly mobile Mexicans did not generally take on a 'Spanish' identification." The study demonstrated that those who rise in social status "remain loyal to the Mexican identification" and develop or retain a corresponding ethnocentrism. The highest status individuals were second-generation persons who preferred to call themselves "Mexican-Americans." A major change in group identification seems to be under way with increasing pride toward the word "Mexican" and away from the term "Spanish." The upwardly mobile persons studied often preferred, however, to use English rather than Spanish (Peñalosa and McDonagh).

In the final stage of the search for his own identity the once-Mexican-American is acknowledging his kinship, his common origin, with the American Indian. This sinks his roots deep into that very Southwest for 20,000 years, the "Spanish" experience becomes but a cultural graft, and he is Indo-hispanic, indigenous to that soil, the *orgullosa* (proud) *casta indo-americana.*

There are still only relatively few self-designated *Indo-hispanos* in the Southwest, many more, increasingly more Chicanos, Mexican-Americans in perhaps equal numbers with the Chicanos, ever fewer Spanish-Americans. A professor who held on to his self-identification as "Spanish" is blacklisted. Many an Eduardo who allowed himself to be called Eddie at school and even began to sign his name Edward has hurriedly and happily changed back to the original.

Fernando Peñalosa recalls that "Spanish" restaurants abounded in California twenty-five years ago where now only "Mexican" ones are found.

The Question of Color

The swiftly evolving sense of identity, of self-differentiation as a people, is a necessary catalyst for action by an ethnic minority. So it is with the color of the skin. Mexican-Americans are a heterogeneous people quite as disparate in physical appearance as their kin-people south of the Río Bravo. In Mexico, skin color ranges from "white" through *güero* (blond or light-colored), *trigueño, apiñonado, tostado, moreno, cobrizo* and *prieto* to *negro,* which does not mean Negro or black in the American-English sense but "dark," and is commonly applied with a sense of special affection:

> Negra, negra consentida,
> negra de mi vida,
> Etc.

> Negrita primorosa de mi barrio
> que llevas tanta huella de dolor. . .

> Las blancas las hizo Dios
> y a las morenas el cielo;
> quédense con Dios las blancas,
> yo a las morenas quiero.

So go the people's love songs. And so it is that although skin color rarely matters to either people, either could justifiably choose to be called "white" or "dark," or "brown" or "copper." Forced to differentiate themselves, especially in Texas, from the American blacks in order to combat segregation and other forms of racist discrimination—and probably in part as a gesture toward assimilation— Mexican-Americans once chose to be called "white." In 1967 there occurred in Texas an incident which gives one-half of the story.

Certain Office of Civil Rights data collection forms were put to use in Texas and elsewhere to report on compliance with civil rights laws. The forms identified pupils and school staff as "white," "Negro," and "other." In the "other" category respondents were instructed to designate specific racial or national origin groups recognized as such in their communities, e.g., Indian-American, Oriental, Latin, Mexican-American. A rash of newspaper protest broke out complaining that the federal government was requiring that Mexican-Americans not be classified as "white." A raw nerve had been touched, since in Texas in the 1930's (but only in Texas) Mexican-Americans had fought through the courts to establish that they are "white." Robert Ornelas, National President of the LULACs (League of United Latin-American Citizens) led that protest, joined by the PASO organization and the GI Forum, the latter a nationwide Mexican-American war veterans' group. The national Office for Civil Rights immediately had the forms redesigned to use the innocuous misnomer "Spanish-surnamed Americans." Thereafter, all

Caucasians, including Spanish-surnamed Americans, the Office declared, would be listed in the "white" column. The Spanish-surnamed were to be those persons considered in school or community to be of Mexican, Central American, Latin American, Cuban, or Puerto Rican descent. Spanish descent was, ironically, overlooked, and under the circumstances Indo-Hispanic would have been unthinkable. Hector García, a founder and spokesman of the GI Forum, declared that the Mexican-Americans would rather be classified white even if thereby they lost all assistance from the federal government.

The other half of the story, parallel to the symbolic shift from Spanish to Indo-Hispanic described above, is a symbolic shift along the color line, a repudiation of the whiteness of the *gabacho* (a term meaning light-colored in Mexico, which was applied pejoratively to Frenchmen in the time of Benito Juárez and is now a favorite derogatory name for Anglo-Americans in the Southwest) and a fierce allegiance to brownness or the hue of bronze. Here, too, it is not the remaining "Spanish-Americans" and not all Mexican-Americans who see themselves as brown or bronze. Perhaps most of the latter do, and the self-designated Chicanos make it a point of their ideology.

Chicanos now often protest at being labeled "white" even as they often protest and scorn the ambiguous "Latin American" of the conservative LULACs (League of United Latin-American Citizens), a group formed in 1929 when it was much harder to be Mexican in Texas. The LULACs have actively promoted assimilation; English has been the official language of the League; and they have urged their people to continue to speak Spanish in the home, but to speak English in public places.

The shift away from white was marked by unusual irony in Houston and other Texas cities, where the "white" Mexican-Americans found themselves combined with black school children to achieve "racial integration," leaving the Anglo children untouched in their own segregated schools.

In June 1970, Federal District Judge Woodrow Seals ruled that Mexican-Americans are a distinct ethnic group and that school zoning must take their distinctness into account. The Seals ruling overturned the prior 1948 ruling that Mexican-Americans, known as Latin Americans, were to be classified as "white." Despite official classification as "whites" in Houston for purposes of the census, Mexican-Americans there were commonly classified as Latin Americans on police tickets and similar records.

Mrs. Rose Cansino of Albuquerque reported herself "brown" and Mexican-American on the U.S. decennial census form (April 1970) and was told "You're not brown; you are considered white here." Mrs. Cansino later reported to the press, "I told her that the Gringos had always considered us Mexicans but now all of a sudden they want to consider us white—why?" (*El Grito del Norte*).

Legal and Other Authoritative Recognition

This brief essay attempts no more than to relate certain innovations in American education to their social context and present evidence that that context includes a dynamic movement of self-differentiation by the Chicanos. Of special interest as part of the context are certain related official acts by the federal and state governments and by other prestigious agencies. Though often marked by ambivalence, their net result is likely to be a darkening of the line which marks off the affected ethnic groups as distinct cultural entities. The Bilingual Education Act and the census-taking forms mentioned above are examples of such acts.

The Bureau of Indian Affairs, in April 1970, finally yielded to the appeal of the Navajo people to have their own high school, operated by Navajos for Navajo purposes and agreed to transfer, for each of the next three years and thereafter renegotiate in good faith, the sum of $368,068 for 167 pupils which would otherwise have gone for their support in far-away Indian boarding schools. Ramah (New Mexico) Navajo High School is the result (Martinez). The Navajo people already have complete control of the operation of an elementary school (Rough Rock) and have established and control a Navajo Community College. Navajo is taught extensively in both places and also is used as a medium of instruction.

The immensely powerful National Education Association has gone on record as favoring bilingual education, has questioned the fairness and wisdom of efforts toward quick Americanization, and has recommended repeal of state laws specifying English as the language of school instruction (NEA).

An 1894 California requirement that voters be able to read English was eliminated recently when the State's Supreme Court ruled unanimously that any language is acceptable, provided the voter is otherwise qualified and can show access to political information. The suit which produced the new ruling was brought by two Mexican-Americans.

Pope Paul VI has recently elevated a Mexican-American to the rank of bishop. Father Patricio F. Flores, of Houston, is the first Mexican-American to be so named. He will be auxiliary to the Archbishop of San Antonio.[7]

In January 1970 the Assembly of the State of California in its Resolution No. 444 took sympathetic note of the rising protest of Mexican-American organizations against the disproportionate number of children from that group who are assigned to classes for the mentally retarded and requested the proposal of legislation to correct the situation.

There were at that time about 85,000 children in California classified as educable mental retardates and placed in special classes for such children. Spanish-surnamed people were 13% of the population of California, but 26% of the educable mental retardates had Spanish surnames. Mexican-Americans had long protested this statistical impossibility. They investigated the cases of 47 randomly selected Spanish-speaking "retarded" children, half from urban, half from rural backgrounds. When the children were re-examined in the Spanish language by competent Spanish-speaking psychologists, it was found that 42 of the 47 scored above the IQ ceiling of the mental retardate classification. Thirty-seven scored 75 or higher; over half scored 80 or above; 16% scored 90 or more. On February 5, 1970, U.S. District Court Judge Robert E. Peckham ruled that thenceforth school officials would be required (a) to explain any disproportionate assignment of Spanish-speaking children to classes for mental retardates and (b) to have prepared an IQ test normed to the California Spanish-speaking child population; and that such children will be tested in both Spanish and English and be allowed to respond in either tongue. The implications of this ruling for the role of the Spanish language in education in the Southwest are enormous.

In June 1969, President Richard Nixon appointed Martin G. Castillo, of Monterey Park, California as a member and chairman of the Inter-Agency Committee on Mexican-American Affairs (later renamed the Cabinet Committee on Opportunity for the Spanish Speaking). Mr. Castillo, an attorney, did not know how to speak Spanish.

Arnold Leibowitz, in a study of laws in the United States dealing with language and literacy, has shown that "statutes requiring English literacy as a condition to access to . . . areas of American life . . . (other than official government proceedings and promulgations) . . . operate as a mechanism of racial restriction rather than as an educational device. . . ." For that reason recent relaxation of those laws, cited by Leibowitz, are of interest here (Leibowitz).

One word, one symbol, "Aztlán," combines all of the elements of the reality and the dream: Aztlán, place of reeds and herons where the Aztecs, together with seven other tribes of Nahuatl origin, began the pilgrimage southward which ended with the founding of Tenochtitlán, now Mexico City. The original Aztlán is believed to have been in the area of Maricopa County, Arizona; the symbolic one is all the land ceded by Mexico after the War of 1848, or more generally, the entire American Southwest.

To say Aztlán is to proclaim identity with the original Americans, the aborigines and lay claim to roots thousands of years deep in southwestern soil. Aztlán acknowledges brotherhood no less with the Mexican, also Indian by weight of blood and numbers. Aztlán is any place in the United States where a Chicano— or any other member of *la Raza*—finds himself. There is a map of Aztlán and a flag, red, white, and green—like Mexico's flag—with a three-faced mestizo: Spanish father, Indian mother, and the resultant Chicano mestizo. A new scholarly journal *Aztlán—Chicano Journal of the Social Sciences and the Arts,* has begun publication under the auspices of the Mexican-American Cultural Center, University of California, Los Angeles. *La Verdad,* one of the forty newspapers of the Chicano Press Association is published with the dateline in San Diego, Aztlán. *El Plan de Santa Bárbara* (v. page 160, above) originated in Santa Barbara, Alta California Aztlán.

Finally, there is the *Plan Espiritual de Aztlán,* adopted at the first national Chicano Youth Liberation Conference, sponsored in Denver in March 1969 by Rodolfo Gonzales' Crusade for Justice. At the second national conference in March 1970, attended by over 3000 young Chicanos representing five score organizations from 18 states, work on implementation of the *Plan* continued.

El Plan Espiritual de Aztlán

In the spirit of a new people that is conscious not only of its proud historical heritage, but also of the brutal "gringo" invasion of our territories, we, the Chicano inhabitants and civilizers of the northern land of Aztlán, from whence came our forefathers, reclaiming the land of their birth and consecrating the determination of our people of the sun, declare that the call of our blood is our power, our responsibility, and our inevitable destiny.

We are free and sovereign to determine those tasks which are justly called for by our house, our land, the sweat of our brows and by our hearts. Aztlán belongs to those that plant the seeds, water the fields, and gather the crops, and not to foreign Europeans. We do not recognize capricious frontiers on the bronze continent.

Brotherhood unites us, and love for our brothers makes us a people whose time has come and who struggle against the foreign "gabacho" who exploits our riches and destroys our culture. With our heart in our hands and our hands in the soil, we declare the independence of our mestizo nation. We are a bronze people with a bronze culture. Before the world, before all of North America, before all our brothers in the bronze continent, we are a nation, we are a union of free pueblos, we are AZTLAN.

Key words and phrases from the official explication of the *Plan* elaborate the theme. ". . . social, economic, cultural and political independence is the only road to total liberation from oppression, exploitation and racism. . . . Nationalism . . . transcends all religious, political, class, and economic factions or boundaries . . . economic control of our lives . . . by driving the exploiter out of our communities, our pueblos, and our lands . . . ignore (reject) materialism and embrace humanism . . . co-operative buying and distribution of resources and production . . . . Lands rightfully ours will be fought for and defended . . . . Education must be relevant to our people . . . history, culture, bilingual . . . . Community control of our schools . . . Institutions shall serve our people . . . on the basis of restitution, not handouts. . . . Restitution for past economic slavery, political exploitation, ethnic and cultural psychological destruction and denial of civil and human rights . . . love and carnalismo. . . . For the very young . . . no longer . . . acts of juvenile delinquency, but revolutionary acts. . . . Our cultural values of life, family, and home will . . . defeat the gringo dollar value system. . ."

The Plan Espiritual de Aztlán has been adopted as the platform of the Raza Unida (Mexican-American) national political party, organized in May of 1969. The Raza Unida party has nominated candidates for state and local offices in Colorado and Texas and in the latter has already had some minor victories, notably in Crystal City.

On November 28, 1969, Wilfredo Sedillo, Vice President of Reies Tijerina's *Alianza Federal de los Pueblos Libres,* sent to President Richard M. Nixon a map of the *Republic of Aztlán,* which he proposed as a way of terminating the Mexican-American war of 1848, "that seems," he said, "to make Indo-Hispanos of the Southwest subjects of a foreign nation (the United States of America)."[8]

NOTES

1. Title VII of the Elementary and Secondary Education Act of 1967, Public Law 90-247. Revised and expanded in 1974.

2. In a letter to Senator Joseph Montoya of New Mexico dated November 15, 1974, the Commissioner of Education, Terrell H. Bell made the following statement of policy: "I maintain that the proper goal of federally-supported Bilingual/Bicultural Education Programs is precisely that stated in the OE (Office of Education) staff paper cited in your letter—namely, 'to enable children whose dominant language is other than English to develop competitive proficiency in English so that they can function successfully in the educational and occupational institutions of the larger society. . . . What we know about the educational process tells us that the most effective and the most humane way to achieve this English language competency is through a Bilingual/Bicultural approach.' "

3. Amendments to the Bilingual Education Act in 1974 retained the original criterion of emphasis on the "relative numbers of persons from low-income families sought to be benefitted. . . ."

4. The description of the role of MECHA comes from the MECHA publication No. 3 listed under "Chicano Studies" in the references.

5. In the intervening years since 1969 the number of Chicano studies programs and interest in them had declined seriously.

6. "Anglo" in this context in the Southwest loses its original sense and means all Americans except Mexican-Americans and other members of *la raza*.

7. In 1974 a second Mexican-American, Monsignor Gilbert Chavez, became a Catholic bishop. His assignment is the diocese of San Diego, California.

8. The National Council of the Episcopal Church, against the wishes of Episcopal Bishop of New Mexico and West Texas, C. J. Kinsolving, III, granted substantial funds to the *Alianza* for community action projects in New Mexico. The *Alianza* was also funded (1972) by the "Campaign for Human Development," an organization of the U.S. Catholic Conference.

REFERENCES

Chicano Coordinating Council on Higher Education, *El Plan de Santa Bárbara.* Santa Barbara, California: La Causa Publications, P.O. Box 4818. The moving force behind this remarkable document was the student organization MECHA (Movimiento Estudiantil Chicano de Aztlán). MECHA, in 1969 had chapters in at least 40 colleges, junior colleges, and universities.

"Chicano Studies." Booklets published by Montal Systems, Inc., 600 Federal Bldg., 1522 K Street, N.W, Washington, D.C. 20005.

1. *Criteria for Employment of Chicano Studies Staff,* René Núñez. Centro de Estudios Chicanos, San Diego State College.

2. *The Role of the Chicano Student in the Chicano Studies Program,* Manuel I. López. University of Colorado, Denver.

3. *The Role of the Chicano Student in the Chicano Studies Program,* Movimiento Estudiantil Chicano de Aztlán (MECHA). California State College, Long Beach.

4. *La Raza Community and Chicano Studies,* Lionel Sánchez, Director, Farm Workers United. Fort Lupton, Colorado.

5. *Guidelines for Employment in Chicano Studies,* Marcela L. Trujillo. Chicano Studies Program, University of Colorado, Denver Center.

6.   *What Are the Objectives of Chicano Studies?* Manuel H. Guerra. Arizona State University.

7.   *Research and Scholarly Activity,* Ernesto Galarza and Julián Samora. University of Notre Dame.

8.   *Objectives of Chicano Studies,* Reynaldo Macías, Juan Gómez-Quiñones, and Raymond Castro. The Mexican-American Cultural Center, University of California, Los Angeles.

9.   *Chicanismo,* Thomas A. Martínez.

10. *The Establishment and Administration of a Master's Program in Chicano Studies at the University of Colorado,* Salvador Ramírez. University of Colorado, Boulder.

11. *Critical Areas of Need for Research and Scholastic Study,* Sergio D. Elizondo. California State College at San Francisco.

12. *The Establishment of a Chicano Studies Program and Its Relation to the Total Curriculum of a College or University,* Richard H. Wilde. Dean, California State College, Long Beach.

13. *Chicano Resource Materials,* María Quezada, et al.

CPA. The following newspapers were members of the Chicano Press Association (1969). Most have discontinued publication. Mail addressed to those marked with an asterisk is returned "not forwardable."

Arizona:
CORAJE, c/o Mexican American Liberation Committee, Tucson
EL PAISANO, P. O. Box 155, Tolleson 85353

California:
*BASTA YA, P. O. Box 12217, San Francisco
BRONZE, 142 Pickford Avenue, San José 95127
CARTA EDITORIAL, P. O. Box 54624, Terminal Annex, Los Angeles 90054
CHICANO STUDENT MOVEMENT, P. O. Box 31322, Los Angeles
EL CHICANO, 1669 Vine Street, San Bernardino 92410
EL MALCRIADO, P. O. Box 130, Delano 63215
*THE FORUMEER, 990 Elm Street, San José 95110
*INSIDE EASTSIDE, P. O. Box 63273, Los Angeles 90063
*LA CAUSA, 4715 E. Olympic Blvd., Los Angeles 78040
LA RAZA, P. O. Box 31004, Los Angeles
LA VERDAD, P. O. Box 13136, San Diego 92113
NEW-MISSION-NUEVA, 2204 Bryant Street, San Francisco

Colorado:
EL GALLO, 1567 Downing Street, Denver 80218

Florida:
NUESTRA LUCHA, 110 NW 5th Avenue, Delray Beach 33444

Illinois:
LADO, 1306 N. Western Avenue, Chicago 60622

Indiana:
Noticiero hispano, 1337 Van Buren, Gary

Kansas:
VIVA! P. O. Box 2181, Kansas City 66110

Missouri:
*ADELANTE, 2019 Summit St., Kansas City
THE PEOPLE'S VOICE, 2019 Summit St., Kansas City 64108

New Mexico:
*EL GRITO DEL NORTE, Route 2, Box 5, Espanola 87532
EL PAPEL, P. O. Box 7167, Albuquerque 87104

Texas:
*COMPASS, P. O. Box 8706, Houston 77009
EL AZTECA, 701 Santa Getrudis, Kingsville
EL DEGUELLO, P. O. Box 37094, San Antonio
EL GOLPE AVISA, P. O. Box 2321, Waco
*EL REBOZO, P. O. Box 37207, San Antonio
*EL YAQUI, P. O. Box 8706, Houston 77009
*YA MERO, P. O. Box 1044, McAllen 78501
HOY, Pharr
*INFERNO, 719 Delgado Street, San Antonio 78207
LOS MUERTOS HABLAN, 1903 Bruni Street, Laredo 78040
*LA NUEVA RAZA, 2815 W. Commerce, San Antonio
LA REVOLUCION, Box 1852, Uvalde
LA VOZ DE LOS LLANOS, 1007 A Ave. G., Lubbock
THE VALLEY OF THE DAMNED, 2020 Santa Rita Avenue, Laredo 78040

Wisconsin:
LA GUARDIA, 635 S. 5th Street, Milwaukee
*LA VOZ MEXICANA, P. O. Box 101, Wautoma 54982

Haugen, Einar. "Bilingualism, Language Contact, and Immigrant Languages in the United States: A Research Report 1956-1970." To be published in *Current Trends in Linguistics,* ed., Thomas A. Sebeok, vol. 10. The Hague: Mouton.

Leibowitz, Arnold. "English Literacy: Legal Sanction for Discrimination," *Notre Dame Lawyer,* 45 (Fall 1969), No. 1, p. 7-67. He finds that passage of the Bilingual Education Act "affords another reason to question the reasonableness of State legislation limiting the language of instruction to English," p. 44.

El Grito del Norte (Espanola, New Mexico), Apr. 13, 1970. p. 1.

Martinez, Juan. President, Ramah Navajo School Board, Inc., Box 7, Ramah, New Mexico 87321.

El Chicano (San Bernardino, Calif.), March 15, 1970 letter to ed.

NEA. *The Invisible Minority Pero no vencibles.* Washington, D.C. National Education Association (1966).

Peñalosa, Fernando, and Edward C. McDonagh. "Social Mobility in a Mexican-American Community," *Social Forces,* 44 (June 1966), No. 4, p. 504-05.

USOE. *Manual for Project Applicants and Grantees—Programs Under Bilingual Education Act (Title VII, ESEA)* Washington, D.C.: U.S. Office of Education publication (draft), March 20, 1970.

Vecoli, Rudolph J., Professor of History, Univ. of Maine. Quote from paper published in the Hearings before the General Subcommittee on Education . . . on H.R. 14910 (The Ethnic Heritage Studies Centers Bill). Washington: Government Printing Office (1970), p. 71.

11

THE DILEMMAS OF CULTURAL PLURALISM

ABSTRACT   *The thesis of this essay is that current thinking in the United States about "cultural pluralism" is ambivalent to the extent that the concept is indistinguishable from social justice plus ethnic studies. A kind of cultural pluralism which rejects acculturation and assimilation is defined and examples of it are given.*

Any discussion of "cultural pluralism" must begin with an understanding of what we are talking about. Sharp ambivalence or, in folksier terms, fuzzy thinking about the meaning of the expression is everywhere manifest. What is cultural pluralism, either in relation to society at large in the United States, or more narrowly, to its elementary and secondary school education?

It might be well to begin by distinguishing between cultural pluralism and social justice, for the confusion of these two lies at the center of the question. Social justice is everyone's concern, irrespective of social level or ethnic affiliation. The struggle for social justice is one thing that certain minorities, the under-represented, so-called "disadvantaged" minorities, have in common. The point here is that social justice can be sought and achieved within a context or framework of complete assimilation—social and cultural—to the dominant majority.

Witness the Norwegian-Americans, who were once immigrants, at least a million of them and whose achievement of social justice now includes only nostalgic, museum-piece vestiges of their own original language and culture. Social justice means equal opportunities, freedom from discrimination, unrestricted intermarriage, etc.

Cultural pluralism, on the other hand, implies social justice, but goes far beyond. It is the thesis of this piece that if cultural pluralism is to be anything but a new name for the melting pot the term should mean co-existence, preferably in a status of mutual respect and encouragement, within the same state or nation, of two or more cultures which are significantly distinct one from the other in their patterns of belief and behavior, including, as the case may be, different languages. It implies a kind of cultural autonomy for each such group. Thus cultural pluralism is not an assimilative posture; it is a negation of assimilation. It is a posture which maintains that there is more than one legitimate way of being human without paying the penalties of second-class citizenship, and that this pluralism would enrich and strengthen the nation. Social justice, alone, means a fair share of the pie; as a goal in the United States it has usually meant an assimilative attitude. Cultural pluralism, on the contrary, calls unavoidably for a pluralistic viewpoint; it demands the same fair share *plus the right not to assimilate.* Both attitudes are legitimate and praise- and support-worthy, but they are different and in an essential sense contradictory.

Admittedly, each person is free to assign to the term whatever meaning he chooses, but to equate it with social justice is to say that the several ethnic groups which have blended into the generally undifferentiated "dominant majority" now live in a status of cultural pluralism. This equates the thing with its opposite.

It is useful to make a distinction between acculturation and assimilation. As used here the former means merely the adoption by one ethnic group of the cultural patterns, the beliefs and behaviors, of another group. The blacks in the United States are in this sense acculturated (relatively little of their African cultural heritage has been retained), but they have not been assimilated. The latter term is used to mean the virtually complete merger through both acculturation and unrestricted mixing, including inter-marriage, of one group with another.

The ambivalence of the blacks, the Chicanos and Puerto Ricans, the native American Indians, and perhaps others in regard to all this is both clear and clearly understandable. The dominant majority has expected them to become acculturated. It has wanted them to want to assimilate, but it has—in varying degrees—always denied them that alternative. Now, with sharply-awakened consciousness of the excellence and worthiness of their own ways, some members of these ethnic groups are asking themselves if it would not have been a great loss and a mistake anyway. They are thinking seriously—not all but some of each of them—of putting their own houses in order on their own terms. Thus the contradictions: Peoples who are already partially or largely acculturated to the mainstream but not assimilated, yet who are nevertheless now demanding equal time and treatment for their own cultural characteristics, and—for the most part—in a framework of

ever-closer integration! They are talking about cultural pluralism without regard
for the contradictions and without a vision either of the new social pattern that
would result or of the means required to secure it.

   The irony of it is that their former segregated and semi-segregated statuses—
separate schools, churches and other institutions, separate enclaves—together with
the markedly different culture and status of the dominant majority—was already
a clear example of cultural pluralism. Except that it was cultural pluralism at its
worst: an enforced and grossly unequal separatism, without mutual respect or
encouragement, and one which effectively denied those peoples the right to live
and develop fully in harmony with their own special genius and heritage.

   How would cultural pluralism manifest itself? By what forms and what
substance would we recognize it? As the terms are used here, it would be a
rejection, to the extent possible, of both acculturation and assimilation. The
Amish are an example in the United States of cultural pluralism. They live,
unacculturated and unassimilated, in keeping with their own significantly different
heritage of beliefs and behaviors. The fact that they are neither poor nor disadvantaged has no direct bearing on the case. Their marked preference for their own
way of life is the essence of the matter. Navajo Indians in the Navajo "nation" are
another example of cultural pluralism in this country. They, in contrast to the
Amish, are often both poor and disadvantaged. The Hasidim, extreme exponents
of orthodox Jewry, provide still another example. All three of the peoples cited,
the Hasidic Jews, the Amish and the Navajos, struggle successfully to resist
acculturation. The Jews and Amish must also resist assimilation.

   What would cultural pluralism in the United States mean in the cases of the
blacks, the Puerto Ricans, the Chicanos, the native American Indians? Ethnic
studies departments in the nation's universities and a fair share of the pages in its
school books would not constitute pluralism. They are merely social justice, the
correction of distortions and omissions. Mere "community control" of schools is
not cultural pluralism. It is apple-pie American. Would cultural pluralism mean
support for the closely-knit, extended family and a different view of competitive-
ness, two characteristics which Dr. José Cárdenas, a prominent Mexican-American
educator, attributes to his people? There is among the Spanish speakers an
increasing demand for "bilingual-bicultural education," but the demand is always
coupled with insistence upon ever-closer integration with the "Anglo" community.
These are essentially contradictory postures. A study of the prospects of Spanish
as a language of the people in the United States (Chapter 9) shows that the sociocultural factors which are controlled by the Spanish speakers themselves already
tend to encourage the shift to English rather than to resist it.

   In the case of the blacks, how far would cultural pluralism go beyond
support for "the values of democracy, love, peace, and brotherhood" espoused by
Dr. Martin Luther King, Jr., and for "the extended black family, . . . its belief in
individualism, its confidence in education, and its faith in Christianity," set forth
as the characteristics of black people by Barbara Sizemore and Anderson
Thompson? These admirable qualities do not differ markedly from those long

professed by the major segment of American society, hence would not be a sufficient basis for pluralism.

Application of the principle of parity in the management of public schools (full participation in all decision-making of all groups concerned: students, parents, teachers, the schools, the university) is clearly an example of democratically-shared authority and of social justice. It is clearly not an example of the rejection of acculturation and assimilation which must characterize cultural pluralism.

Among the formal participants in a national conference on cultural pluralism in education, sponsored by the U.S. Office of Education (1971), Vincent Harding and Eduardo Seda Bonilla expressed the clearest view of cultural pluralism. Harding, a black, sought "release from essential identification with the goals and purposes of America." He rejected "white-painted universalism," . . . "those empty universalisms which regularly break forth from the lives of those whose identity is lost, strayed or stolen." He seeks "the spirit and roots of the mother continent" and would create new, black institutions. His pluralism would "circumvent and subvert the White nationalist purposes. . . ." Education must "become highly political," and is part of the struggle for the power which must undergird self-determination for the blacks.

Seda Bonilla, a Puerto Rican, distinguishes clearly (as does Hardy by implication) between the "visible" and the "white" minorities and their fate in the melting pot of America. The latter were acculturated, Anglo-Saxonized, lost their ancestral cultures when their roots were severed, and became "full-blooded Americans." The former group, the visible ones, Seda Bonilla finds, have been excluded on racist grounds. He rejects acculturation, "the noxious identity" which would destroy his group's autonomy and vitality. He distinguishes between the concepts of acculturation and assimilation. Both of these together, Seda Bonilla finds, are bad enough, but the first without the second is "empty space," "marginality." These facts, he says, lead to the demand for cultural pluralism, "independent cultural assertion." Acculturation, alone, spells ruin. Despite his clear perceptions, Seda Bonilla stops far short of the "separatism" which Hardy does not mention but strongly implies. Seda Bonilla asks only for relief from ethnocentrism and recommends strong ethnic studies programs for teachers and other professional persons who deal with Puerto Ricans. He also wants "bilingual-ism," including teaching through the medium of Spanish. His recommendations fall far short of matching his perceptions of the problem.

Barbara Sizemore (1972), former Director of the Woodlawn Experimental School Project in Chicago and later Superintendent of the District of Columbia's public schools, points up the dilemma. She wants "integration" and means by the term that "all barriers to association would have been leveled except those based on ability, taste and personal preference." She rejects both segregation and desegregation (moving people about to achieve "racial balance"), since both of these are imposed on the blacks. Sizemore pushes beyond mere "community control" to "separate" schools for blacks, "the development of alternative black institutions which will reflect the needs and aspirations of black people."[1] Yet she sees such separatism as merely a stage on the way to full "inclusion," i.e., (quoting Talcott Parsons) "full participation in the American social order with complete preservation of distinctive ethnic and cultural differences."

An example typical of most Mexican-American pronouncements on the subject: Art Ruiz, Professor of Psychology, University of Missouri-Kansas City, limited his recommendations on educational programs to promote cultural pluralism to two: ". . . dissemination of information about Mexican-Americans to all segments of American society . . . revised textbooks . . . about the contributions of Mexican-American society and culture," and the establishment of "departments of Chicano studies."

It should be clear from the above that black studies, Puerto Rican studies, Chicano studies, are at best only a first step toward cultural pluralism. The inclusion of these in school or college curricula is like adding the long-missing pages and chapters to every American's history book. In the larger context, of course, it is evident that cultural pluralism, were it to exist, would mean a heavy emphasis upon the special history—in the broadest sense—of each partner in the plurality, but many other changes also would be entailed.

The two clearest efforts aimed at cultural pluralism—as it is understood here—are two projects under way in the field of bilingual education.[2] One is directed by the Navajos, the other by the Sioux. The projects support intensive literacy training in Navajo for teachers who speak it natively and in Lakhota for Sioux teachers, so that both groups can then develop textbooks in those languages, eventually—they hope—for all school subjects, and so offer to their children formal schooling in the parents' own language. They rest upon the emerging view of bilingual schooling which rejects the notion that it must be justified by experimental research and asserts instead the age-old proposition that every people has the incontrovertible right to rear and educate its children in its own image—and language. In these cases bilingual education is viewed not merely as innovative pedagogy, but as a sociological innovation with far-reaching effects outside of the schoolhouse. Such examples are extremely rare in the United States.

In sum, there is little cultural pluralism in the United States and there are very few evidences that the extent of the nation's pluralism will increase. In education, most of the demands now made under the label of cultural pluralism are in fact strongly integrative. This can be said of all of the following:

The teaching of ethnic studies

Revision of school textbooks to give a more honest and complete version of the nation's history, economics, sociology, etc.

More nearly "open social arrangements, wherein every individual has an opportunity to make a multitude of voluntary contacts with any other human being based only on personal taste, ability and preference" (Sizemore and Anderson)

The rights of people to live, work, and go to school anywhere (Sizemore and Anderson, 242)

Parity of all concerned in educational decision-making

Community control of schools

Increase of the number of teachers, professors, administrators, etc., drawn from the ethnic minorities

Cultural pluralism (in the sense that the term is used here) might indeed offer relief from the "noxious identity," the "empty space" and "marginality" that has been the lot of those groups who are losing their own heritage through acculturation only to find that the other heritage is denied them to the extent that they are denied full assimilation. Since cultural pluralism is a repudiation of integration, of "togetherness," it will not be attained by integrative activities and the condition of marginality is likely to persist.

Both the federal district courts and the U.S. Supreme Court have demonstrated that equal opportunity to be educated can be sought for disadvantaged children in the United States through reinterpretation of existing law and practice in the light of the Constitution.[3] What follows here is a rationale for attempting through such legal action to establish educational policy which would be maximally supportive of educational cultural pluralism as this term is used here. The rationale is based on common observation buttressed by the findings of research.

1. *The basic proposition.* School children are most "successful" (i.e., learn more, and more readily, and develop the strongest sense of their own worthwhileness and ability to control their destinies) in a school (and school system) which is based upon and maintains the strongest mutually-reinforcing relationship in all respects with the parents of those children and with their encompassing sub-society. Mutually reinforcing means that the school reflects and sustains patterns of belief and behavior, the values, and the social order which predominate and are extolled in that sub-society; and in turn the sub-society affirms the importance and supports the functions of its self-reflecting school. Examples of such schools are Groton, Choate, and the suburban ones serving middle- and upper-middle-class families. Children attending such schools can be said to have unexceptionable educational opportunity.

2. The above proposition is echoed in the common observations that the children of the segment of society that controls the schools are the most successful learners; that—a seeming paradox—"good" students make good schools even more than "good" schools make good students (Who can doubt that the Choate School, moved without its student body and rebuilt in New York City's Spanish Harlem, with every brick, book, teacher, and penny of the endowment intact, would within six weeks become a "problem school"?); that student achievement in school correlates highly with social status; and that by and large the United States' schools have been least successful with—indeed have in large measure failed—the children of the very lowest socioeconomic strata.

3.   The commonsensical observations seem, in turn, to be strongly supported
     by the research of James S. Coleman and others, Christopher Jencks and
     others, and Seymour Sarason, who have sought to identify the policies,
     practices, attitudes, rules, traditions, etc.—largely outside of the awareness
     of school people—which combine to assure that success in school will
     correlate highly with social status.

4.   If the proposition elaborated in 1-3 above is valid, it follows that unless a
     school is controlled, organized, staffed, and administered so as to assure the
     mutually-reinforcing relationship described above—including, in the case of
     children with a non-English mother tongue

     a. primacy to that tongue as the medium of instruction (even as English is
         given primacy with children for whom it is the mother tongue);
     b. predominant employment of teachers and other school personnel
         representative of the pupils' parents and sub-society and able to teach
         through that non-English medium (in the same way that this is done for
         middle- and upper-middle-class English mother-tongue white children);
     c. predominant attention to the history, beliefs, behavior, values, etc., of
         that sub-society taught through that same medium (equal to the extent
         that this occurs for the more favored children); and
     d. control of the school—pedagogical, administrative, and fiscal control—by
         the sub-society—

     the school is manifestly failing to offer educational opportunity equal to
     that provided to middle- and upper-middle-class children. The proposition
     here is that such a school violates its pupils' civil rights.

     It is important to note that what is being proposed is nothing more than
equality of educational opportunity, and that nothing less than what is being
proposed would constitute equality.
     The May 1972 U.S. Supreme Court decision in the case of the Amish
(Wisconsin vs. Yoder) seems to support this rationale. That decision was, in effect,
that the Amish could not be compelled to send their children to secondary schools
which teach attitudes, goals and values which are markedly at variance with those
held by the Amish, which therefore carry "a very real threat of undermining the
Amish community and religious practice as it exists today . . ." and which force
the choice either to "abandon belief and be assimilated into society at large or be
forced to migrate to some other and more tolerant region."
     Lau vs. Nichols (1974) found that "there is no equality of treatment merely
by providing students with the same facilities, textbooks, teachers, and curriculum;
for students who do not understand English are effectively foreclosed from any
meaningful education." *Lau* rejected the notion of "cultural neutrality" and
required boards of education to relate their programs to the specific deficiencies
of children. *Lau* was based on the Civil Rights Act of 1964. An earlier finding,

similar to *Lau* (Serna vs. Portales Municipal Schools, 1972) makes it plain that the same ruling can be made on constitutional grounds.

ASPIRA vs. Board of Education (1973) was terminated by a consent decree which is resulting in Spanish-medium instruction throughout the New York City public schools for children whose command of English is found by testing to be inadequate. This is a long step beyond *Lau.* The significance of these cases lies in the constitutional underpinning given to existing statutory rights to education and the sweeping relief ordered by the courts to assure provision of "adequate" education "suited" to each child's needs.

The basis for further legal action becomes clearer.

Meanwhile, if acculturation, concomitant loss and displacement of the original culture by the dominant one and, in the case of the visible minorities, Seda Bonilla's noxious void are inevitable unless they are resisted with a form of separatism, what is to be that form and its degree? Among the Chicanos the nearest-to-radical elements have reached (and only at the symbolical level) the stage of defining themselves as a "pseudo-species" (*la raza,* Indo-hispanic, bronze, brown), have identified a territory (symbolic Aztlán), and are moving toward a sense of their own "nationalism" and the reactive rejection of all outsiders. They have begun to establish their own schools (Colegio Tlatelolco in Denver, etc.), colleges (Colegio Jacinto Treviño in Mercedes, Texas, Colegio César Chávez in Mount Angel, Oregon, etc.) and a political party (*la Raza Unida*). Only time can tell what this gathering of strength means. At this moment it seems to mean only the power to demand social justice and eventual inclusion.

The dilemma remains: how to achieve cultural pluralism except by some form or measure of separatism, unless pluralism is somehow made compatible with integration and eventual assimilation. Realization of this dilemma helps in understanding the opposition of a number of black leaders of the national Black Political Convention (1972) to their Black Political Agenda's resolution condemming "forced racial integration of schools."[4] Put in extreme language it is a case of the segregationist doing the right thing for the wrong reasons; the integrationist doing the wrong thing for the right reasons. In this view, busing school children to receive integration is, as James Stines has said, "the long arm of the melting pot."

REFERENCES

Coleman, James S. et al. *Equality of Educational Opportunity.* Washington, D.C.: U.S. Government Printing Office (1966).

Harding, Vincent, "Black Reflections on the Cultural Ramifications of Identity," in *Cultural Pluralism in Education: A Mandate for Change* (Madelon D. Stent, William R. Hazard, Harry N. Rivlin, eds.). New York: Appleton-Century-Crofts (1973), p. 103-13.

Jencks, Christopher et al. *Inequality—A Reassessment of the Effects of Family and Schooling in America.* New York: Basic Books (1972).

Parsons, Talcott. *The Negro in America.* Talcott Parsons and Kenneth B. Clark (eds.). Boston: Houghton Mifflin (1965), p. 721-22.

Ruiz, Art. Panel Session on Cultural Pluralism in the Teaching of American Studies. Midcontinent American Studies Association, Parkville, Mo., March 24, 1972 (mimeo transcript), p. 14.

Sarason, Seymour B. *The Culture of the School and the Problem of Change.* Boston: Allyn and Bacon (1971).

Seda-Bonilla, Eduardo. "Ethnic and Bilingual Education for Cultural Pluralism," in *Cultural Pluralism in Education: A Mandate for Change.* (Madelon D. Stent, William R. Hazard, Harry N. Rivlin, eds.). New York: Appleton-Century-Crofts (1973), p. 115-22.

Sizemore, Barbara. "Is there a Case for Separate Schools?" in *Phi Delta Kappan* (January 1972), p. 281.

Sizemore, Barbara, and Anderson Thompson. "Separatism, Segregation, and Integration," in *Educational Leadership* (December 1969), p. 240.

12

LA CENTRALIDAD DEL IDIOMA ESPAÑOL COMÚN

ABSTRACT   *An attempt to state and ponder the factors which underlie discussions of the legitimacy, pedagogy, and politics of the variants of Spanish spoken in the United States.*

Se celebró en agosto de 1973 en la ciudad de México, D.F. un "simposio internacional sobre el porvenir del idioma español en los Estados Unidos." Lo patrocinaron la Liga Nacional Defensora del Idioma Español (véase el capítulo 15) y la Asociación Americana de Profesores de Español y Portugués. Participaron representantes de los pueblos puertorriqueño, chicano y cubano de los Estados Unidos juntos con mexicanos, puertorriqueños de la isla y otros latino-americanos. Como era de esperarse, el simposio suscitó discusiones acaloradas cuyo fondo— disimulado las más veces por las exigencias de la diplomacia—no dejó de ser la cuestión de la legitimidad, la pedagogía y política de las distintas variantes del español que se hablan en los Estados Unidos. Se reveló a través de las deliberaciones todo un mundo de preocupaciones personales y de realidades psicológicas en conflicto con otras realidades. Surgieron cuatro tesis contradictorias en cuanto al porvenir del idioma: (1) el peligro que corre nuestro español es enorme; (2) no existe tal peligro; (3) sí sabremos defender el idioma; y (4) el caso no tiene remedio. Lo que sigue es un resumen de algunos de los factores que se han de tomar en cuenta.

El hispanismo—o indohispanismo—renascente en los Estados Unidos tiene al menos cuatro bases. Mejor dicho, se basa sobre cuatro realidades.

1.   La realidad de la injusticia que se manifiesta institucionalizada en las esferas económica, educacional, y social. De esta realidad ha surgido la lucha cada vez más econada—paulatina y seguramente triunfadora—por la rectificación de esa injusticia. Esta lucha involucra señaladamente a los chicanos (mexiconorteamericanos) y los puertorriqueños.

2.   Las multiples facetas de la verdad histórica de los pueblos hispanoparlantes a través de los años—siglos en el caso chicano—vividos dentro del territorio que es actualmente los Estados Unidos.

3.   Las raíces y los otros ramos del gran conjunto cultural hispánico en las tierras ancestrales y en las demás naciones hermanas.

4.   La centralidad del idioma español, el cual es a la vez la manifestación principal del hispanismo, el vehículo principal de toda cultura, y el elemento aglutinante, cohesivo que lo unifica todo.

No cabe aquí hablar de la lucha por la justicia social, aparte de reiterar que por cien caminos y en otros tantos frentes el movimiento va triunfando.

Respecto a la necesidad e importancia apremiantes de investigar, recopilar y divulgar los hechos de la historia, la sociología, etc., de los pueblos hispanos en contacto con la nación norteamericana, la unanimidad es completa.

En cuanto a los lazos étnicos y culturales entre el hispano de los Estados Unidos y sus congéneres en los demás países hispanohablantes, se puede decir—con regocijo—que a tientas, con recelo y muchas reservaciones, poco a poco van estableciéndose y afirmándose esas relaciones por lo menos entre chicanos y mexicanos.

Al nivel foklórico—héroes populares, fechas y fiestas nacionales, canción y baile, todo lo nostálgico—la hermandad (a cierta distancia) es perfecta. A otros niveles, entre escuelas, entre universidades y universitarios, entre escritores y artistas, hombres de política, grupos feministas, etc., las tentativas para estrechar esos lazos aumentan año tras año y son cada vez más prometedoras.

En cuanto a la centralidad del idioma español, existe probablemente un consenso—al menos al nivel del manifiesto político y de la retórica de arenga. A ese mismo nivel y a todos niveles, sin embargo y aun sin resolución, está el problema de precisar de cual idioma se trata: ¿se trata del *español común* (común a todos los países hispanoparlantes), o de una sola variante dialectal, o de todas las variantes dialectales que se oyen en los Estados Unidos? El habla del pueblo hispano estadounidense varía desde ese español común característico de la clase media de Puerto Rico, México, Cuba y otros países hispanos (hablado hermosamente por miles sin contar de individuos) hasta el extremo del "pachuco" o caló secreto ininteligible para el hispanoparlante mismo no inciado. Y en el habla del bilingüe se destaca la influencia del inglés, desde el empleo consciente, de cuando en cuando, de una vóz inglesa o un anglicismo hasta el fenómeno del vaivén continuo entre el inglés y el español, ora inconsciente, ora contra la voluntad del hablante, ora adrede y con orgullo; infrecuente en algunos casos, constante en otros.

Esto que hemos llamado "problema" no lo es, desde luego, al momento de la intercomunicación personal. Solo surge lo problemático cuando de las escuelas se trata—la educación de los niños—o cuando se trata de esa continuidad cultural con aquellas raíces y ramos en México, Puerto Rico y las demás naciones hermanas. Es la tesis de este ensayo que esa continuidad dejará de existir—aparte de sus vestigios foklóricos y nostálgicos—en la medida en que se rechazare ese español común, el idioma de todos, el eslabón, el aglutinante esencial.

No es difícil comprender—entre todos los resultados y manifestaciones de la larga historia de discriminación que han sufrido—por qué los hispanohablantes de Estados Unidos aprecian y estiman tanto lo que Angel Rosenblatt ha llamado (refiriéndose al habla de los rioplatenses) sus "peculiaridades lingüísticas." (Conste, entre paréntesis, que esas peculiaridades se deben directamente a esa discriminación y a la consiguiente dominación económica.) Véase como constancia de esto la historia en este sentido paralela del pueblo franco-canadiense (Bouthillier y Meynaud, 1972). Las chozas en que viviera la familia de "migrantes" durante su peregrinación anual entre campos de cosecha, la abandona esa familia con regocijo el día que se logre un poco de prosperidad. La dieta inadecuada se enriquece. La lucha por mejorar la educación de sus hijos es constante. Los estereotipos y otras falsificaciones del pasado histórico se sustituyen por verdades históricas. El sentido de minusvalía, legajo cruel en algunos niños de sus profesores racistas, se corrige inculcándoles a esos niños sentimientos nobles de orgullo y de confianza. En cambio, al idioma estropeado y empobrecido se aferran, no obstante el hecho de que sus aberraciones nunca fueron intencionales, sino el resultado directo o indirecto de una política social que procuraba destruir y acabar con el español en los Estados Unidos. Y se vuelve símbolo de su orgullo el decir (es un ejemplo al parecer insignificante) *la sistema* en vez de *el sistema.*

La explicación y la justificación de esto son, en parte, muy fáciles. Por principio de cuentas, como nos enseña el sociolinguista Lachman Khubchandani, el concepto académico—lo comparte el vulgo también—del idioma como entidad fija, acabada, entera, conoscible y conocida no es más que una abstracción, o peor aún un mito. "La matriz [matrix] entera del habla de una comunidad lingüística será probablemente un conglomerado de variantes distintas—muchos estilos, registros, códigos [codes], dialectos, jergas, etc.—con estructuras diversas y heterogéneas (Weinreich; Labov; Herzog, 1968)." Por lo tanto, el concepto tan arraigado de una lengua como "entidad cristalizada" con su "perfil de tradiciones" bien diferenciado puede ser tan sólo un mito, el resultado de la propensión de las comunidades lingüísticas a apreciar e idealizar todas las variantes de su habla como partes de una sola tradición que comparten todos, o la mayor parte, o al menos la mejor parte de sus hablantes. En otras palabras, la sociolingüística ha demostrado que no existe y jamás ha existido en la realidad del habla cotidiana lo que solemos llamar "el español puro o correcto," "el inglés puro," "el francés puro," etc. El concepto de una lengua como entidad uniforme, homogénea y de perfiles nítidos, descriptible en su totalidad y, en el caso de lenguas como el español y el inglés, descrita de hecho en uno o más tratados de gramática, con sólo una sintaxis, una morfología, y éstas dos sujetas a reglas fijas y conocidas—ese concepto es una ficción, una arbitrariedad perpetrada con fines estéticos, pedagógicos, patrióticos y políticos.

Asimismo, la lingüística científica ha demostrado que en términos absolutos un lenguaje—llámese idioma o dialecto o comoquiera—vale tanto como otro para los fines de communicación entre los individuos que lo utilizan. Habrá pueblos primitivos, pero ningun lenguaje es primitivo.

En términos pedagógicos, los chicanos (y en menor grado los puertorriqueños) insisten sobre el empleo del español, tal como lo hablan ellos, como medio de instrucción para sus hijos en la escuela primaria. Esto lo justifican alegando que el no utilizarlo así equivale al rechazo psicológico del niño mismo. (Lo que no dicen es que si logran imponer ese criterio en las escuelas bilingües aseguran con ello que sólo ellos en esos casos pueden servir de profesores.)

Finalmente hay realidades psicológicas que deben tomarse en cuenta. El idioma es la manifestación principal de la personalidad del que lo habla, y por lo tanto las dos cosas—idioma y personalidad—suelen entrelazarse de tal modo que se confunden. "Lo que digo, eso soy." De ahí el fervor con que se defienden las peculiaridades lingüísticas. Además, es mucho más fácil sustituir la "carcacha" de los tiempos aquellos de la "migra" por un auto nuevo que cambiar *la sistema* por *el sistema.*

No obstante todo lo anterior, los decretos de lingüistas y sociolingüistas y los plañidos de la psiquis ultrajada no bastan para resolver el problema, porque hay otras realidades que tampoco se han tomado en cuenta. Si es verdad que cualquier habla—llámese idioma o llámese dialecto—es igual y perfectamente adecuada para expresar lo que suele pensar y decir el pueblo—o el individuo o el niño—que la utiliza, no es menos verdad que si desea pensar y discurrir de modo más amplio, elaborado y discerniente tendrá que ensanchar y elaborar su idioma. El habla del agricultor le basta al agricultor, pero no alcanza satisfacer las necesidades lingüísticas del abogado o del economista. Será ésta una realidad sociológica.

Y hay otra realidad pedagógica: si se han de rechazar las normas lingüísticas y del buen decir y si un modo de hablar vale tanto como otro (léase: si se rechaza el concepto de un español comun y de un español ideal) síguese y resulta que en las escuelas ya no puede haber instrucción sobre lenguaje y escritura, ¡pues el modo como discurre y escribe cada alumno ya está perfectamente bien!

Y una realidad estética: si se rechazara el concepto del ideal lingüístico ¿qué serían de los valores estéticos en la literatura? Pues resultaría que el peor cagatintas valdría estéticamente lo que un Darío o un Martí. No habría modo de distinguir entre ellos.

Una realidad política: al nazi-facista Heinreich Himmler se le atribuye el haber concebido el "currículum Himmler," en el cual se respetaba total y perfectamente la condición subdesarrollada (respecto al dominio sobre el idioma y a lo demás que había de estudiarse) de ciertas clases de estudiantes precisamente para que no salieran de su condición de inferioridad y pudieran así ser más fácilmente explotados.

Un hecho internacional: para los fines de comunicación con los demás pueblos hispánicos, para facilitar la utilización de la riqueza cotidiana de lo que se publica en español en otras partes—la prensa, las revistas, los libros, la investigación, los materiales escolares—y para poder acoger y disfrutar la herencia cultural secular del mundo hispano, es obligatorio servirse del español común a todo ese mundo.

Y para acabar, un hecho lingüístico. Los partidarios del "pocho" y los "pochismos" (el empleo en una frase esencialmente en español, de elementos fonológicos, sintácticos o léxicos tomados del inglés) no se dan cuenta de que están facilitando la sustitución completa del español por el inglés. Uriel Weinreich lo ha dicho así: "Heavy borrowing shows an advanced state of acculturation. It is used for that purpose."

13

ANÁLISIS CRÍTICO DE *PEREGRINOS DE AZTLÁN*

En el sudoeste de Estados Unidos, de la pluma e ingenio de un mexicoamericano muy chicano—chicano por excelencia—ha surgido una novela que por sí sola nos permite decir por fin que en este país, con sus diez a doce millones de hispano-parlantes, sí que hay una literatura nuestra en español y de primera clase. *Peregrinos de Aztlán** apareció en mayo de 1974, en Tucsón, Arizona, y la escribió Miguel Méndez M., arizonense de nacimiento, "desde [su] condición de mexicano indio, espalda mojada y chicano." Digámoslo de una vez: como literatura es una joya; como novela no es sin tacha; como escritor y humanista Miguel Méndez M. es un gran talento.

Los peregrinos son los chicanos (otrora californios, hispanos, latinos, mexicanos, *Mexicans, Spanish-Americans, Spanish,* y últimamente indohispanos). Los vemos peregrinantes en medio de los demás elementos humanos que determ-inan y presencian su vía dolorosa: los angloamericanos, lor negros, y los mexicanos mismos en las ciudades fronterizas. Aztlán, "lugar de juncos y garzas," simboliza a la vez la realidad y el ensueño. Se supone que desde el Aztlán original—en la región del condado de Maricopa, estado de Arizona—los aztecas, con otras tribus de origen nahua, emprendieron aquel peregrinaje que acabó con la fundación en 1325 de Tenochtitlán, ahora capital de los Estados Unidos Mexicanos.

Aztlán no se limita a aquella región original, sino que es—simbólicamente— todo el territorio cedido por México después de la guerra de 1848. Más allá del

*Editorial Peregrinos, 2740 Aurora Drive, Tucson, Arizona 85706.

sudoeste, Aztlán es cualquier lugar en los Estados Unidos donde se encuentre un chicano o una chicana. Quien dice Aztlán proclama también la identidad esencial de los chicanos y los pueblos indígenas americanos, y por lo tanto el origen multimilenario del chicano en el suelo americano. Hay un mapa de Aztlán y una bandera—rojo, blanco y verde como la de México.

Miguel Méndez es, ante todo, maestro consumado del idioma español. Su dominio abarca desde lo más castizo hasta lo más extravagante, neológico, y averiado. Entre estos extremos despliega ora sutilezas, ora vulgaridades, lo más delicado, lo más realista. Todos los dialectos los maneja sumisos a su visión de chicano preclaro. Lo que lo caracteriza sobre todo es su don poético y capacidad ilimitada de crear e hilar imágenes: una tras otra, frescas, airosas, diáfanas; burdas, vulgares, soeces; humorísticos, irónicos, satíricos.

La novela de Méndez es como el segmento de sociedad que despliega tan minuciosamente ante nosotros: el desfile de todo un modo de ser humano, un conjunto algo caótico de situaciones y verdades, pero como la vida misma, no tiene enredo ni por qué tenerlo. Le dan integridad unas cuantas vidas entrelazadas más bien por azar, y el clamor bronceado de protesta e indignación del autor contra la injusticia endémica, institucionalizada que azota al chicano en los Estados Unidos. El viejo yaqui, Loreto Maldonado, lavador de coches; el buen Chuco, espalda mojada, campeón en los juegos olímpicos de la pizca; el joven Frankie Pérez, ni aun despierto a lo que es la vida cuando lo mandaron a Vietnam; Jesús (Chuy) de Belem; Lorenzo Linares, el "torrente de alegría y de dolor, encauzado en un río de añoranzas." Veinte más. En el fondo, observándolo todo, la omnisciencia del narrador, que por casualidad había trabajado bastante—como Miguel Méndez—en la "construcción."

Haciendo caso omiso de la "tacha" a que nos referimos arriba, lo que hay de trama en la novela lo tiene que ir urdiendo el lector. Si no encuentra perfiles nítidos y sucesos encadenados lógicamente hacia un desenlace fulminante de tesis, es que la vida no es así. Méndez nos da viñetas y, de pronto, vistas panorámicas, y si nos confunde saltando sin previo aviso de un lado a otro de la frontera aquella entre los "Estados" y el "macizo," saltando a través de las generaciones, e interrumpiendo de pronto sus relatos para empezarlos súbitamente de nuevo, es que la vida también es así, un tanto caleidoscópica. No se crea por lo anterior que la obra de Méndez no sea novela de tesis. La tesis la defienda a martillazos; el chicano ha sido víctima de un sistema de explotación socioeconómica que no desaparecerá "hasta que la vida ya no nos importe nada."

La tacha, veámosla de una vez, es una sola, pero aparece varias veces. De cuando en cuando, contrastando severamente con la autenticidad y pureza de la novela como totalidad, aparecen escenas en las que los personajes son caricaturas estereotipadas, las situaciones inverosímiles y trilladas, y el efecto es el del teatro de golpe y porrazo de las carpas de vecindad. Es inaceptable el suponer que un escritor de la sensibilidad exquisita de Miguel Méndez no se haya dado cuenta de la incongruencia y falsedad de esos trozos incrustados en la superficie lustrosa de su prosa.

Son al menos cuatro estos episodios de carpa. Tres de ellos giran alrededor de individuos "anglos" de los Estados Unidos. Son tres casos inmaculados de malevolencia, perversidad, hipocresía, y cinismo. Inmaculados por la pureza sin tacha de su maldad. Es lo de menos que pinte al "anglosajón" como escoria humana o que lo vea exclusivamente como caricatura, pero es incongruente que sean personajes y situaciones totalmente trillados, gastados. Conste que no se trata tan sólo de una ofuscación por desdén incontenible hacia el gringo, porque en otro de los episodios, igualmente inverosímil, los personajes son hispanos. Lo único que importa decirse de la tacha de inverosimilitud e incongruencia es que a la larga, tomando en cuenta el carácter episódico de la novela, no importa nada. Los fallos de juicio y criterio estético ocasionados se limitan a lo de menos: el "qué pasó" de la obra. El pensamiento de Méndez, visionario, justiciero, y su lenguaje, tropel de imágenes, siguen arrollando, tan poderosos como siempre.

Puesto que su lenguaje se distingue tan notablemente por esa capacidad inagotable de embellecer, precisar y profundizar lo que dice mediante imágenes metafóricas, no está de más ver unos cuantos ejemplos. Las hay sencillas como cuando habla de ese viejo que era "antítesis cabal de la dignidad simulado": ". . . no le quedaba tela para cortar sonrisas. . ." ". . . escupía por los ojos. . ." Esperaba el anciano aquel momento cuando ". . . el tiempo roe la carroña con boquitas de gusanos." "Fui huracán," dice, "y ahora soy ojarazca podrida. . ." Sencillas y conmovedoras como cuando explica lo bien accompañados que iban los espaldas mojadas ". . . el hambre, combustible de ilusiones . . . el hambre deseperado . . . se ha echado por las carreteras que llevan hacia el norte."

Las hay juguetonas: "Las tripas le maullaban chillonas como gatas violadas en la oscuridad." "Desde sus pies se alzaba la fetidez cacheteando olfatos." Humorísticas, como esta visión de una mujer: ". . . alta cual carrizo, descarnada como cuaresma . . . la manifiesta ausencia de nalgatorio daba al triángulo del pubis un realce arrogante de frente de chivo que se apresta al ataque arremetedor; con osamenta fácil de numerarse a ojo pelón: un chiflido." Protestan: "Yuma . . . Arizona . . . ¡Cómo te ensañas con mi raza! Sudarios en los algodonales, calvarios de lechugas. ¡Viñedos rebozando racimos de lágrimas!"

Las más son pura poesía: " ¡Desierto! Cadáver de mar disecado; páramo donde caben los misterios de la mente; sórdido refugio de heroicos reptiles . . . . . . mezquites esqueléticos que pintaban sombras desnutridas . . . . . . ¡Desiertoooo! Marcharemos sobre tu vientre esteril, verdugo de los verdores del campo. . . . ¡Desierto de Yuma! Onomatopeya de los infiernos. Yuma, llema, llanto, llano, Yuma, llama, llamarada, ya nooo . . . aaay . . ."

Su técnica metafórica produce efectos sorprendentes, grotescos, risbles. Lo más patente en cada caso es el control absoluto que ejerce el escritor sobre su pluma. Así es el mundo, ¿para qué negarlo?: ". . . el aliento de los alcohólicos, que con su libar nocturno impregnaban su despertar con hedores de mierda. . . . . . . la atmósfera pletórica de cochinadas. . ." Querámoslo o no, el contraste grotesco de *libar nocturno* con *mierda* y de *pletórica* con *cochinadas* es de la realidad cotidiana del chicano . . . y de todos los demás. Méndez introduce de pronto voces familiares como para descargar la tensión excesiva de su poesía: ". . . los ríos se viboreaban a la tierra, pródigos en nudos y contorsiones, mismamente cual venas varicosas." Tratándose de lo que se trataba, ese *mismamente* no es desliz sino pincelada magistral de ternura.

Lo metafórico en *Peregrinos* no se limita a palabras y frases evocadoras. Hay episodios, vidas enteras, que son pura imagen. El caso de Jesús (Chuy) de Belem (Sonora, República Mexicana) nos reitera la vieja historia bíblica de nuestra inhumanidad, con toques inimitables de hilaridad grotesca y la franqueza acídula del que ya no se deja "pendejear." Es a la vez símbolo inquietador de la peregrinación de los yaquis, de los indígenas todos del continente, y del chicano. Jesús, "puro yaqui crudo" que "le andaba peinando a los 33," sabía curar cuerpos y almas afligidas pero sabía aun más. A la hora de la hora pidió a Diosito que perdonara a los verdugos que lo amarraron contra al sahuaro, "porque bien saben lo que hacen." La hermosa historia de Chuy sería imposible de contar si Méndez no dominara magistralmente el claroscuro de todos los modos de hablar español.

Vemos, pues, que las "voces inoportunas, feas por toscas y deformes" a que se refiere Méndez en su prólogo, no las emplea contra su voluntad o inconscientemente sino de intento y a muy buen propósito. Señaladamente le permiten lograr un efecto estético no desemejante al contraste filosófico tan notable en el Quijote: un claroscuro que combina y contrasta lo castizo y lo vulgar, el idealismo y el realismo. En eso precisamente está la tesis más fundamental de su obra: lo chicano abarca todo lo humano, en todos sentidos; y en cuanto al lenguaje del chicano, no hay matiz del idioma español, al nivel que sea, que no le pertenezca, que no forme parte de su partrimonio.

Felizmente, el lenguaje y estilo de Miguel Méndez no se ciñen dentro de los límites del español común, o sea "el idioma común de la gente culta, sin notables regionalismos o matices locales, en todos los países de habla espanola." Afortunadamente su paleta es infinitamente más rica que la de aquel lenguaje imprescindible para los materiales de escuela y documentos oficiales. Se le notan cuatro vetas principales. Ya hemos visto su don poético y como lo inclina hacia la expresión metafórica.

Otro rasgo estilístico que, al parecer de quien esto escribe, tiene más de Méndez que de mexicano y que por lo tanto puede ser una característica chicana, es el empleo constante de los llamados diminutivos y aumentativos a todos los niveles lingüísticos (ricachitos, jotolingo, gringuito, comilludo, viejunote, tontolón). En México—y conste que el lenguaje de Méndez así como el español de cualquier otro chicano es esencialmente el habla de México—se emplean esos sufijos, pero con estas diferencias: son las mujeres y los niños quienes más se sirven de ellos; se oyen mucho y se escriben menos; y en todo caso raras veces aparecen en escritos formales o entremezclados con el español más castizo y formal. Los personajes de la novela de Méndez—hombres casi todos—y el narrador omnipresente, poeta y filósofo que es Méndez mismo, salpican tanto su habla como su prosa con esos sufijos que son el elemento más variable y más fácil de personalizar del idioma español.

Semejante al empleo inusitado de aquellos sufijos es otra característica, su afán creativo: la formación y empleo constante de neologismos (alambrista, triperío, cacaraquear, camellar, gringuía, nalgatorio), la substantivación del participio pasado (una alimentadita, una contratada), la formación de verbos nuevos a base de substantivos (centavear, encigarrar, mitotear), y una preferencia marcada por la terminación *era* (entendederas, tembladera, rechinadero, chifladera, chingadera, chirilonera, máquina tostonera).

El cuarto rasgo es una como jocosidad irresistible que se nota en un sinfín de locuciones donairosas: levantar la pata (orinar), la de caimán (la boca), jalarle al corcho (tomar), pelar los dientes (sonreír), cara de metate (indio), mochar el llorido (dejar de llorar), pelar los chícharos (fijarse), colgar los tenis (morir).

En resumen, el lenguaje y estilo de Miguel Méndez son de una exuberancia extremada, incontenible, un contraste continuo de delicadezas y crudezas. No le basta el lenguaje ya hecho y derecho. Quiere poner algo de su parte, domar el habla, volverla a inventar, jugar y regocijarse plenamente con ella. El resultado es un torrente barroco, o más bien—y más mexicano—churrigueresco.

Peregrinos de Aztlán no es totalmente accesible al lector hispano común y corriente. Ni siquiera es accesible al lector chicano que no domine esa habla fantasmagórica que es el "pachuco." La novela no está escrita en ese dialecto, ni mucho menos, pero por fortuna nuestra lo hablan algunos de sus personajes—entre ellos el segundo en importancia y quizás el más chicano de todos, el buen Chuco, Jorge Curiel. Sirvan los apuntes y el glosario que siguen para dar al no iniciado la clave indispensable para comprender al admirable buen Chuco y sus carnales. Sirvan a la vez como elemento fundamental de la tesis de este análisis crítico, tesis que se esbozará en los párrafos finales del mismo.

El lenguaje llamado pachuco ya existia entre ciertos grupos de mexico-americanos en las ciudades fronterizas de siquiera Tejas, Arizona y California hace mas de treinta y cinco años, y durante ese período unos elementos léxicos del pachuco se han extendido y son conocidos entre muchos jóvenes chicanos—principalmente los citadinos—por todo el sudoeste. Pero conste ante todo que el lenguaje de los chicanos no se limita al pachuco, sino que éste es apenas un dialecto limitado de un número limitado de individuos y la mayoría de ellos entienden y pueden hablar de otros modos también.

Un análisis somero del pachuco tal como aparece en la novela de Miguel Méndez revela tres elementos distintivos o privativos: la frecuente sustitución aliterada de un vocablo por otro de significado aparentemente diferente; el redoblamiento jocoso y a veces rimado de las sustituciones; y el empleo frecuente de voces apocopadas, a las que se aplica también a veces el mecanismo de la sustitución aludida. Aparte de estos tres elementos—que podrían también llamarse mecanismos—se notan varias características no menos esenciales sin que sean privativas del pachuco. Estas son la propensión desmesurada al uso de un número limitado de alusiones sexuales e injurias—limitado en cuanto a su contenido, pero interminablemente variado de forma; el empleo rutinario de aquellas aberraciones morfológicas endémicas entre hispanohablantes analfabetos de todos los países hispanos—y por demás en algunos casos arcaicas; ciertas preferencias sintácticas; un acopio generoso de vocablos que se oyen también en el habla secreta del hampa criminal de México; y, esparcidos acá y acullá, anglicismos y hasta palabras inglesas enteras, cual injertas o trasplantes que el corpus hispano no acierta ni a digerir ni a rechazar.

Desde luego, comparte el pachuco muchos elementos del habla popular mexicana. Para los fines del análisis, postulamos la esencial unidad y continuidad de los pueblos mexicano y mexiconorteamericano o chicano en cuanto al idioma español. Esta postulación no niega los cambios occurridos debido al contacto del idioma inglés con el español en condiciones sumamente desfavorables a éste, ni niega tampoco que el dialecto pachuco—visto como conjunto—es de los Estados Unidos y es un resultado de ese contacto desfavorable.

Combinados, los mecanismos y características producen un lenguaje que responde—como todos los demás lenguajes—a las necesidades prácticas y psicológicas de quienes lo hablan. Da vuelo libre a la inmensa pujanza, alegría, y creatividad juveniles; es a la vez una manifestación de desafío, rebeldía y rechazo contra las normas de esa sociedad que a su vez ha rechazado al joven pachuco; y es un lenguaje secreto que excluye a los no iniciados. En fin, una jerigonza.

Los casos que siguen son ejemplos, escogidos para aclarar el mecanismo o la característica.

SUSTITUCIONES ALITERADAS

Se trata de un mecanismo para sustituir palabras de uso común por otras comprensibles o inteligibles únicamente al interlocutor iniciado. Se emplean voces que empiezan con el mismo sonido—una sílaba o dos—que la voz sustituida:

Concepto	Sustitución	Ejemplo
1. año	abro	"torció el abro pasado."
2. caliente	calota	"una rabia . . . muy calota"
3. callado	calletano	"Calletano, y la gallina es tuya."
4. camarada	camarón, carnaval	"Aliviáname con un toleco, camarón."
5. ¡chale! (¡No! ¡Vaya!)	chaleco	" ¡Chaleco!"
6. chingar (tener coito con una mujer)	chihuahua	"Chi . . . huahua!"
7. duro	durazno, a	"Está durazna la movida."
8. ése (camarada)	ésele	"Esele, aliviáname . . ."
9. basta	estufas	"Ya estufas, me estoy poniendo trancas."
10. gabacho (anglo)	gabardina	
11. lado	laredo, ladero	"Cantoneamos pa'este laredo."
12. madre	madera	"Es pura pinchi madera."
13. mes	mezquite	"Me metían al tari por un mezquite."
14. México	Mexicles	
15. no	nel	"Nel, carnal, uno es como . . ."

Concepto	Sustitución	Ejemplo
16. paso, pasó	pasiones, pasadenas	"¿Qué pasiones? ¿Qué pasadenas?" "Andan de pasadena."
17. pasado	peseta	"Me caes peseta."
18. quieras	querétaros	". . . en donde querétaros, chavalo."
19. sabes	sábanas, sabinas	"Tú, ya sábanas . . ."
20. sí	simón, sirol	"Simón, ése, semos chicanos."
21. solo	sóliman	
22. suave	suavena	"Pásela suavena . . ."
23. visto, vemos	vidrios	"No la había vidrios."
24. volada	volonia	"Anda de volonia."

VOCES APOCOPADAS (APOCOPE Y AFERESIS)

Concepto	Apocopación	Ejemplo
1. California	califa	
2. camarada	camita	"Chale, camita, ¿Qué pasiones?"
3. compadre	compa, compita	
4. cuenta	cola	"No se dió cola."
5. Estados Unidos	Estados	
6. gabacho	gaba	". . . un cantón como tienen los gabas."
7. gobierno	govern	
8. hermano	mano, manito	
9. Los Angeles	los	"Me metieron al tari en Los."
10. Tijuana	Tijuas	
11. vacilada, vacilón	vacil	"Puro vacil, ése, ya no tiro guante."

REDOBLAMIENTO

Aquí, al parecer, se trata de agregar otra voz—algunas veces a una de las sustituciones de los mecanismos anteriores—para despistar aun más al que no pertenece a la hermandad o pandilla pachuqueña, o simple y alegremente porque "suena más bonito." A veces el redoblamiento aparece rimado; otras veces se prescinde de la rima. El vocablo añadido suele no cambiar el sentido de la frase.

Sustitución	Redoblamiento	Ejemplo
1. codo (avaro)	recododuro	
2. ése (camarada)	ése guy (voz inglesa)	"Simón, esé guy." (Sí, hombre.)
3. ésele (por analogía con ándele)	ésele bato	Equivale a ¡Oiga, hombre!
4. estufas (basta)	estufas y calentones	"Ya estufas y calentones con este bato."
5. iguanas (igual)	iguanas ranas	"Está uno iguanas ranas,"
6. pasadenas (pasó)	pasadenas califa	"¿Qué pasedenas califa, ése?"
7. pelona (madre)	pelona chirriona nona	
8. simón (sí)	simón lion	"Simón lion." (Sí.)
9. mero (mejor, principal, etc.)	el mero mero	"No en vano era el mero mero."

Sustitución	Redoblamiento	Ejemplo
10. nel (no)	nel chaleco	" ¡Nel, chaleco!" (¡No!)*

*En el caló del hampa en la capital mexicana el mecanismo de la sustitución aliterada es fundamental, como se nota por los ejemplos siguientes, escogidos entre otros muchos. (Carlos G. Chabat. *Diccionario de caló–el lenguaje del hampa en México.* 2da ed. México: Francisco Méndez Oteo, 1964)

acá: acámbaro, acántaros, acantos; agua: aguacate; algo: algodón; diez: dientes; duro: durazno; lado: ladero, ladrillo; mil: milagro; no: niguas, naranjas, narices, negros; pagador: Pablo; por atrás: por atrasines; presta: prestigios; quinientos: quimera; sí: cirilo, simón, simondor, sábana; solo: solano; suave: suavena.

Del mismo caló, dos ejemplos del mecanismo de apocopación son libertad: li, liebre; y compadre: compa. Un redoblamiento: espérate: (cálmala) que se vuelve calmantes montes.

INJURIAS Y ALUSIONES SEXUALES

La gran mayoría de las injurias e insultos en el habla popular de México (y por ende en la de los chicanos y en la jerigonza pachuqueña) atribuyen inmoralidad sexual a la madre del individuo insultado. El tema de segunda importancia y frecuencia es la atribución de feminidad al hombre insultado. Los dos temas han dado origen a todo un léxico de verbos, locuciones, y dichos con sus eufemismos correspondientes.

El intercambio es *decirse de madres, echarse madres, mentársela,* o *rayársela*; el insulto máximo mienta a la madre del adversario: ¡Chinga a tu madre! o ¡Hijo de la chingada! Se habla comúnmente del insulto con eufemismos: *darse en la venerable abuelita, darle en la jefa (o jefita).* En vez de *hijo* se oye a menudo *jijo de la chingada* o sencillamente ¡*jijo!* La madre, *ésa que mientan tanto,* es *la chingada* o *rechingada, la tiznada* o *retiznada, la retostada,* y *la pelona.*

Aparte de los insultos, *chingar* puede significar arruinar, fastidiar, fregar, maltratar, molestar, matar, etc. *Desmadrar* es destruir, golpear, dañar, envilecer, etc., y el sustantivo *desmadre* es como vileza o desastre. *Dar en la madre* equivale a *desmadrar.*

Darse en la madre o *en toda la madre* quieren decir pelearse y esforzarse. Hay una serie de locuciones, generalmente enfáticas, de negación y desaprobación, y otra de afirmación y aprobación: "No puedo ver ni madre" (no puedo ver nada); "un chavalo de a madre" (muy bien chico); "un chico a toda jefa" o " ¡Qué amigo tan a toda jefa es usted, ése!" " ¡Qué a toda, carnal!" (qué bueno, hombre). "Están dados a la madre" (echados a perder); "No tenían ni madre en donde caise muertos" "Pa madre los necesitamos" (para nada).

Para expresar enojo, asombro, consternación: " ¡Me lleva la chingada!" o con más énfasis aún: "Me llevaba tía chingada de cruda." (véase en el glosario).

Irle a uno bien (o mal) puede ser *dar el madrazo* o *el chingazo, chingadazo* o *chingamadrazo.* "Escriben la chingadera y media en las paredes" es así como "escriben cosas muy feas . . ." "Mucho" puede ser *un chingo* o *de a chingo*: "un chingo de gente," "La raza le apaña pisto de a chingo" (los chicanos le compran mucho licor). El individuo "chingón en el jale" es experto o muy asiduo en su trabajo.

Para atribuir al adversario feminidad y por extensión cobardía se utiliza el concepto de la grieta, por alusión a la fisiología de la mujer. De ahi vienen *rajarse, cuartearse, maderearse* o *maderiarse*. Por extensión significan también delatar, acusar, someterse, no cumplir la palabra dada, flojear, etc. "Se rajó con la jura" (la policía); "Ya sabe lo que es el que se raje." Palabras como *argolla* y *aro,* no obstante su sentido antiguo en España, son en México alusiones sexuales también.

Hay que hacer constar que aunque esta retahila monótona es un componente principal del habla pachuqueña, lo es también en menor grado del habla popular de todo México. Los ejemplos expuestos arriba son de la novela de Méndez; no se pretende que representen toda la batería de injurias, imprecaciones, insultos y alusiones sexuales del pachuco, del chicano, y mucho menos del mexicano.

No está de más llamar la atención sobre una actitud muy arraigada en el habla popular de México—y al parecer en el habla de los peregrinos de Méndez—y que resulta directamente del empleo desmesurado y constante de la palabra madre en alusiones sexuales y para insultar. En efecto, ha cobrado tanta fuerza y se ha generalizado tanto la connotación grosera de la palabra que se sustituye preferentemente por mamá. *Peregrinos de Aztlán* no desmiente esta afirmación; se encuentra un ejemplo perfecto de ella en la novela. El narrador, hombre culto, le dice al buen Chuco, "Platíqueme de su familia, de su mamacita, sus hermanos." Nótese que le habla "de usted"; no lo tutea. No obstante, hubiera sido afrentosa la palabra madre. En México se observa este tabu a veces hasta en los periódicos. Entre personas "del pueblo" que no se conocen bien, que no son de confianza, no se dice "su mamá," sino "su mamacita" o "su madrecita," siendo éstas en tal caso las formas de cortesía y formalidad.

En cambio, la voz padre, término general de aprobación, es sinónimo de excelente, fino, grande, bueno, etc. "Qué cruda tan padre se traería el pobre desgraciado." En México, a una joven mujer: " ¡Estás padre, madre!"

Un rasgo notable en la novela de Miguel Méndez es que al reproducir los modos de hablar—los dialectos—de individuos iletrados por ambos lados de la frontera, y señaladamente al reproducir el habla pachuqueña, prescinde casi totalmente de desplegar aquellas aberraciones morfológicas tan características del habla de la gente analfabeta en los países hispanos. El lector preguntará para sí ¿por qué prefirió Méndez hacer caso omiso del desfile de los *vivites, comites, hablates, trabajates* y sus fieles variantes, *vivistes, comistes, hablastes* y *trabajastes?* ¿Qué pasó con *tábanos, íbanos, cómanos, sépanos, vénganos, váyasen* y *véngasen?* ¿Con la retahila inocente y tristona de las *paderes,* el *idomia,* el *estógamo, muncho, anque* y *toos?* Hay cientos más por el estilo.

Mendez los pasó por alto—así lo creo y espero—porque afean la lectura, ofenden el oído, entristecen al hispanófilo, y *no son privativos del habla chicana y pachuqueña.* Se oyen en todas partes del mundo hispano, dondequiera que exista, muy arraigado, el analfabetismo. Por supuesto, cuando se encuentra el analfabetismo en contacto bilingüe con otro idioma más fuerte política y económicamente, las aberraciones son aun más extravagantes.

Valiéndose de sus privilegios de observador y creador todopoderoso, Méndez prefirió limpiar un poco, fijar un tanto, y darle algo más de esplendor a lo que decían sus interlocutores.

Ya he dicho que para mí la tesis más fundamental de la obra de Miguel Méndez es que lo chicano abarca todo lo humano, en todos sentidos, y en cuanto al lenguaje del chicano no hay matiz del idioma español, al nivel que sea, que no le pertenezca, que no forme parte de su patrimonio. Me parece que Méndez lo ha verificado y confirmado plenamente. Importa muchísimo hacer entender esto por todo el mundo.

Nos enseña la sociolingüística dos verdades (entre otras muchas) respecto del lenguaje que vienen muy al caso nuestro. La primera es que no existe y jamás ha existido *en la realidad del habla cotidiana* lo que solemos llamar "el español puro o correcto," "el inglés puro," "el francés puro," etc. El concepto de una lengua como entidad uniforme, homogénea y de perfiles nítidos, descriptible en su totalidad y, en el caso de lenguas como el español y el inglés, descrita de hecho en uno o más tratados de gramática, con sólo una sintaxis, una morfología, y estas dos sujetas a reglas fijas y conocida—ese concepto no es más que una ficción, una abstraccion, una arbitrariedad. La segunda verdad es que esa ficción y arbitrariedad, ese concepto de la lengua idealizada *es terriblemente importante* porque responde a nada menos que los imperativos de la estética, la pedagogía, el patriotismo y la política.

Un análisis muy somero pero ilustrativo del lenguaje de cualquier pueblo nos da la lista siguiente de categorías o niveles lingüísticos.

La clasificación corresponde franca y necesariamente a aquellos imperativos de la estética, la pedagogía, el patriotismo, y la política.

La poesía
La literatura buena (y mala)
Lenguaje del gobierno, las cortes, la iglesia
Lenguaje de las ciencias
Las revistas buenas (y malas)
Los materiales de ensenanza
Los periódicos buenos (y malos)
La gente educada
La gente de poca educación formal
La gente analfabeta
Las jergas (estudiantil, de los oficios, del ejército, etc.)
Las jerigonzas (v. g., el caló del hampa)

Se nota en seguida que el lenguaje de los chicanos abarca e incluye—con una excepción—*todas las categorías de la lista.* (De la categoría "gobierno, cortes, iglesia" habrá poco en la actualidad, pero sí existe.) La excepción parece ser la categoría "ciencias." Si no hay aún periódicos excelentes en español en el sudoeste, hay siquiera artículos buenos; las revistas ya son excelentes–aunque preponde- rantemente en inglés–pero sí aparecen en ellas ensayos y estudios en español; se lucha con mil mañas en contra de los buenos materiales de enseñanza en español, pero se utilizan algunos. Que existe literatura buena iluminada por un don poético excelso nos lo demuestra la obra de Miguel Méndez.

Lo que sucede es que a muchos de los hispanos en el sudoeste de los Estados Unidos–siendo víctimas de una política escolar que ha hecho todo lo posible por destruir su idioma materno y relegar al analfabetismo a sus hablantes–les falta el criterio necesario para juzgar y defender su idioma. Por falta de conocimientos técnicos y de la perspectiva que resulta de esos conocimientos, no saben si hablan "bien" (respecto de las normas del español común en todos los demas países hispanos) o si hablan "mal." Por consiguiente, cuando se enfrentan con los ataques etnocéntricos y denigrantes del pueblo mayoritario, y de los llamados "profesores de español," optan muchas veces por la autodenigración. Yo he presenciado esa auto-denigración, ese rogar avergonzado "que me perdonen la pobreza de mi español, que es apenas el Tex-Mex," en boca de individuos que hablaban muy bien, hasta hermosamente.

Lo que sucede con los dos idiomas principales en el sudoeste de los Estados Unidos se ve esbozado aquí abajo. El esquema no pretende representar una fórmula matemática sino que es una aproximación hacia una realidad sociológica. Debido precisamente al hecho de la dominación político-económica del pueblo hispano por el de habla inglesa, y uno de sus resultados, esa política escolar, la curva que representa el idioma español está sesgada adversa y desgraciadamente hacia un lado. No obstante esto, dejando aparte la cuestión de la proporción del total que corresponde a cada categoría, y haciendo caso omiso de la categoría "ciencia," las dos curvas abarcan todos los niveles de elaboración lingüística. Repítase por segunda vez la tesis; en cuanto al lenguaje del chicano, no hay matiz del idioma español, al nivel que sea, que no le pertenezca, que no forme parte de su patrimonio.

La cuestión de los niveles de elaboración lingüística es extremadamente importante. Importante sobre todo cuando de un movimiento de reivindicación y renacimiento se trata. Suele preguntarse ¿Qué es el lenguaje del chicano? ¿Cómo debe ser? ¿Es o no es el español común? Las respuestas varían según conteste aquel avergonzado de quien ya hablamos, o un maestro hispano en un programa de educación bilingüe de aquéllos que no han leído jamás un libro en español, o un inocente de los que alaban el vaivén continuo entre el inglés y el español (sin darse cuenta de que ese vaivén indica y apresura el desplazamiento completo del español por el inglés), o un pachuco, o un escritor como Miguel Méndez. Que no responda nadie que no haya ponderado bien la relación estrechísima entre el nivel de elaboración conceptual y el nivel correspondiente de elaboración lingüística. No existe uno sin el otro. Van siempre a la par. Quien quiera concebir (es decir, pensar) de un modo más elaborado, diferenciado y preciso necesita un lenguaje igualmente elaborado. Por eso es por lo que importa tanto que en las escuelas bilingües se les enseñe a los chicos hispanos el idioma español en toda su plenitud.

La Gama Lingüística Normal

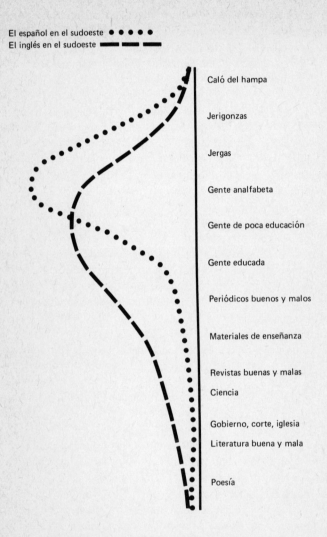

El español en el sudoeste ● ● ● ● ●
El inglés en el sudoeste ▬ ▬ ▬ ▬ ▬

Caló del hampa

Jerigonzas

Jergas

Gente analfabeta

Gente de poca educación

Gente educada

Periódicos buenos y malos

Materiales de enseñanza

Revistas buenas y malas

Ciencia

Gobierno, corte, iglesia

Literatura buena y mala

Poesía

Alabado sea Miguel Méndez, "ni más ni menos canario dando serenata al creador."

GLOSARIO DE VOCES Y LOCUCIONES DIFICILES
EN *PEREGRINOS DE AZTLAN*

El glosario que sigue se enfoca sobre los vocablos y locuciones más difíciles e inaccesibles del dialecto pachuqueño en *Peregrinos de Aztlán.* No obstante ese enfoque se han incluido otras voces poco comunes, voces familiares y populares, para facilitar su lectura y para hacer constar que ningún modo de hablar español es exclusivo de los demás modos, sino que cada uno (estilo, dialecto, jerga, jerigonza) comparte elementos con los demás. Así como los jóvenes chicanos, de la clase social que sea, reconocen y emplean términos del pachuco, sería rarísimo el mexicano que no supiera algo del caló del hampa de su país y mucho del lenguaje popular y más común. En verdad, el idomia español es uno e indivisible no obstante sus multiples manifestaciones.

El objeto del glosario es facilitar al lector el acercarse a Frankie Pérez y al buen Chuco y sus carnales. He indicado en muchos casos si la voz o locución se oye también en México o en España. Estas indicaciones—en conjunto con las que aparecen en el ensayo crítico—ayudarán al lector a juzgar hasta qué punto el lenguaje de los chicanos sea privativo de ellos.

ABREVIATURAS

adj.	adjetivo
adv.	adverbio
aum.	aumentativo
dim.	diminutivo
f.	substantivo femenino
interj.	interjección
loc.	locución
m.	substantivo masculino
p.	participio
pl.	plural
s.	substantivo
sing.	singular
U.t.e.E.	Usase también en España
U.t.e.M.	Usase también en México

Glosario de pachuquismos y otras voces poco comunes

A

abro.   s.   año

abuelita.   loc.   *darse en la venerable abuelita,* variante eufemística de *darse en la madre* (Véase)U.t.e.M.

abusado.   adj.   listo, atento, avisado, aguzado. U.t.e.M.

acharolado.   adj.   rico (dícese de una persona). U.t.e.M. En España acharolado es lustroso.

agabacharse.   v.   ir adquiriendo la mentalidad, los puntos de vista, etc., del gringo. U.t.e.M. En España se refiere al francés.

agringarse.   v.   portarse como el gringo. U.t.e.M. En España se refiere al inglés.

agua.   s.   orina; *tirar el agua,* orinar. U.t.e.M. y E.

¡aguas!   interj.   para avisar que se acerca la policía. U.t.e.M. En México: ¡Agua, agua! o ¡Aguate! *Darle a uno su agua* es herir, golpear; *echar aguas* es vigilar. Caló del hampa en México.

agüela.   s.   variante de abuela. U.t.e.M.

agüitado.   adj.   deprimido, flojo, desanimado, débil; "No se me ponga tan agüitado." U.t.e.M.

agüitarse.   v.   darse por vencido, achicopalarse. U.t.e.M. Caló del hampa.

agüite.   loc.   disgusto: de puro agüite.

aire.   loc.   *darle a uno el aire,* despedirlo del trabajo.

ajusilen.   fusilen. U.t.e.M.

alambre.   s.   espalda mojada, mexicano que atraviesa ilegalmente la frontera con EE. UU. para trabajar.

alambrista.   s.   individuo que atraviesa la cerca de alambre que señala la frontera entre México y los. EE. UU.

alazo.   loc.   *darle a uno el alazo,* agradar. U.t.e.M.

alba.   loc.   *al alba,* loc. de aprobación: fino, bueno, de primera clase; *bato muy al alba,* muy buen muchacho; "*Al alba con los frajos, ése.*" Qué buenos frajos, hombre.; alegre: *Póngase al alba, mi buen.* alégrese, hombre; interj. muy bien; interj. de asombro, enojo, admiración, etc.; ¡cuidado!; loc. de saludo amistoso; *ponerse al alba,* ponerse listo; *ser al alba,* tener razón.

alimentadita.   s. dim.   de *alimentada,* comida; *darse una alimentadita,* comer, alimentarse. U.t.e.M.

alivianar.   v.   variante de *aliviar,* ayudar. prestar; *aliviáneme con un toleco,* préstame cincuenta centavos. U.t.e.M. En España es apresurarse, hurtar.

alma.   loc.   *mal alma* s.   malvado; *gringos mal almas*

aluego.   adv., conj.   variante de *luego.* U.t.e.M.

aluzar.   v.   amanecer, alumbrar; "ya el alba aluzaba" U.t.e.E.

amarrárselas.   loc.   *ahora sí me las amarré.*   Lo dice el adicto a las drogras que se libra de su adicción. En México amarrarse es enamorarse. U.t.e.E.

amasomado.   adj.   bronco, tímido

amolar.   v.   arruinar, destruir, echar a perder. U.t.e.E. y M. *¡no la amueles!* ¡no me digas! expresión de asombro o de consternación.

amolarse.   v.   arruinarse, lastimarse

ancho.   loc.   *dar el ancho,* hacer lo que se espera de uno. U.t.e.M.

antojo.   loc.   *mal de antojo,* referencia jocosa a la propensión de las mujeres a volverse antojadizas y caprichosas en el comer cuando están encintas. U.t.e.M. y E.

apalabrar.   v.   hablar. En España es convenir de palabra.

apañar.   v.   robar, agarrar, conseguir; comprar, sentir; *apañar avión,* sentirse
eufórico, ebrio; *apañar güergüenza,* sentir vergüenza; *apañar de volada,*
arrebatar; "Toda la raza, ése, le apaña pisto de a chingo" Todos los chicanos,
hombre, le compran mucho licor. U.t.e.M.

apenitas.   adv. dim.   de apenas. "apenitas si gano pa mal comer." U.t.e.M.

aperrunarse.   v.   llegar a tener las características del perro. En España es
apretujar.

aquella (muy de)   loc.   de aprobación. Aplícase a términos masc. y fem. ". . . *le
apaño un chante muy de aquella*": le pongo una casa muy buena; bueno,
fino, etc.; *muy de aquellas,* un bato muy de aquellas: un muchacho muy
bueno.

ariete.   s. m.   ". . . el ariete del burlador . . ."

aro.   loc.   *entrar al aro,* someterse, hacer algo por fuerza. En España se dice
entrar por el aro. U.t.e.M.

arrane.   loc.   *tirar arrane,* copular. En el caló del hampa en México, arranar es
dormir.

arrebatinga.   s.   escándalo, zafarrancho; "Se armó una arrebatinga . . ."

arriera.   loc.   *ponerle a uno una arriera.*

arriscada.   s. loc.   "*Se pegó una arriscada*" se encrespó, se enfureció. En España
arriscar es encresparse o enfurecerse.

asina.   variante de *así.* U.t.e.M.

atacador.   s.   pretendiente bravucón

atontiar.   v.   variante de atontar

atornillado.   adj.   sujeto, "La cabrona ilusión nos tenía allí, bien atornillados."

atravesado.   adj.   intrépido, alocado

aventarse.   v.   sobresalir; *aventarse para trabajar,* sobresalir en el trabajo

aventón.   s.   una llevada gratuita. U.t.e.M.

azonzar.   v.   atontar

B

baba.   s.   cosa o razón insignificante "Me cateo por cualquier baba." Caló del
hampa en México.

bailar.   v.   sentenciar, condenar; germ. española, hurtar.

baisa.   s. f.   mano. Usase también en el caló del hampa en Méx. *chocar la baisa,*
estrechar o dar la mano.

baraña.   s.   mañana, amanecer

bartolina.   s.   cárcel, calabozo estrecho. U.t.e.M.

bartolo. s. hombre, tipo. En España es perezozo, apático, indolente.

bato. s. hombre, hombre joven, camarada. En España, hombre rústico y de pocos alcances. En el caló del hampa de México es hombre o la víctima.

bichi. loc. *volverse la bichi en bicicleta.*

bironga. f. cerveza

birote. adj. *un pan birote,* bollo

birria. s. cerveza. En España es cosa grotesca o ridícula.

bizcocho. s. y adj. "No seas bizcocho," no te desanimes.

blanco. s. individuo del color de la gente europea. Del punto de vista del indígena americano, puede aplicarse a mexicanos y españoles.

bocabajiado. adj. deprimido, triste. En México dícese del que ha perdido algún amparo, amigo, etc.

bocabajear. v. insultar, humillar

bocaza. s. aum. de boca. En España es persona que habla más de lo que aconseja la discreción.

bola. s. muchedumbre, montón, U.t.e.M.; dólar; *dar bola,* bolear, limpiar y lustrar zapatos. En España embolar es lustrar el calzado. *hacer bola.* loc. confundirse. ". . . hechos bola en la misma borregada . . ." En el caló del hampa de México es el peso plata.

bolillo. s. gringo, norteamericano, persona que no sea de "la raza." U.t.e.M. Es un término despectivo que bien puede referirse a su color "blanco insípido" y su supuesta falta de pasión viril.

boludo. adj. con hinchazones

borlo. s. baile. En México borlote es ruido, desorden, algazara.

borlotero. s. pendenciero

borrachales. s. masc. sing. y pl. individuo borracho

borrarse. v. irse, morir; "Bórrate con tus pinches llantas . . . ." vete con tus pinches llantas (véase).

bote. s. masc. lata de marijuana; cárcel. U.t.e.E. y M.

briago. adj. ebrio, borracho. U.t.e.M.

bruja. adj. masc. y fem. sin dinero, muy pobre. "Estoy bruja." U.t.e.M. *Andar brujas.* loc. m. y f. "Ando brujas." Caló del hampa en México.

buqui. s. masc. niño (voz del idioma yaqui)

burra a. cárcel; *montarse en la burra,* empezar a emborracharse.

burrada. s. los hijos. "Vino con su mujer y toda la burrada."

buti. adj. y s. mucho. "Tengo butis carnalitos." Tengo muchos hijos. "Le tengo escame de a buti." Le tengo mucho miedo. Caló del hampa en México.

C

caballo.   s.   guardia en una prisión o cárcel

cabrona.   s. f.   término despectivo por analogía con cabrón. U.t.e.M. y E.

cacaraquear.   v.   blasonar, gritar

cacharpas.   s. pl.   monedas de escaso valor. Caló del hampa en México.

cachetear.   v.   abofetear, dar cachetes. U.t.e.M.

cadena.   loc.   botársele a uno la cadena. (Cadena es cabeza.)

cafeses.   variante de *cafés*

cáfiro.   s.   *echar un cáfiro*

caimán.   loc.   *la de caimán,* la boca

cairse.   v.   variante de caerse

calco.   s.   zapato. Viene de la germanía española. Caló del hampa de México.

caldearse.   v.   enojarse. En España es afervorizar, entusiasmar.

califa.   s.   variante de California

calota.   adj. fem.   caliente

calletano.   adj.   variante por aliteración de callado. "Calletano y la gallina es tuya."

camarón.   s.   variante por aliteración de camarada

camellar.   v.   trabajar

camello.   s.   trabajo; *darle al camello,* trabajar. En el caló del hampa en México es peón o bracero.

camita.   s. masc.   variante por aliteración de camarada

canería.   s.   de la voz inglesa *cannery*: fábrica donde se enlatan legumbres, fruta, etc., para el comercio.

cantón.   s.   casa; choza. Caló del hampa en México.

cantonear.   v.   habitar (una casa); ser: "ansina cantoneo yo." Así soy yo.

canuzco.   s.   algodón

carajazo.   s.   aum. de carajo, estallido (de metralladora)

carcanchón.   s.   automóvil viejo, en mal estado. En México *carcacha* es automóvil viejo, gastado, destartalado.

carga.   s.   heroína

carnal.   s.   (fem. *carnala*) camarada, especialmente otro individuo chicano o de "la raza." Caló del hampa de México.

carrancear.   v.   (de Carranza). robar; "avanzarse." Véase.

catear.   v.   pelear a golpe de mano: "yo me cateo contigo a baisa pelona." Me pelearé contigo a puñetazos. Viene de la germanía española. En México se dice "darse de cates." Caló del hampa en México.

catota.   s.   canica. U.t.e.M.

centavear.   v.   ganar centavos; ganar miserablemente

cincho.   s.   éxito seguro. ". . . su gran ejército llevaba cincho." Tenía la victoria asegurada.   adv.   *de cincho,* seguramente, con toda seguridad; "De cincho que me van a dar en la jefa" Sin duda me van a dejar mal. En el caló del hampa en México cinchar es amarrar, asegurar.

clandestina.   s.   prostituta

coco.   s.   Dícese del chicano vendido: color de café (chicano) por fuera y blanco (como los gringos) por dentro.

cododuro.   adj. y s.   avaro, tacaño, agarrado. En México codo, avaro, es del caló del hampa.

cogedor.   s. y adj.   varón que tiene coito con una mujer; macho

cola.   loc.   *darse cola,* darse cuenta. Es variante aliterativa.

colero.   s.   individuo que come y bebe de gorra, de mogollón

comillo.   s.   astucia; *de mucho comillo.* Dícese de la persona que no se deja engañar fácilmente.

comilluda.   adj. f.   astuta. U.t.e.M.

compa.   s.   variante apocopada de *compadre.* En México, caló del hampa.

compita.   s. masc.   variante *de compadre*

corbata.   s. loc.   *llevarse una cosa de corbata,* llevársela arrastrando o colgando

conseguirse.   v.   tener relaciones sexuales ". . . capaz de conseguirse a la misma muerte . . ."

contratada.   s.   acción de contratar a los trabajadores para hacer la cosecha.

corcho.   loc.   *jalarle al corcho,* tomar (alcohol), emborracharse.

corte.   loc.   *dar corte,* procesar, juzgar.

coscolina.   s.   prostituta. U.t.e.M.

count.   voz inglesa. cuenta ". . . no se daba count . . ."

coyote.   s. m.   El que hace de intermediario para arreglar asuntos, muchas veces ilegales, en las dependencias del gobierno o las casas de comerco. U.t.e.M.

cruda.   s.   malestar que se siente después del consumo excesivo de alcohol u otra droga: "Qué cruda tan padre se traería . . ." U.t.e.M.

cuacha.   s.   excremento, estiércol

cuadrar.   v.   gustar. En España significaba agradar en el siglo XVI.

cuate.   s. masc.   compañero íntimo, amigo, gemelo. U.t.e.M.

cuatro.   s.   trampa. "Le pusieron un cuatro." U.t.e.M.

cucho.   adj.   ". . . le cortó la jeta de arriba, dejándolo cucho," labio hendido

cueriza.   s.   paliza, derrota; "Les dieron tal cueriza . . ." U.t.e.M.

cuerote.   s. y adj.   muchacha o mujer linda, de buen cuerpo. U.t.e.M. "Estás cuero," estás buena, hermosa. En México *cuero* es hembra de placer. Caló del hampa en México.

cuico.   s.   policía. U.t.e.M.

culebra.   s.   pene; ano (el culo)

cursiento.   adj.   que tiene cursos o diarrea: ". . . cara de chango cursiento." U.t.e.M.

CH

¡chale!   interj.   de enojo, asombro, saludo, etc.: ¡No! ¡Vaya! ¡Hola!

chaleco.   variante de chale (véase). En México *a chaleco* es de balde.

chamuchina.   s.   los niños, los hijos (de chamaco, niño). "La chamuchina se silenciaba al verlo . . ." U.t.e.M.

chanate.   s. m.   café; "No le hago al chanate" No me gusta el café. Caló del hampa en México.

chancla.   loc.   *tirar chancla,* bailar

chancho.   s. y adj.   puerco, sucio. U.t.e.M.

changarro.   s.   tendajón. U.t.e.M.

chanía.   s.   Dios en chanía

chante.   s. masc.   casa. Caló del hampa en México.

chanza.   adv.   de la voz inglesa *chance.* tal vez; "chanza hubiera manera de . . ."

chaparrito.   s. y adj.   dim. de chaparro. bajo de estatura. U.t.e.M.

chavalada.   s.   conjunto de amigos o compañeros (los chavales)

chavalón.   s.   aumentativo de chaval, muchacho. Chaval es voz española. Caló del hampa en México

chavalona.   s.   aumentativo de *chavala,* muchacha. Chavala es voz española.

chi.   s. loc.   *hacer chi,* evacuarse. U.t.e.M.

chicano.   s. y adj.   individuo mexiconorteamericano; idioma de los chicanos. U.t.e.M.

chicos.   adj.   úsase solamente en plural. grandes. "Te clavan chicos estacones . . ." U.t.e.M.

chícharos.   s. pl.   ojos; "Pela los chícharos" Estáte pendiente, ten cuidado.

chifladera.   s.   cosa de poca importancia. En México es monomanía y cierta acción de chiflar o silbar.

¡chihuahua!   interj.   de asombro, etc., que recuerda la palabra chingar. Véase. U.t.e.M.

chihui.   s. m.   niño

chilla.   s.   pobreza; *estar en la chilla,* no tener dinero; ". . . en la más vil de las chillas." U.t.e.M. Es americanismo.

chinga.   s.   sufrimiento, esfuerzo, pena; "Lleva uno esas chingas tan padres." Pasa uno esos trabajos tan duros. "Con el summer se acaban las chingas." En México es paliza.

chingadazo.   s.   variante de *chingazo* (véase); golpe. U.t.e.M.

chingadera.   s.   lo malo. "La chingadera es que él paga. . ." Véase *chingar.* U.t.e.M. Locución general de desaprobación. "Escriben chingadera y media en las paredes." U.t.e.M.

chingada.   p. p.   de chingar (véase)   s.   mujer que ha tenido relaciones sexuales (término soez); úsase en innumerables expresiones insultantes, de enojo, de consternación, etc. "me lleva la chingada." me lleva el diablo. U.t.e.M.

chingamadrazo.   s.   golpe. Véase *chingar* y *madre*

chingar.   v.   tener coito con una mujer; joder, arruinar, maltratar, molestar, golpear, fastidiar, matar; salir bien; ganar. ¡Chinga a tu madre! (el peor y más común de los insultos); *chingar paleta,*   loc.   tener éxito. "Ya chingamos paleta, manito." *¡Chínguele!*   interj. de aprobación o desprobación general. U.t.e.M.

chingazo.   s.   golpe, desastre. "Me llevan a los chingazos." Me llevan a la guerra. U.t.e.M.

chingo.   s.   número o cantidad grande; "un chingo de gente"; *de a chingo,*   loc. adv.   de afirmación, aprobación, etc. "La raza le apaña pisto de a chingo." Los chicanos le compran mucho licor.

chingón.   s. y adj.   experto, diestro, bueno; *chingón en el jale,* experto en el trabajo. "Chiquito de cuerpo pero chingón de alma."

chirilonera.   s.   chismosa

chismolera.   s. y adj.   chismosa

chiva tatemada.   s. f.   (En el caló del hampa de México chiva es droga, y un individuo que sirve a la policía sin ser agente oficial de ella.)

chola.   s.   muchacha o mujer chicana

cholo.   s.   joven chicano de los que andan en pandillas

chorizo.   s. loc.   "de chorizo brinca": En México es malvado, travieso.

chota.   s. masc.   un policía; fem. la policía "Vienen los chotas pa' 'ca." Caló del hampa en México.

chucha.   s.   perra

D

dale que dale.   loc.   dándole

dañisto.   adj.   dañino, travieso

denantes.   loc.   *en denantes,* anteriormente. En España desde el XVI.

desaije.   s.   accion de entresacar (plantas, etc.)

desgarriate.   s. m.   destrozo, desastre. U.t.e.M.

desidia.   s.   negligencia, indiferencia

desmadre.   s. m.   desastre, desbarajustre, matanza, etc. ". . . el alma llena de nudos de ver tanto desmadre." U.t.e.M.

desplumadero.   s.   prostíbulo

desvalagado.   adj.   disperso, apartado

determinado.   adj.   dispuesto, resuelto; (de la voz inglesa *determined*)

dientes.   loc.   *pelar los dientes,* hacer una mueca; sonreír. U.t.e.M.

domás.   adv.   variante de *no más*; sólo.

durasno.   adj.   variante por aliteración de *duro*. (También durazno.) Caló del hampa de México.

E

echarse.   v. loc.   ganar, vencer: "Se los echó" Les ganó; los venció; "Se lo echó al plato" Lo venció. *echarse una mujer,* tener con ella relación sexual

ella.   loc.   *a toda ella,* expresión enfática de aprobación. "suave a toda ella." buenísimo

embarrado.   adj.   culpable. U.t.e.M.

empelotar.   v.   desnudar. U.t.e.M.

empeloto.   adj.   desnudo. U.t.e.M.

encanicado.   p. p.   de encanicar. enamorar: "burro encanicado"

encigarrar   v.   darle a uno un cigarro: "encigárrenme la plática"

enjuanetudo.   adj.   que tiene juanetes en los pies. En España se dice enjuanatado.

enjuntar.   v.   secar; adelgazar (probablemente de *enjuto*)

ensartar.   v.   acuchillar

entendederas.   s. pl.   entendimiento. "corto de entendederas." Voz española del XVII.

entrarle.   v.   trabajar duro: ". . . ponen batos que le entren como caballos." En México entrarle a una cosa es acometerla.

entregar el equipo.   loc.   morirse. U.t.e.M.

darse un entrón.   loc.   pelearse. "Vamos dándonos un entrón." U.t.e.M.

¡Epale!   loc.   exclamación de asombro, enojo, etc.

escame.   s. m.   miedo, recelo. En España escamar es hacer que uno entre en recelo o desconfianza.

escante.   s.   momento, poco tiempo: "Huáchame la birria un escante." ". . . un escante de feria," un poco de dinero

escarbadera.   s.   trabajo de escarbar, abrir un hoyo en la tierra: "Estaba pelona la escarbadera." En España es escarbadura.

escondidas.   loc.   el juego de las escondidas, jugar al escondite. U.t.e.M.

escuincle.   s. masc.   niño. U.t.e.M.

ése.   s.   voc. amigo, hermano, hombre; "*Chale, ése*": ¿Qué tal, amigo? *ése bato,* voc. redundante, *ése guy* voc. redundante. *Ese* (camarada, amigo, etc.) combinado con *guy* (voz inglesa: camarada, amigo, etc.)

engarruñado.   adj.   encogido. U.t.e.M. En España es engurruñado.

Esos.   voc. muchachos

espinero.   s.   abundancia de espinas. Americanismo de Venezuela.

espuelear.   v.   variante de espolear. U.t.e.M. y otros países americanos.

esquitera.   s.   variante del mexicanismo esquitero: estallido

estados.   loc.   *los estados,* los Estados Unidos

estufas.   loc. v.   basta: "Ya estufas . . ." Ya basta. . . "Ya estufas y calentones," Ya basta (forma redoblada, redundante)

hacer del excusado.   loc.   eufemismo por evacuarse. U.t.e.M. y E.

expectante.   adj.   dícese de la mujer encinta

F

fairo.   s.

ficha.   s.   dinero.   loc.   "Se me borró la ficha."

fifirichi.   adj. masc.   variante del mexicanismo *fifí*: petimetre, enclenque, presumido.

fila.   s.   cuchillo, navaja

fileriar.   v.   inyectarse con heroína

files   s. pl.   de la voz inglesa *fields.* campos de cultivo

flaca.   s.   muerte (personificada) U.t.e.M.

fondío.   s.   variante de fondillos.

forje.   s. masc.   tamaño.

frajo.   s.   cigarro. Caló del hampa de México.

fregada.   p. p.   de *fregar.* molestar, chingar (véase);   s.   eufemismo de *chingada* (véase). En México fregada es suceso adverso, contingencia desagradable. Es americanismo. U.t.e.M.

fregadera.   s.   fregada (véase)

friega.   s.   molestia, fastidio: ". . . que friega pa tu vieja"

fundío.   s.   variante de fundillo, *fundo.* las nalgas, el trasero

funnies.   s.   voz inglesa: tira cómica que sale en los periódicos; raros

G

gaba.   s. masc.   variante de gabacho (Véase)

gabacho.   s.   hombre blanco, anglosajón, norteamericano que no sea de "la raza" U.t.e.M. En España es término despectivo aplicado al individuo francés.

gabardina.   s. masc.   variante aliterativa de *gabacho.* Véase.

gacho.   s. y adj.   de desaprobación general: malo, torpe, tosco, feo, etc. "*La regué buti gacho.*" muy mal; "*Se hizo el gacho . . .*" Se portó mal, feo, etc. En México gacho es fastidioso, chocante. Caló del hampa de México.

gallina.   loc.   *la gallina es tuya,* Vas a ganar, triunfar.

gallo.   loc.   "Se le durmió el gallo."

ganster.   s. masc.   de la voz inglesa *gangster.* criminal del hampa

gente.   adj.   fino, de la clase media, decente, bueno (dícese de individuos) "un doctorcito muy gente." "Se portó muy gente conmigo." U.t.e.M.

greñero.   s.   greñas; cabello revuelto

grifa.   s.   droga estupefaciente, marijuana; *hacerle a la grifa,* endrogarse. Caló del hampa de México.

gringuía.   s.   los Estados Unidos

guachapori.   s. m.   "toboso"

guacho.   s.   (despectivo) mexicano de cierta región

guaino.   s.   de la voz inglesa *wino*: individuo que se emborracha de vino

guango.   loc.   *venirle a uno guango,* no importarle nada. Me viene guango. Es mexicanismo. En México es también ancho, demasiado holgado.

guante.   loc.   tirar guante, pelear a puñetazos

guardar.   v.   encarcelar. "¿Te tenían guardado?"

guasanga.   s.   (o guazanga) bulla, algazara. U.t.e.M. Es americanismo.

güesamenta.   s.   variante de osamenta. Usase también en Venezuela.

gueva.   s. masc.   variante de *huevón*; dícese del hombre sumamente flojo

güevito.   loc.   a güevito, a la fuerza (de huevo, testículo)

güevo.   s.   variante de huevo, testículo. U.t.e.M. y E.

güevón.   s. y a.   (de huevón), flojo, haragán, aletargado. U.t.e.M.

güevoncito.   s. y adj.   (hombre) valiente. "Pa' que aprendan a ser más guevoncitos."

guey.   s.   variante de buey, estúpido, embrutecido. U.t.e.M.

güiri güiri   loc. s. masc.   parloteo, garrulería, conversación. U.t.e.M.

guy. s. masc. la voz inglesa *guy* (pronúnciase *gai*); hombre, *"ése guy,"* vocativo redundante: hola

H

hacerle. v. úsase en locuciones. "Si le hacemos buti a la teórica. . ." Si hablamos tanto, mucho, demasiado; "No le hago al chanate" No me gusta el café. "Lo hemos hecho de buti feria" Le hemos producido mucho dinero; es duro "hacerle al santo" es difícil ser santo.

hambreado. s. hambriento

¡Hijue puchi! interj.

hilacha. s. ropa vieja, gastada; *darle vuelo a la hilacha.* loc. pasearse bailando, tomando, etc. U.t.e.M.

hojas. loc. a pocas hojas, en seguida; poco después

hoyo. s. cierto barrio en Tucsón, Arizona

hua. v. contracción de *voy a*

huacavaqui. s. platillo yaqui semejante al puchero español

huachar. v. del inglés *watch*: mirar, ver, verse; "Huáchame la birria," Cuídame la cerveza. "Se huacha menso," Parece zonzo.

huango. variante de *güango.* Véase U.t.e.M.

huarachudo. adj. y s. que calza huaraches. U.t.e.M.

huella. loc. *pintar la huella,* ganar suficiente; hacer lo que se espera de uno

huellar. v. dejar huella

huesitos. s. singular, fem. la muerte (personificada) U.t.e.M.

huesuda. s. la muerte (personificada); *calmar la huesuda:* posponer la muerte; seguir viviendo, comer. U.t.e.M.

huichaca. s. parloteo, conversación; "Cálmense la huichaca," Dejen de hablar.

huilo. adj. estropeado, acabado. En México huilo es tullido, inválido.

huiri-huiri. loc. s. m. parloteo, garrulería. "Está huiri-huiri" Está hablando excesivamente. U.t.e.M.

huisa. s. muchacha, amada; dícese de la amiga predilecta; *ponerse a las huistas,* enamorar a las muchachas. Caló del hampa en México.

I

iguanas. a. variante aliterativa de igual; *iguanas ranas*: otra variante con añadidura rimada: "Está uno iguanas ranas."

indiada. s. banda o conjunto de indios.

J

jalar.   v.   trabajar, funcionar; *jalarle al corcho,* tomar; *jalarle el pescuezo al gallo,* tomar (de botella); masturbarse

jale.   s.   trabajo, empleo, truco, engaño, maniobra; *atorarle el jale,* trabajar enérgicamente (dícese del ser humano)

jalonear.   v.   jalar (véase)

jambar.   v.   robar

jando.   s.   dinero. U.t.e.M. en el caló del hampa.

jariar.   v.   estar excitado sexualmente ". . . las dejan jariando . . ." En el caló del hampa en México, jaria es hambre.

jefa.   s.   esposa, mujer, madre; *a toda jefa,*   loc.   de aprobación, "Qué amigo tan a toda jefa es usted, ése," *darle a uno en la jefa,* variante eufemística, humorística de dar en la madre (véase). Caló del hampa de México.

jefita.   s. dim.   de *jefa* (véase)

jefitos.   s.   padres

jeta.   s.   labio grueso, carnoso

¡jijo!   s. interj.   variante de *hijo.* Recuerda al oyente la locución ¡Hijo de la chingada! U.t.e.M.

jipi.   s. masc. y fem.   de la voz *inglesa* hippie

joder.   v.   fastidiar, arruinar, hacer perder, "¿Qué bien jodes!" "Cómo jode ese viejo cabeza de vejiga." U.t.e.M.

jodete.   s.   puñetazo, manotada

jodido.   p. p.   de joder.   s.   individuo malo, malvado, indigno, etc. U.t.e.M.

jodidos.   loc.   equivale a *diablos* en expresiones como ". . . no sé qué jodidos. . ." "cuándo jodidos," "por qué jodidos" U.t.e.M.

jodida.   s.   variante eufemística de *chingada* (véase) ". . . me está llevando la jodida." Me va mal.

joma.   s. fem.   joroba

jomuda.   adj.   jorobada

jonuco.   s.   vivienda o casa pequeña y pobre; casucha

joto.   s.   homosexual, hombre afeminado; hombre que explota a las mujeres, prostituyéndolas. U.t.e.M.

jotolingo.   s.   variante jocoso de *joto.* Véase.

juera.   v.   variante de *fuera.*

juiliar.   v.   de la voz inglesa *wheel*: rodar; dar vueltas

jura.   s. f.   la policía. Caló del hampa en México.

jusilar.   v.   fusilar

L

ladero.   s.   variante por aliteración de lado. Caló del hampa de México.

lambizcón.   adj.   servil, adulador U.t.e.M.

lana.   s.   dinero. U.t.e.M. y E.

laredo.   s.   variante por aliteración de lado; "pa este laredo"

lengoneada.   s.   calumnia, chismografía, acción de denostar

leño.   s.   cigarro de marijuana

lidiar.   v.   vender heroína

lija.   s. loc.   *darse su lija,* presumir, darse pacote

lisa.   s.   camisa

locación.   s.   de la voz inglesa *location,* lugar

Los.   s.   Los Angeles, California

lucas.   a. mas. y fem. fing.   loco; *tirarle a uno de a lucas,* despreciarlo. U.t.e.M.

luegito.   dim. de luego, un poco más pronto que luego, "Luego, lueguito aprendió a hablar . . ." U.t.e.M.

luego.   loc. adv.   *a luego,* en seguida. U.t.e.M.

lengua.   s.   variante de *lengua*

lader.   s.   variante por aliteración de *lado.*

lurias.   a. masc. y fem.   loco. U.t.e.M. y E.

LL

llanta.   s.   especie de churro en forma de aro (inglés: *doughnut*)

llégueles.   v. loc.   "pos llégueles," pues, que lleguen, que vengan

llorido.   s.   llanto: "para que mochara el llorido" para que dejara de llorar

M

macizo.   s.   México

macucho.   s.   cigarro (cigarrillo) de hoja

madrazo.   s.   insulto calumniando a la madre; *dar el madrazo,* dar el golpe, U.t.e.M.

madre.   s.   elemento del insulto máximo: *chinga a tu madre,* y por lo tanto palabra vedada; úsase comúnmente en expresiones insultantes, negativas, y de énfasis; *echar madres,* insultar; *dar en la madre,* golpear, maltratar arruinar; *darse en la madre,* pelearse, esforzarse mucho: "me doy en la madre contigo"; *dado a la madre,* echado a perder; *ni madre,* negación enfática: "No tenían ni madre en donde caise muertos": "No puedo ver ni madre"; *a toda madre,* loc. de aprobación, excelente, de primera, muy bien: "una mujer a toda madre"; *de a madre,* bueno, excelente: "Chavalo de a madre, ése" Hombre, es muy buen chico; *pa' madre,* para nada: "Pa' madre necesitamos a esos perros hijos . . ." U.t.e.M.

manazo.   loc.   dar el manazo, tener éxito, salir bien: "Me voy a dar el manazo con una huisita muy cuerote." Voy a conquistar a una muchacha muy linda. U.t.e.M.

manito.   s. masc.   dim. de *mano*: hermano. Caló del hampa de México.

mangonear.   v.   mandar excesivamente. En México, mandonear.

mariguanada.   s.   acción de fumar marijuana: . . ."las mariguanadas que contentaban al general . . ."

matasellos.   s. masc. sing.

matazón.   s. f.   guerra

mayate.   s. masc.   individuo negro

mayugue.   v.   variante de *magulle*

meados.   s. pl.   orina

mecha.   s.   fósforo

mechudo.   s.   hombre (de cualquier edad) de pelo largo

medias.   loc.   *andar a medias,* estar medio borracho

mendingar.   v.   variante de *mendigar*

mentársela.   v. loc.   insultar a otro calumniándole la madre

mero mero   loc. masc.   jefe, campeón

mesalina.   s.   prostituta. U.t.e.M.

metate.   loc.   despectiva, *el cara de metate,* indio. U.t.e.M.

metichi.   s. m. y f.   entrometido. U.t.e.M.

mezquite.   s.   variante por aliteración de *mes.*

migra.   s.   de *migración*: los oficiales del servicio de migración que vigilan la frontera entre México y EE. UU.

mijitos.   contracción de mis hijitos

mismamente.   adv.   exactamente, U.t.e.M. y E.

mitotear.   v.   armar escándalo, alborotar. U.t.e.M. En México mitote es alboroto, pendencia, baile.

mole.   s. m.   sangre. U.t.e.M.

mona.   f.   borrachera U.t.e.M. y E. *dormir la mona,* dormir por efectos del alcohol

moqueo.   s.   sonido producido al aspirar o sonarse los mocos

mordelón.   s. y a.   policía u otro oficial que exige sobornos, "mordidas" U.t.e.M.

mordida.   s.   soborno. U.t.e.M.

mosquero.   s.   enjambre de moscos

mota.   s.   marijuana. Caló del hampa de México.

moterío.   s.   las motas (de algodón)

movida.   s.   actividad clandestina, estrategia: "Por ese lado les tenemos agarrada la movida," En ese sentido les ganamos la jugada; actividad; negocio; equipo de cocina; muebles

N

nalgatorio.   s.   nalgas

narco.   s.   policía (a veces secreto)

nel.   adv.   no; de ningún modo

nidada.   s.   nido

naiden.   variante de nadie

O

oficialiada.   s.   conjunto de oficiales.

ojeruda.   adj.   variante de ojerosa. U.t.e.M.

olfatos.   loc.   *cacheteando olfatos,* ofendiendo la sensibilidad

oquis.   loc. adv.   *de oquis,* variante de de oque, de balde; sin pagar. U.t.e.M.

¡Orale!   loc.   de saludo. hola;   interj.   de aprobación: muy bien, está bueno, ándele. U.t.e.M.

orita.   adv.   variante de ahorita, ahora: dentro de poco tiempo o hace poco tiempo, ahora mismo. U.t.e.M.

P

pablear.   v.   pagar. En el caló del hampa de México al individuo que paga se le dice "Pablo."

pachuco.   s.   chicano del suroeste de EE. UU. de los que hablan el dialecto pachuco. En México es persona que se viste exageradamente o es cursi en su manera de vestirse. En el caló del hampa es explotador de mujeres, y billete de a peso.

padre.   adj.   expresión de aprobación, asombro, etc.: "Qué cruda tan padre." "Vi a una mujer padre." U.t.e.M.

pa' grande.   s. masc.   lenguaje infantil, abuelo

pajuelazo.   s.   trago de alguna bebida alcohólica.

palanca.   s.   influencia; tener palanca, tener influencia, o amigos de influencia, en la política, los negocios, etc. U.t.e.M.

pa' lante. loc.   (para adelante); en adelante

paleta. loc.   *chingar paleta,* ganar, salir bien: "Ya chingamos paleta, manito!"

paloma. s.   pene; loc. "Tóquenme la paloma," juego de palabras de doble sentido, *La Paloma* (obra musical) y el pene. En México es pene del niño o genitales de la niña; *dormírsele a uno la paloma,* descuidarse

panicilín. s. pl.   la penicilina

panza. s.   estómago, abdomen

paparrucha. s.   aum. de *papa*: mentira

pasadenas. v.   variante por aliteración de paso o pasa. ¿Qué pasadenas? ¿Qué pasó? ¿Qué pasadenas califa? juego verbal del mismo sentido que agrega califa (California) o sea Pasadena, California; *andar de pasadena,* andar de paso o de paseo.

pasiones. loc.   ¿Qué pasiones? variante por aliteración de ¿Qué paso?

pata. loc.   *levantar la pata,* orinar

patas. loc. s.   el *cuatro patas,* perro

patín. loc.   *agarrar patín*

patuleco. s.   individuo que camina tropezando

pedo. s.   cosa, cuento, etc., en la locución "Ese es otro pedo."

pegostiada. adj.   pegajosa

pelado. s.   individuo ruin, de baja categoría moral

pelar. loc. v.   *Pela los chícharos,* Estáte pendiente; ¿Qué le pela? ¿Qué le hace? ¿Qué más da?; pelar, ir, llegar: ". . . pelamos hasta Mexicali"; pelarse, morirse, abandonar, dejar: "No se me pele, cuatecito." U.t.e.M.

pelo. loc.   *de este pelo,* de este tamaño U.t.e.M.

pelón. adj.   difícil, duro, feo, etc. "Estaba pelona la escarbadera." Era muy difícil escarbar el hoyo; de escasos recursos económicos; *pelona* es variante eufemística de *chingada,* por ejemplo "hijos de su pelona madre"; s.   la muerte personificada; soldado raso. Caló del hampa en México.

peluza. s.   conjunto de compañeros, pandilla

pendejo. s.   estúpido, individuo que se deja engañar. U.t.e.M.

perro. s. masc.   policía. U.t.e.M. *tirar a perro,* rechazar: "¿Pos no dices que te tiró a perro?"

petróleo. loc.   referencia a la expropiación por México en 1938 de la industria petrolera, propiedad hasta entonces de compañías extranjeras

picarle. loc.   apurarse, animarse: "Cállese y píquele . . ."

pichelazo. s.   cantidad de un licor que cabe en un pichel (véase)

pichonear.

pilón. loc.   *de pilón,* por anadidura

pinchi.   adj. y adv.   de desaprobación. mal, malo: ". . . se los va a cargar pinchi con todo y la tía de las chavalonas," Les irá muy mal.

pinto.   s.   individuo encarcelado

pistear.   v.   tomar (bebida alcohólica)

pisto.   s.   trago, licor alcohólico. U.t.e.M. en el caló del hampa.

pizcar.   v.   recolectar a mano la cosecha, esp. algodón, frutas, etc. U.t.e.M.

placa.   s. f.   la policía

pocho.   s.   Dícese del individuo de ascendencia mexicana que se ha aculturado, en cualquier grado, a la sociedad norteamericana. U.t.e.M.

ponerle.   v. loc.   compartir: "Si le queda jando, pos le pone . . ." si le queda dinero, pues lo comparte . . . ; "Pónganle al jale," pónganse a trabajar.

ponerse.   loc.   "ponerse a las huisitas," enamorar a las muchachas; *ponérsele a uno.* ocurrírsele, parecerle, antojársele: "Se le había puesto que miraba a la muerte." ". . . no más porque se les pone."

popof.   adj. masc. y fem.   pretencioso, de la alta sociedad: "gente popof" U.t.e.M.

probe.   adj.   variante de *pobre*

puerta   loc.   *dar puerta,* dícese de la mujer que está sentada con las piernas entreabiertas; mostrar algo. Caló del hampa en México.

Q

quebrada.   s.   de la voz inglesa *break.* respiro, período breve de descanso; *pasar quebrada.*

quesque.   loc.   según dicen, según dices, etc.

¿Que no?   loc.   ¿Verdad?

querétaros.   loc. adv.   variante por aliteración de quieras

quijadón.   s.   aum. de quijada

quiquiar.   v.   de la voz inglesa *kick.* amarrárselas (véase)

¿Quihubo! (o *¡Quihúbole!*)   loc.   de saludo: Hola, ¿qué tal?

R

rajarse.   v.   delatar; acusar. En México rajarse es no cumplir lo convenido; hacerse para atrás por miedo (U.t.e.E.) Rajarse y todos los demás términos que expresan la idea de abrir una grieta, v. g., cuartearse, rajón, leña, etc., son susceptibles de servir para atribuir feminidad al adversario, por alusión a la fisiología de la mujer. Caló del hampa de México.

rana.   loc.   *por un pelito de rana,* por poco. U.t.e.M.

ranfla.   s.   cama; automóvil

raspado.   s.   bebida refrescante que lleva raspaduras de hielo

rayar.   v.   entender, percibir (en locuciones, como ¿La raya usté, carnal? ¿Se ha fijado, hombre?; retar, insultar, v.g., *rayarle a uno la madre,* mentarla; *rayarse,* recibir el salario U.t.e.M.; s. loc. *pasar de la raya,* ponerse insufrible, hacer algo ilegal U.t.e.E.

rayo.   loc.   de énfasis. ". . . le cai suave al rayo" le caí muy bien; en el caló del hampa de México, *al rayo* es pronto.

raza.   s.   la raza; los chicanos, los hispanos; individuo chicano, hispano. "¿Es raza?"; "Eramos puritita raza."

reborujo.   s.   bulla. En México reborujar es juntar en desorden.

recle.   s. m.   tiempo: "Hace recle que estoy aquí"; loc. *al recle,* al rato; poco después; *pa'l recle,* en seguida. En España recle es tiempo que se permite a los prebendados no asistir al coro para su descanso y recreación (Alonso).

reclito.   s.   dim. de recle. momento, tiempo

recododuro.   adj.   de *codo* (véase) avaro, tacaño

rechinadero.   s.   batahola de rechinamientos; "rechinadero de llantas"

rechingada.   a. y s.   variante enfática de *chingada* (véase); ¡me lleva la rechingada! loc. interj. de consternación, enojo, asombro, etc.

red.   adj.   de la voz inglesa *red,* rojo

refín.   s. masc.   comida; alimentos

refinar.   v.   comer. Caló del hampa de México.

rejuego.   loc.   *de rejuego,* de aventura, de ronda

rengo.   s.   individuo que cojea

resacado.   adj.   rebelde, agresivo

retacar.   v.   llenar, embutir; "Retáquense a sus pinchis leyes en el ojete."

retachar.   v.   volver, regresar; "*Orita me retacho pa tras*" al momento vuelvo. Caló del hampa de México. En Guatemala retachar es rebotar un cuerpo elástico.

retache.   loc. adv.   *de retache,* de regreso, de vuelta

retajodido.   adj.   variante superlativa de *jodido*

retiznada.   s.   variante enfática de *tiznada* (véase *madre*)

retostada.   s.   variante eufemística de *chingada.*

rial.   s.   ". . . se compuso de ahí pa'l rial." Se dirigió hacia el camino. (de camino real)

rocanrolero.   s.   aparato fonográfico que toca discos cuando se le mete una moneda; sinfonola *rodear.*   v.   rodar

rolar.   v.   dormir; enrollar (un cigarro)

rorrona.   s.   aum. de *rorra*: mujer de vida alegre

rostizarse.   v.   asarse. Del inglés, *roast*

ruca.   a. y s.   mujer. En Amer. Centr. es viejo, inútil (aplicado especialmente a las caballerías).

ruidajo.   s.   aum. de *ruido*. (En Colombia es ruido pequeño.)

ruperto.   s.   zorro, individuo astuto: En el caló del hampa de México es ladrón o ratero.

S

sábanas.   v.   sabes (otra variante: sabinas) En el caló del hampa de México es sí.

sanababichi.   s.   de la locución inglesa *son of a bitch*

sangrón.   s. y adj.   dícese del individuo antipático y pesado. U.t.e.M.

save.   v.   del inglés *save*: ahorrar dinero

semos.   variante de *somos*

simón.   adv.   variante de sí. U.t.en el caló del hampa de México.

simón lion.   variante rimada de *simón*, sí; eso sí

solano.   adj.   solo. Caló del hampa de México.

sombrerudo.   s.   hombre que lleva sombrero grande

sonar.   v.   pegar; "no me suenes" "Le sonó en las narices." U.t.e.M. y E.

sopa.   s.   condena

suavena.   adj.   variante de *suave*. bien, bueno; "¿Ta suavena?" ¿Está bien? Caló del hampa de México.

sura.   adv.   variante de zurra. *caerle a uno sura,* caerle mal; s. moneda de veinticino centavos

T

talón.   s.   trabajo; empleo

taloniar.   v.   trabajar enérgicamente; andar a pie. Caló del hampa en México.

tan.   adv.   a tal grado; "y tan se hicieron tontos . . ."

tanate.   s. m.   mochila, zurrón de cuero o de palma; U.t.e.M. *hincharse los tanates,* ir cada vez peor, empeorar; "Se nos están hinchando los tanates."

tandaraleola.   s.   (En México tandariola es ruido, escándalo.)

tari.   s. masc.   la cárcel

tatemar.   v.   quemar, oscurecer (la piel) por el sol; *tatemar los sesos*, esforzarse mucho pensando. U.t.e.M.

tecato.   s.   individuo adicto a la heroína.

tejerse.   v.   pelearse; golpear; "le tejí buti chingazos" "se tejieron a golpes."

tenis.   s. loc.   *levantar los tenis* o *colgar los tenis,* morir. Es de la voz inglesa *tennis* (shoes).

teórica.   s.   plática, discusión; "Si le hacemos buti a la teórica . . ." Si hablamos mucho, demasiado . . .

teoricar.   v.   hablar, discutir, decir

teoriquear.   v.   hablar (variante de teoricar)

tía chingada.   loc. adv.   de énfasis. "Me llevaba tía chingada de cruda" Sentía en demasía el malestar que viene después de la borrachera.

timar.   v.   estafar, robar. (Voz de la delincuencia española.)

tiquete.   s.   boleto. U.t.e.M.

tirada.   s.   maniobra

tironear.   v.   variante de estironear. romper, produciendo tiras

tiznada.   variante de *chingada* (véase)

toda.   loc.   *a toda,* variante apocopada de *a toda madre* (véase) "Qué a toda, carnal" Qué bueno, camarada.

en todavía.   todavía U.t.e.E.

toditititita.   adj.   variante enfática de toda. "Les dió en todititita la madre."

toleco.   s.   moneda mexicana de a cincuenta centavos. Caló del hampa en México.

tomada.   s.   acción de tomar alcohol; trago

tomado.   adj.   ebrio; "Estás tomado." Estás borracho. U.t.e.E. y M.

tontolón.   adj.   aum. de tonto

tooth.   loc.   de la voz inglesa *tooth. pelarle a uno el tooth,* sonreír.

topetiar.   v.   variante de topetear, topetar, topar

torcer.   v.   irse "no tengo jefita; torció el abro pasado.": No tengo mujer; se fue (me abandonó); encarcelar (caló del hampa en México).

tostón.   s.   moneda (mexicana) de cincuenta centavos

tostonera.   adj.   de tostón. *máquina tostonera,* rocanrolero (véase)

totacha.   s.   el idioma inglés; *teoriquear pura totacha,* hablar únicamente inglés

traiba.   v.   variante de traía

tramados.   s. pl.   *pantalones; tramado de coludo,* traje de etiqueta

trancas.   adj. sing.   borracho. En el caló del hampa de México es piernas de mujer.

tranzar.   v.   variante de *transar*: transigir. (". . . habíanse negado a tranzar en todo arreglo . . .")

tres.   loc.   *darse las tres,* darse cuenta. Darse las tres en México es fumar marihuana.

trola.   s.   fósforo, calcetín. Caló del hampa de México.

tronar.   v.   tronar el pico. Imitar al cuervo.

troniditos.   s.   diminutivo irónico: el sonido de las balas mortíferas

troque.   s. m.   camión de carga

trotear.   v.   trotar; "Cómo he troteado": Cómo he andado apurado, trabajando. (En España es correrse juergas.)

trucha.   adj. m. y f.   listo, manioso, avispado. U.t.e.E. y M.

trujo.   v.   variante de *trajo*

V

vaca.   s.   "llantas con chanate con vaca." Donas (de la voz inglesa *doughnut*) y café con leche.

vacil.   s.   variante de *vacilón* o *vacilada* (véanse)

vacilada.   s.   burla, choteo

vacilar.   v.   burlar, chancear; comportarse ligeramente con personas del otro sexo

vacilón.   adj.   burlón

valecito.   s.   dim. de *vale*: amigo

vendido.   s. y adj.   Dícese del chicano que se ha asimilado al "gringo" al punto de no interesarse vivamente por la lucha de "la raza" por la justicia social.

ventiar.   v.   variante de *ventear*

vido.   v.   variante de vió

vidrios.   v.   variante por aliteración de vemos y visto; "No la había vidrios por ese laredo." No la había visto por ese lado.

vieja.   s.   mujer U.t.e.M. y E.

vinacho.   s.   trago de vino; *echarse un vinacho.*

virulo.   adj.

volada.   loc. adv.   *de volada,* a toda prisa, en seguida; "Qué de volada, ése" Cómo vas de prisa, hombre.

volado.   s.   fanfarrón

volársela.   loc.   arruinarse, amolarse

volonia.   loc. adv.   variante aliterativa de *volada* (véase)

voltear.   v.   someter a sodomía

Y

yesca.   s.   marijuana (Caló del hampa en México.)

14

LAS CONSECUENCIAS
DEL BILINGÜISMO COLECTIVO

ABSTRACT   *A presentation on the consequences of bilingualism, at the* Congreso de la lengua, cultura y educación, *an assemblage of Puerto Ricans, South Americans and Spaniards at the Universidad de Puerto Rico, Mayagüez campus, January 24, 1975. The case is made that collective Spanish-English bilingualism is the prelude to complete disintegration of Puerto Rico's Spanish language and culture.*

Al pararme ante Vds. me azota una ráfaga de sensaciones mixtas: un tanto de humildad por la pobreza y condición algo atrofiada de mi español, otro tanto de orgullo por ser hispanófilo, y una carga muy pesada de presunción, porque voy a tener que decir unas verdades muy duras.

Entre paréntesis—como suele decirse—me molesta un poco el que no haya entre nosotros los ponentes ninguna mujer. Por eso voy a hacer algo inusitado. Voy a dedicar mis cuatro palabras, muy respetuosamente, a una mujer puertorriqueña excelsa, preclara, cuyas palabras sobre este mismo tema me han sido de mucha inspiración: Doña Margot Arce de Vásquez.

Me invitaron a hablar de las consecuencias del bilingüismo en la personalidad de los hispanoamericanos. Cuanto antes voy a extender el tema para abarcar a toda la humanidad. Asimismo, como no soy psicólogo, en vez de hablar de la personalidad individual, pienso enfocar mis observaciones sobre la personalidad colectiva, o sea sobre la cultura entera de un pueblo. Para mí y para los fines de esta charla, una cultura es—simultáneamente—causa y resultado del conjunto de la interacción de todas las personalidades individuales de un pueblo o sociedad a través de su historia. Así pues el enfoque es la consecuencia del bilingüismo sobre la personalidad colectiva de un pueblo.

Existe una gran confusión—por no decir ignorancia—respecto del bilingüismo. Se oyen muchas aseveraciones y declaraciones respecto al dominio del hombre sobre dos idiomas, pero suelen carecer de seriedad porque casi nunca se especifica el tipo exacto de bilingüismo de que se trata. Se oyen comparaciones entre uno y otro país ("La Suiza es un país bilingüe, ¿por qué no nosotros también?") como si hubiera tan sólo un tipo de bilingüismo. Como si todos los pueblos en los que se desarrolla este fenómeno lingüístico fueran idénticos. Por ende me ocuparé primero de distinguir entre los dos tipos fundamentales de bilingüismo y de asentar, a grandes rasgos, los factores constituyentes de la dinámica del fenómeno. El primer tipo es el famoso bilingüismo elitista, académico, individual, y sobre todo voluntario. Se manifiesta por todo el mundo. Se adquiere por propia voluntad del individuo que ha de ser bilingüe o por voluntad de sus padres, mediante tutores, criados, familiares, estancia en el extranjero, escuelas particulares, o simplemente por el estudio de una lengua extranjera.

El segundo tipo fundamental de bilingüismo se distingue por su carácter obligatorio. Se manifiesta no al nivel individual sino como fenómeno colectivo y se produce del contacto y conflicto de dos pueblos dentro de un mismo estado o nación o bajo un mismo gobierno: un pueblo dominante y el otro dominado y subordinado. La diferencia esencial entre los dos es el carácter voluntario del fenómeno individual y el carácter obligatorio, ineludible, del fenómeno colectivo. Ineludible y obligatorio por la dura necesidad de comer.

Saltan fácilmente a la memoria ejemplos de ambos tipos de bilingüismo. Los sudamericanos o españoles bilingües en español y francés o español e inglés ejemplifican el fenómeno voluntario. Otro caso, más famoso aunque no muy típico: los rusos de la alta sociedad a fines del siglo 18 en tiempos de Catarina, por capricho y esnobismo se daban el lujo de hablar francés entre si mismos. Esto es el bilingüismo voluntario, por libre elección.

Al contrario, en los Estados Unidos los millones de hispanos bilingües en español e inglés; en Sudamérica y México los indígenas bilingües en la lengua materna y español; los bretones en Francia; en España los catalanes y los vascos— todos estos son ejemplos del fenómeno obligatorio. Y, de paso, Puerto Rico, isla bendita (o como ha acertado a decir don Salvador Tió Montes de Oca, punto neurálgico del choque de dos culturas), el bilingüismo español-inglés en Puerto Rico es obligatorio. Y esto no obstante el que crean algunas familias que si mandan a sus hijos a escuelas de lengua inglesa lo están haciendo por su propia voluntad y elección.

Ya que hemos asentado las dos rúbricas básicas bajo las cuales se clasifica el bilingüismo, es menester tomar en cuenta que hay siquiera 54 tipos esencialmente distintos por la dinámica sociopolítica que los caracteriza. No es ésta la ocasión para identificar y analizar detalladamente las 54 clasificaciones pero sí es imprescindible para nuestros fines identificar siquiera los principales factores constituyentes de esa dinámica.

1.   *Un pueblo o dos pueblos.* Importa mucho precisar si el bilingüismo colectivo proviene del contacto y conflicto de dos pueblos y dos idiomas bajo un mismo gobierno (Bélgica: holandeses y franceses; el Canadá: anglófonos y francófonos; la República de Sud Africa: *afrikaans* e inglés) o si se trata de un solo pueblo con dos idiomas (Egipcia: árabe vernacular, árabe coránico; Grecia: *katerévusa* y *dimotikí*; la Suiza alemana: germanosuizo y alemán). En estos últimos casos, tratándose de un solo pueblo no suele haber conflicto porque no hay con quienes contender y porque cada uno de los idiomas se utiliza por voluntad de sus hablantes bilingües para fines totalmente distintos. El germanosuizo, por ejemplo, es el idioma de la intimidad, las relaciones familiares, el compañerismo, mientras que el alemán se utiliza como medio de instrucción escolar, y para los fines formales.

2.   *Política asimilista o política pluralista.* Desde luego importa mucho si la política lingüística del país donde conviven dos o más pueblos es asimilista (con el objetivo de hacer desaparecer el idioma y la cultura de la minoría) o si es pluralista (con el objetivo de establecer y proteger la autonomía cultural de cada uno de los pueblos en convivencia). Países de política asimilista (entre muchos) son los Estados Unidos, Francia, España, y los de Sud América (con la excepción notable de Paraguay). Algunos países de política pluralista son Bélgica, Checoeslovakia, Yugoeslavia, la Unión Soviética, y Paraguay.

3.   *El poder político-económico.*

4.   *El prestigio del idioma.* Conviene sopesar y ponderar juntos estos dos factores porque se encuentran algunas veces en juego uno con el otro de modo—a primera vista—contradictorio. Por regla general, pesa mucho más el poder político-económico, pero en algunos casos no es así. Basten tres ejemplos para aclarar esto. En la República de Sud Africa los *afrikaaners,* cuya habla es una variante del holandés, gozan de hegemonía política, económica y demográfica sobre sus conciudadanos angloparlantes. No obstante esto es tan poderoso el prestigio del inglés que se han tomado medidas específicas para delimitar y evitar el bilingüismo afrikaans-inglés, pues de otro modo se teme que sea algún día reemplazado totalmente el afrikaans por el inglés. Asimismo en Bélgica los de habla holandesa predominan pero su idioma no resiste el empuje poderoso del francés, idioma de envergadura mundial. En ciertos países africanos suelen ser pequeñísimas las minorías bilingües, pero su segundo idioma, el francés o el inglés, es de prestigio enormemente superior al de los vernáculos.

5.   *Extensión demográfica del bilingüismo.* Importa muchísimo este factor por lo que se dirá a continuación del carácter esencialmente autodestructor del

bilingüismo colectivo en un pueblo subordinado a otro. (Dicho sea de paso que en estos casos únicamente se vuelve bilingüe el pueblo dominado. Unicamente en el idioma del pueblo dominado se verifica la llamada interferencia lingüística: jamás sufre la lengua dominante la inundación de su léxico, la deformación de su sintaxis.)

A la base y raíz de todo lo que he expuesto hasta ahora se encuentra un hecho sencillísimo: el bilingüismo colectivo de un pueblo subordinado a otro es un fenómeno lingüístico por naturaleza inestable y transitorio. Tiende irremisiblemente a destruirse. Mientras más bilingües menos necesidad hay del bilingüismo. Esta clase de bilingüismo es un medio de comunicación intermediario entre dos pueblos monolingües. Cuando lleguen todos o la mayor parte a ser bilingües no hay más necesidad de ello. Ningún pueblo jamás ha necesitado dos idiomas para los mismos fines.

En muchos países del mundo se dan perfecta cuenta de esto y por lo tanto, en aquellos estados donde conviven dos o más pueblos de hablas distintas si quieren asegurar la justicia social y la convivencia pacífica de esos pueblos se promulga siempre una serie de leyes para delimitar y en la medida que sea posible evitar el bilingüismo. Se procura, por todos los medios razonables, evitar la agresión de un idioma contra otro y asegurar la autonomía cultural de cada pueblo. Se procura asegurar el unilingüismo al nivel de la colectividad.

Una advertencia: Quiero hacer constar que al exponer todo esto no me estoy refiriendo a Puerto Rico. Me refiero a Bélgica, a Québéc, a Checoeslovakia, a Chipre, a España, a mi querido Nuevo México, mi estado natal, y al estado de Wisconsin, donde nació mi padre, hijo de inmigrantes noruegos. De Puerto Rico hablaré después.

Ahora bien, habiendo asentado, aunque a grandes rasgos, los factores principales de la dinámica del bilingüismo, podemos enfrentar la cuestión de sus consecuencias en la personalidad colectiva de un pueblo. Ya podemos precisar de qué clase de bilingüismo se trata.

Les ruego por lo tanto que tengan bien en cuenta que no hablamos de ese bilingüismo—el aprendizaje voluntario de otro idioma—que produce al paraguayo o mexicano que domina el inglés o el francés o el ruso. En esos casos las consecuencias son entera y únicamente benéficas: Se le ensancha el horizonte intelectual. Se le aumenta su caudal estético. Adquiere una doble perspectiva valiosísima sobre la condición humana. Es motivo de legítimo orgullo y hasta puede resultar de beneficio profesional y económico.

Ahora, por fin llegamos a lo cruento. ¿Qué hemos de decir de ese bilingüismo colectivo, obligatorio, ineludible, que se desarrolla en un pueblo—con o sin la intervención del sistema escolar—en un pueblo que existe subordinado en convivencia con otro?

¿Qué decir de un bilingüismo que acaba por destruir y reemplazar a la lengua materna?

El bilingüismo colectivo no es ni mas ni menos que la manifestación principal del proceso de la asimilación. Dejarse asimilar—querámoslo o no—es entregarse.

Dejarse asimilar es dejar de ser lo que se es. ¿Qué hemos de decir de esto y sus consecuencias?

   ¿Qué diremos del bilingüismo que acaba por generar ese esnobismo que se ufana de discurrir en el idioma invasor para menospreciar, rechazar y diferenciarse de su propio pueblo?

   ¿Qué será la consecuencia cuando el bilingüismo colectivo—como suele occurrir—engendra en la juventud esos dialectos de desafío, enajenación y menosprecio hacia todas las normas de su cultura? Esto suele ocurrir, y les pongo por ejemplos *le joual,* ese triste francés bastardo de ciertos grupos en Québec, y el *pachuco,* la jerigonza de extensos grupos de la juventud mexicanonorteamericana.

   Pensemos un momento en el efecto de la traducción continua sobre la mentalidad de un pueblo—dizque bilingüe—dominado por otro cuando una gran parte de lo que se publica *en el idioma materno*—periódicos, revistas, libros, materiales de enseñanza, televisión, radiodifusión, cine—es una traducción del original en el idioma invasor. ¿Qué será el efecto cuando en vez de crear todo esto lo recibe un pueblo todo de segunda mano traducido o doblado?

   Vuelvo a hacer constar que no estoy hablando del bilingüismo voluntario, elitista, académico. No me refiero al aprendizaje de lenguas extranjeras. Me refiero al bilingüismo que surge lenta e ineludiblemente cuando un pueblo se encuentra subordinado a otro.

   Lo cierto es que en estos casos la agresión cultural acaba por paralizar a la lengua subordinada. Se encuentra amurallada. Se momifica. Se les acaban, en quienes la hablan, las fuerzas creadoras. Toman la defensiva; se preocupan más de protegerse que de crear. Surgen varias formas de auto-engaño. Se adormece y se consuela el pueblo con la triste ilusión de ser un pueblo superior porque habla dos idiomas. Jactarse de ser un país bilingüe en estas condiciones es como vanagloriarse de ser tuberculoso. Y si no digo canceroso es porque según dicen, el cáncer no tiene curación y la tuberculosis sí la tiene. En nuestros días sí que la tiene.

   Empiezan las capas altas de la sociedad a despreciar su lengua. Los pobres, ciudadanos de segunda clase en su propio territorio, dirán "¿Qué más da?Primero es comer." Y acabarán menospreciándola todos, aun al punto de parecerles indigna de ser escrita, impropia para los empleos formales. Luego las familias empiezan a utilizar ambos idiomas en casa para criar a sus hijos, y se acerca el fin. A la próxima generación se reemplaza; se sustituye el idioma materno por el otro. Ha pasado todo esto muchas veces en la historia de los pueblos.

   Voy terminando, pero no sin hacer hincapié en la preponderancia del factor político-económico en todo esto. Las palabras claves son *poder*—poder político-económico—y *prestigio,* prestigio relativo de las dos lenguas en pugna. En algunos casos, casos muy especiales, el prestigio pesa más que el poder. Ya les puse el ejemplo de Bélgica, donde gozan de superioridad económica, política y demográfica los flamencos, los que hablan holandés. Conviene reiterar que el empuje y prestigio relativos del francés, hablado por los valones, el otro pueblo bélgico, son tan fuertes que no obstante el poder de los holandéshablantes, se ha notado a través de los años *un glissement* (deslizamiento) continuo de familias flamencas que se volvían primero bilingües y después valonas. Para evitar esa agresión de un idioma contra otro, existe ahora en Bélgica una defensa de leyes que protegen el unilingüismo y la autonomía cultural de los dos pueblos.

Lo esencial para nosotros es reconocer que en la mayoría de los casos pesa más el poder que el prestigio. Esto me recuerda un dicho—o más bien dicharacho—español que les ofrezco como *aide-mémoire*: Jalan más tetas que carretas. Jala más, mucho más el idioma del taller con que se gana la vida que el idioma de la escuela. Para nada nos sirve echarles la culpa a los maestros de escuela y los profesores universitarios. Sí importa el prestigio del idioma y por lo tanto las escuelas sí tienen un papel importante en esta lucha, pero es una ilusión peligrosísima suponer que en las escuelas está el remedio.

Terminaré esta divagación refiriéndome directamente a Puerto Rico. La toma de posesión de Puerto Rico—isla bendita—aconteció en 1898. Fecha nefasta. No hubo conquista. Conste a todos que no hubo conquista. Ténganlo bien en cuenta: Puerto Rico no es un país conquistado, y quieran los dioses y el destino que jamás lo sea. Pero si llegara algún día a ser conquistado Puerto Rico, sería por medio de un proceso lento que duraría muchos años—tal vez todo un siglo—y el instrumento, al parecer tan inofensivo, en verdad insidioso como pocos, el instrumento de la conquista sería el bilingüismo colectivo.

15

ESTABLISHMENT OF THE *LIGA NACIONAL DEFENSORA DEL IDIOMA ESPAÑOL*

ABSTRACT   *The documents which follow set forth the preliminary plan of organization, the objectives, and some proposed activities of the* Liga Nacional Defensora del Idioma Español *(National League in Defense of the Spanish Language). The special significance of this activity is that, insofar as its founders know, this is the first attempt in the United States to organize a national effort to strengthen and increase the uses and prestige of Spanish as a language of the people.*

En marzo de 1973 se estableció la primera organización en los Estados Unidos de América dedicada a la defensa y mantenimiento del idioma español como idioma del pueblo. Es la *Liga Nacional Defensora del Idioma Españòl.* Su fundación se debió a la iniciativa de un "comité provisional fundador" de veinticinco personas, representativo de los grupos principales de hispanohablantes en el país: trece chicanos (mexicanonorteamericanos), seis puertorriqueños, cuatro cubanos, y otros dos hispanófilos.

No es una organización académica, sino que el enfoque principal de sus actividades es el empleo y el prestigio del español más allá de las aulas escolares y universitarias. Tampoco es anti-académica y decidamente no es anti-intelectual, pero no se interesan sus miembros directamente ni por las jergas callejeras que se hablan en este país, ni por la obligación—un poco ilusoria dada la extensión del analfabetismo—de limpiar, fijar y darle esplendor a esa lengua. El fin de la Liga es a la vez más sencillo y más profundo: despertar en los hispanohablantes una visión de su idioma como símbolo precioso de su modo de ser humano.

El documento siguiente es la "carta-invitación" que mandó el comité provisional fundador por todo el país para solicitar expresiones de interés y adhesión. Unas trescientas personas se hicieron miembros en seguida.

En agosto de 1973 la Liga organizó y patrocinó (con la colaboración generosa de la Asociación Americana de Profesores de Español y Portugués) un simposio internacional en México, D.F., sobre el porvenir del idioma español en los Estados Unidos. Asistieron representantes de Puerto Rico, de la comunidad puertorriqueña continental, de los cubanos emigrados, de los mexicano-americanos, juntos con varios mexicanos distinguidos, representantes de los sectores de más prestigio de aquel país. Está en vías de editarse un libro que dará a conocer los resultados de ese simposio.

En octubre de 1974 se inauguró en Kean College, estado de New Jersey, el primer capítulo regional de la Liga, comprendiendo los estados de Connecticut, Pennsylvania, New York y New Jersey. Asistieron quinientos hispanos a la ceremonia inaugural.

La lista subsiguiente de actividades en pro del español representa la tarea inmensa con que la Liga pretendía enfrentarse.

LA CARTA-INVITACION

4225 N. 23rd Street
Arlington, Virginia 22207
a 10 de marzo de 1973

Saludos.

Nos dirigimos a todos aquellos individuos hispanoparlantes que se interesen por el porvenir en los Estados Unidos del español como idioma del pueblo. Por una confluencia de circunstancias inusitadas—

*la resurgencia de los pueblos chicano y puertorriqueño luchando con éxito cada vez más grande por la autodeterminación económica y cultural;

*la ola fuerte y creciente de inmigrantes del pueblo cubano y otros pueblos latinoamericanos;

*la presencia en este país de casi diez millones de individuos cuyo idioma materno ha sido el de Madero, Martí y Bolívar, de Darío, Neruda y Sarmiento, de Hostos, Chávez, Unamuno y Santa Teresa y de los demás próceres del mundo secular hispánico-latinoamericano.

por esas circunstancias y otras, parécenos haberse presentado el momento histórico de decidir si se ha de mantener el español como idioma del pueblo norteamericano con su papel y prestigio crecientes y cada vez más estables, o si ha de desaparecer poco a poco en este país, perdiendo terreno y reduciéndose constantemente el número de los que lo utilizan. Nos dirigimos sobre todo a los que aún se sirvan del español en casa, con sus hijos y sus padres, y con sus amigos; pero llamamos la atención igualmente a los que profesen la enseñanza del idioma español o que lo hayan aprendido, felizmente, por cualquier motivo.

Se trata de la organización de una liga nacional defensora del idioma español, idioma del pueblo, en los Estados Unidos. Los objetivos de la liga son dos:

*Trabajar a fin de aumentar por todos los medios posibles el empleo y el prestigio del español en todas las esferas de la vida personal y pública del país.

*Lograr que se establezca entre el inglés y el español una relación de estabilidad permanente en la que se reconozcan, respecto a la vida de quienes los hablan, los distintos dominios de cada uno de los dos idiomas.

Nosotros, los individuos cuyos nombres van a continuación, formamos el Comité Fundador Provisional de la Liga y serviremos como tal hasta que sea posible asentarle una base más firme y consultar la voluntad de sus miembros asociados respecto a la elección de un grupo dirigente.

Sr. Francisco Briones, Director de Estudios, Colegio Jacinto Treviño, Mercedes, Texas

Dr. José Cárdenas, Superintendent, Edgewood School District, San Antonio, Texas

Mr. Henry J. Casso, Director, Bilingual-Bicultural Project, School of Education, University of Massachusetts, Amherst, Massachusetts

Dr. Jesús Chavarría, Center for Chicano Studies, University of California, Santa Barbara, California

Dr. Dolores Gonzales, School of Education, University of New Mexico, Albuquerque, New Mexico

Dr. George González, Department of Elementary Education, University of New Mexico, Albuquerque, New Mexico

Mr. Adalberto Guerrero, Assistant Dean of Students, University of Arizona, Tucson, Arizona

Dr. Carlos Lozano, Chairman, Department of Foreign Languages, California State College, Bakersfield, California

Mrs. Olivia Muñoz, Supervisor, Foreign Language Instruction, Houston Public Schools, Houston, Texas

Dr. Cecilio Orozco, Director, Bilingual Education, New Mexico Highlands University, Las Vegas, New Mexico

Dr. Américo Paredes, Center for Mexican-American Studies, The University of Texas, Austin, Texas

Mr. Jorge M. Pérez Ponce, International Programs, American Association of Community and Junior Colleges, Washington, D.C.

Dra. Esperanza Medina Spyropoulos, The President's Committee on Opportunities for Spanish-Speaking People, Washington, D.C.

Sister María Goretti, Bilingual Education Unit, New York State Education Department, Albany, New York

Dr. Medardo Gutiérrez, School of Education, State University of New York, Albany, New York

Mrs. Sylvia Herrera de Fox, Executive Director of ASPIRA, Inc., Chicago, Illinois

Ms. Hilda Moreno, 6405 Sligo Parkway, Hyattsville, Maryland

Miss Awilda Orta, Director, Bilingual Education, School District No. 4, New York, New York

Mrs. Antonia Pantoja, Director, Puerto Rican Research and Resources Center, Washington, D.C.

Mrs. Herminia Cantero, Department of Bilingual Education, Dade County Public Schools, Miami, Florida

Ms. Rosa Guas Inclán, Division of Bilingual Education, Dade County Public Schools, Miami, Florida

Mr. José M. Infante, Supervisor of Foreign Language Instruction, North Carolina State Department of Education, Raleigh, North Carolina

Dr. Carlos M. Raggi, Department of Foreign Languages, Russell Sage College, Troy, New York

Dr. Joseph I. Michel, Foreign Language Education Center, The University of Texas, Austin, Texas

Dr. Bruce Gaarder, U.S. Office of Education, Washington, D.C.

Solicitamos calurosamente la cooperación en esta empresa de toda persona que reúna estos tres requisitos

Que sea hispanoparlante

Que se suscriba a los dos objetivos estipulados de la liga.

Que esté dispuesto a servirse del idioma español para los fines oficiales y públicos de la liga.

La liga nace a la vida pública sin experiencia por parte de sus fundadores y sin fondos. No obstante esto, pues nos consta que la necesidad de luchar por los objetivos de la liga es apremiante, estamos resueltos a emprender la tarea. Dentro de treinta días escribiremos nuevamente a todos los que se sirvan contestar a nuestra carta.

A fin de que este llamamiento e invitación llegue a la atención del mayor número posible de individuos interesados, les rogamos que se sirvan hacer siquiera cinco copias de estas hojas y las manden a otras cinco personas que, a su parecer, reúnen los requisitos especificados.

CONSTANCIA DE ADHESION

Cada uno deberá hacer constar su adhesión a los objetivos de la Liga Nacional Defensora del Idioma Español mediante su firma en el lugar indicado abajo. Devuélvase esta hoja firmada al

> Comité Fundador Provisional
> Liga Nacional Defensora del Idioma Español
> Bruce Gaarder, Secretario Provisional
> 4225 N. 23rd Street
> Arlington, Virginia 22207

Por mi firma hago constar mi adhesión a los objetivos estipulados de la Liga Nacional Defensora del Idioma Español.

Firma: _____

Otra identificación (título, organizacion, etc.):_____

_____

Dirección: _____

NOTA BENE:

Sírvase indicar abajo la actividad o el tema que más le interese o que le parezca más importante. Mediante el *Boletín de Defensa* trataremos de formar pequeñas "redes" de individuos con intereses mutuos.

_____

_____

_____

ACTIVIDADES QUE LA LIGA PUEDE INICIAR Y LLEVAR A CABO, DIRECTA O INDIRECTAMENTE

1. Buscar un modo de identificar, animar y apoyar a individuos hispanos, principalmente los que han nacido en los Estados Unidos, que aspiren a expresar su genio creativo mediante el español escrito. Se trata particularmente de estimular la creatividad literaria en cualquiera de sus formas tradicionales: poesía, drama, novela, o cuento.

Existe desde hace más de veinte años un modelo para hacer esto que ha tenido mucho éxito. Existen también—al parecer—varias posibilidades de conseguir los fondos necesarios. Lo que parece hacer falta es un esfuerzo colectivo para llevar a cabo las gestiones necesarias.

2. Organizar y llevar a cabo una serie de "misiones culturales" ante los gobiernos y los elementos culturales más prestigiosos—el periodismo, las universidades, los escritores y otros artistas, etc.—de España y de los países hispanoamericanos a fin de dar a conocer el resurgimiento de interés por el porvenir del idioma español y la cultura correspondiente en los Estados Unidos, y de pedir su ayuda moral y sus consejos.

3. Editar y publicar un órgano de comunicación y coordinación entre los miembros de la Liga y de publicidad dondequiera, algo como un *Boletín de Defensa.* Será imprescindible una publicación de esta índole si hemos de despertar y aprovechar el interés de todos los que o pública o personalmente no quieran ver disminuir en los Estados Unidos año tras año el prestigio del idioma español y el número de hispanoparlantes.[1]

4. Lograr, en las escuelas y las universidades estadounidenses donde haya contingentes numerosos de estudiantes hispanoparlantes, que se utilice el español como medio regular de instrucción en otras materias además del idioma mismo y sus literaturas. Señaladamente esto podría verificarse en los departamentos y centros de estudios puertorriqueños, chicanos y cubanos. Asimismo el empleo del español como medio de instrucción para la mayor parte de las asignaturas que forman el plan de estudios para la preparación de maestros de español y maestros en nuestras escuelas bilingües.

5. El gobierno federal de EE.UU., por su Government Printing Office, publica en español un número significativo de boletines, anuncios, informes, etc. Desgraciadamente, en muchos casos el lenguaje que se emplea es vergonzoso por descuido extremado de sintaxis y ortografía. Una campaña de protesta servirá a la vez de estímulo para revisar debidamente esas publicaciones y de publicidad para la Liga.

6. Gestionar el establecimiento de más intercambio, a los niveles profesional y estudiantil, entre instituciones docentes latinoamericanas e instituciones docentes de este país. (La Secretaría de Educación Pública en México está dispuesta a emplear en sus escuelas primarias a maestros chicanos que quieran pasar un año o más en aquel país.)

7. Investigar las posibilidades de estimular la organización de unos centros culturales puertorriqueños y mexicanos—tal vez españoles también—por el estilo de la famosa Alianza Francesa (*l'Alliance Française*).

Serían centros de divulgación cultural patrocinados en parte por los gobiernos puertorriqueño y mexicano, y en parte por grupos de individuos en este país. Ofrecerían conferencias, exhibiciones de arte, conciertos de música, enseñanza del idioma y su literatura, una biblioteca, etc.

8. Instituir una campaña nacional pro-alfabetismo entre aquellos hispanoparlantes de todas edades que han sido víctimas de nuestra política escolar, esa política que hasta hace poco ha hecho tanto por destruir el español en este país entre los que lo hablan como idioma materno. (En la Oficina de Educación de los EE. UU. se ha contratado la producción de una serie de 25 películas que se difundirán por televisión para enseñar a leer en español a adultos analfabetos.)

9. Promover en todo el país una discusión del mejoramiento y reforma de la enseñanza de español a estudiantes hispanoparlantes. Se reconoce que tanto en nuestras escuelas como en nuestras universidades y "colleges" el sistema de enseñanza no corresponde sino muy raras veces a las necesidades y condiciones de los alumnos hispanos. Con la colaboración y ayuda generosa de la AATSP (Asociación americana de profesores de español y portugués) se ha preparado ya un plan de reforma: *La enseñanza del español a estudiantes hispanoparlantes en la escuela y en la universidad* (DHEW Publication No. OE 72-135, U.S. Government Printing Office, Washington, D.C. 20402. Precio: 55 centavos.)

    Lo que hace falta respecto a esta publicación es hacer que se discuta el plan de reforma dondequiera que haya alumnos hispanoparlantes, para mejorarlo, adaptarlo a las circunstancias de cada localidad, y lograr que se lleve a cabo la reforma. (La Liga mandará gratis un ejemplar del plan en lengua española a quien nos lo pida.) (Véase el capítulo 5 arriba.)

10. Analizar la educación bilingüe y el bilingüismo a fin de reforzar los esfuerzos de todos los que lo promueven. Lograr que en las "escuelas bilingües" se comprenda la importancia clave de las maestras encargadas de impartir instrucción por medio del español, así como la importancia de darles la preparación necesaria para esa tarea transcendental. Es transcendental, porque actualmente la orientación de esas escuelas es fuertemente asimilativa: son una calle de sentido único hacia el inglés.

11. Llevar a cabo las gestiones a fin de que la Liga sea una sociedad anónima no lucrativa de fines educacionales. Es necesario esto si hemos de conseguir ayuda financiera del gobierno federal y de las fundaciones de beneficencia pública.[2]

EJEMPLOS DE ACTIVIDADES QUE LOS MIEMBROS DE LA LIGA PUEDEN EMPRENDER INDIVIDUALMENTE

12. Organizar una reunión—o mejor una serie de reuniones—de la gente hispanohablante en un pueblo, una vecindad, una iglesia, una escuela, una universidad, para darles cuenta de la Liga a fin de que se pongan a examinar sus recursos y vayan escogiendo un proyecto.

13. Organizar un grupo de niños hispanos y enseñarles a leer y escribir en

español, o un grupo de adultos de todas edades para discutir cualquier tema o para leer y discutir cualquier libro en español.

14. Empezar la recolección y preservación del folklore infantil de su pueblo—canciones, juegos, adivinanzas, cuentos, bailes, etcétera—para darlo a conocer y para utilizarlo en las escuelas. (Es esto uno de los mejores modos de interesar a los adultos y hacer que colaboren con entusiasmo.)

15. Empezar un proyecto de "historia oral," es decir, la recolección de anécdotas, cuentos e historia personal, tal como la recuerdan los adultos—en particular los más viejos—antes de que se pierda al morirse éstos. Para esto se necesita una máquina grabadora de buena calidad. Se transcriben las grabaciones y también se guardan las cintas grabadas.

16. Organizar un viaje a un país hispano para un grupo de jóvenes o adultos hispanos.

17. Conseguir un radio bueno de onda corta que capte emisiones de los países hispanos.

18. Abonarse a un periódico o una revista de lengua española.

NOTES

1. Se publicó el primer número de la revista DEFENSA en marzo de 1976.

2. En 1975 la Liga fue reconocida como sociedad anónima no-lucrativa.

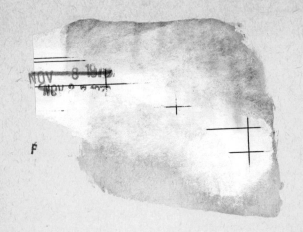

F